ADVANCE PRAISE FOR
THE FLY GIRLS REVOLT

"*The Fly Girls Revolt* plugs long-standing gaps both in the history of women in flight and in American military history. Written with passion, insight, and the perspective only an insider can bring, it furnishes heretofore missing background and detail that overturns much of the conventional wisdom of how women won their own right to fly and fight. Filled with memorable quotes and anecdotes from the women themselves, this book is certain to be a go-to reference for years to come. Eileen Bjorkman, who lived much of the history that she writes, has given her readers a rare treasure."

—**Dr. Richard P. Hallion, United States Air Force Historian, 1991-2002**

"There have been two compelling long-term changes in the military since World War II: racial integration of the forces, and bringing women in as fully equal members. The latter includes elimination of barriers to serve in combat and all other operational and support roles. Eileen Bjorkman has deftly woven her own experiences into the broad story of the hundreds of women and men who fought to make gender equality a reality—despite overwhelming opposition. This is a tale that should be read by every serving member of the armed forces and by all government officials in policy-making positions. A remarkably riveting story."

—**Colonel Scott Willey, USAF (Ret), Book Review Editor,**
Air and Space Power History

"Eileen Bjorkman's book is riveting for any reader but especially for those of us who personally experienced much of the saga she so expertly chronicles. The tenor of my own U.S. Air Force career, which had several touch points with Eileen's, is well captured in this story. I entered the Air Force as part of the first class of women to graduate from the Air Force Academy in 1980 and I retired thirty-five years later as the first woman four star general in the Air Force. Shortly after I retired, I began service as the longest tenured Chair of DACOWITS, a pivotal entity that features prominently in

The Fly Girls Revolt. I can unequivocally state that this is a story that needed to be told, both from an historical perspective and on behalf of the many women who were a part of it. I speak for all of these women in expressing profound gratitude to Eileen for bringing our story to life for others to reflect on, learn from, and act on. As Eileen notes, in order to tap all the talent this country has to offer, much works remains to improve the recruitment and retention of women in our military services. I believe that work is a national security imperative."

—**General Janet Wolfenbarger, USAF, (Ret)**

"Looking back, the opportunity for women to fly combat aircraft seems inevitable, but *The Fly Girls Revolt* shows us how the inevitable was only acquired through the vision and determination of military women who worked stubbornly and tirelessly to drive the changes in policy, rules, and leaders' minds required to gain entry into combat squadrons and cockpits. Eileen Bjorkman skillfully weaves her own career as a flight test engineer into the movement's broader events and challenges to tell a well-researched and compelling story. Must reading for all who aspire to lead change in the American military, or anyplace else."

—**General James M. "Mike" Holmes, USAF (Ret), former Commander, Air Combat Command**

THE
FLY GIRLS
REVOLT

THE STORY OF THE WOMEN WHO KICKED OPEN THE DOOR TO FLY IN COMBAT

EILEEN A. BJORKMAN

To all women military aviators—past, present, and future

CONTENTS

LIST OF ILLUSTRATIONS

INTRODUCTION

As the sun rose one spring day in 2003, I chatted over coffee with four other Air Force colonels in an office near the Pentagon. I was the only woman. We worked in an organization that analyzed combat scenarios for Air Force leadership, and our weekly Friday meeting was our chance to talk freely and blow off steam amongst ourselves without the presence of superiors or subordinates. Three weeks before that Friday, the United States had invaded Iraq, and our conversation turned to the fight.

One of the colonels summarized an incident he'd read in a report: "Two A-10s got attacked a few days ago, and one of them got really shot up. The flight lead told the pilot she could eject if she wanted to, but she chose to fly it back. It took her an hour, but she made it back to her base and landed."

The five of us nodded and murmured appreciatively at what was apparently an exceptional bit of airmanship. Then, as aviators do, we speculated about what had happened. Had she been hit by a missile or anti-aircraft artillery? At what altitude? What parts of her aircraft were damaged?

I was secretly thrilled that no one commented on the pilot's gender. Perhaps the other colonels, three of whom had flown fighters, didn't say anything because of my presence, but they clearly weren't surprised a woman had performed admirably in combat.

This scene would have been impossible when I began my Air Force career in 1980. At that time, women were not allowed to fly in combat. A law passed by Congress in 1948 prohibited that.

The law was repealed in 1991, but even that historic moment didn't immediately open combat aircraft to women. The march to equality was not steady. It was more like a game where the women started ten points behind, and every time they clawed their way forward, the opposing team ran back over them.

Until the end of World War II, only female nurses were permanent members of the U.S. military. Women brought in for emergency service during World War I were quickly discharged at the war's end; those who served during World War II expected the same fate. Senior military leadership and Congress stepped in to make women a small, but permanent, part of each service.

But for the next two decades, those small organizations were subject to the whims of political and military leadership. Support for military women waxed and waned. On more than one occasion, the Air Force tried to get rid of them altogether. The few women who did serve suffered discrimination in promotions and pay for dependents, limited career fields, sexual harassment, and automatic discharges for pregnancy.

In the 1970s, spurred by successful lawsuits, the Equal Rights Amendment, and abolishment of the draft, military women began making permanent gains. The services slowly opened more career fields to women, including those of pilot and navigator. But the combat exclusion laws stymied women's careers. The women aviators were allowed to fly support aircraft such as aerial refueling tankers, but only men were allowed to shoot enemy aircraft out of the sky or drop bombs. Men had a chance to be on the varsity team, while women were relegated to the junior varsity, even though many of them were as good as or better than the men.

By the late 1980s, women aviators were tired of not being able to contribute to the best of their abilities. They wanted a chance to compete on a level playing field. But the desire wasn't just about being "woke" in the name of equality. Allowing women into combat aircraft would also ensure that commanders got the best aviator for a particular job, not just the male aviator who was selected because the woman better than him had to go fly a cargo aircraft instead.

The combat exclusion laws, designed with the World War II-style warfare of total surrender in mind, also didn't work as intended. In the 1980s, women aviators repeatedly flew during

short, high-intensity armed conflicts with limited objectives, entering hostile areas to deliver cargo and troops, refuel airplanes, evacuate wounded personnel, direct air battles, and listen in on enemy communications. Commanders soon realized that it was impossible to keep women away from hostile forces during modern combat, and women did everything men did except for shoot back at the enemy. But a woman's ability to fly into a hostile area often had little to do with her capabilities; instead, individual commanders withheld women from operations deemed too dangerous, while other commanders sent whoever was on the schedule with no thought to gender at all.

The 1990–1991 Persian Gulf War changed everything. The nightly news made it clear that the military needed women to function. The public also realized that women were in combat. U.S. citizens were proud of the women's accomplishments, not horrified that they were at war and that some of them died.

After the dust settled from the conflict, women aviators and their supporters pushed to overturn the laws. The opposition put up a fierce fight; some even continued to advocate for removing women from the military altogether. The laws were overturned within months, but a Presidential Commission to study the issue of women in combat allowed the services to delay the introduction of women into combat aircraft for nearly another two years. The women aviators, consummate professionals, continued to do their jobs until the doors finally opened in April 1993.

There are household names in this story, such as Senators Edward Kennedy and John McCain, and Congresswoman Patricia Schroeder. There are also names well-known in aviation circles, such as Jacqueline Cochran. But most of the women who kicked open the door to fly in combat are not famous. Many were not aviators; some weren't even in the military. Some were vocal about the need for change; others just did their jobs, proving they belonged on the team.

The vast majority of the women aviators in this story would never fly in combat. By the time the laws and policies changed, they were too old to switch careers. But they proved they belonged and fought to get rid of archaic rules that stifled their own dreams, so women after them would have equal opportunities and military commanders would have the best people for the job.

Younger women aviators who have flown in combat have published many memoirs. Likewise, there are many books about a group of women who flew as civilian pilots during World War II. But there are few books about the women military aviators of my generation. These women, who began their service in the 1970s and 1980s, made the final push to open the door to fly in combat.

This is our story.

CHAPTER 1
We Need Women; We Don't Need Women (1940s)

Jacqueline Cochran waited impatiently in her New York City apartment while a group of men in Canada debated her fate. It was June 1941, and she hoped to ferry an American bomber aircraft across the Atlantic and deliver it to the Royal Air Force. The blonde aviatrix, considered the queen of aviation in the United States, was renowned for daredevil record-breaking flights and her cosmetics business, activities that might seem incompatible. But Cochran, who believed that women were just as good at flying airplanes as men, also believed it was "a woman's duty to be as presentable as her circumstances of time and purse permit." Her own time available might only be a few minutes to comb her hair and daub on fresh lipstick at the end of an eleven-hour flight, but Cochran always appeared before the cameras looking as if she had just stepped out of a beauty salon. Except for her fingernails. She never wore polish to avoid attracting attention to her masculine-appearing hands.

Cochran had done everything possible to prepare for the transatlantic flight. She had no experience flying heavy, multi-engine aircraft like the bomber—she had accomplished her aviation feats over the past decade in small, nimble racers—so she'd headed to Floyd Bennett Field on Long Island for several hours of instruction in a Lockheed Lodestar. She then flew to Saint-Hubert Airport, about forty-five minutes from Montreal, home to the Atlantic Ferry Organization, or Atfero. There, she trained on the bomber she planned to

ferry, a Lockheed Hudson. She passed all her check rides, or practical tests, although she had some trouble grasping a hand brake used on the ground. Given her difficulty with the brake, Atfero officials decided she would fly the bomber as a first officer; she could take the controls once airborne, but the other (male) pilot would take off and land. Cochran wasn't happy, but there was nothing she could do.

Many Atfero pilots opposed the flight. About fifty of them formed a band of objectors and called a meeting to discuss the "problem." Cochran's husband, Floyd Odlum, attended to plead her case while she returned to New York.

"She's on a publicity stunt," said one pilot.

It was true that Cochran had leaped at the chance to be the first woman to fly a bomber across the Atlantic, but it wasn't her idea. She had been at a luncheon with Clayton Knight, a World War I aviator who dabbled in all sorts of aviation-related activities, such as illustrating the *Ace Drummond* comic strip written by World War I ace Eddie Rickenbacker. Knight was recruiting U.S. pilots for Atfero; during the luncheon, he asked Cochran, "Why don't you do some of this flying to England yourself to help dramatize the need? The publicity might help."

As Odlum dismissed the publicity concerns, another pilot said, "She'll belittle the rest of us who have been involved in this dangerous work. This isn't women's work. It's for men." This opinion was really a fear that if a woman could do the job, it wasn't all that dangerous. There was a small possibility the Germans might try to shoot down Cochran, but that was a risk she was willing to take.

Yet another pilot hit the bottom line: "Putting a woman into the cockpit of a bomber for ferrying purposes is taking bread out of our own mouths." But Cochran was flying one flight, not storming Atfero with a phalanx of women pilots.

The last pilot to speak told Floyd, "Taking a woman into our organization will be disruptive. We've disapproved of your wife being here from the very moment the question was raised. We've simply been overruled by higher-ups." But he conceded, "We're not running this organization and we've no right to issue an ultimatum to anyone, not even Miss Cochran."

The last pilot was right. The "higher-ups" had spoken, and it was time to follow orders.

Captain Grafton Carlisle was assigned to fly with Cochran. He was mad, not at Cochran but at the other men, some of whom threatened to blackball him from flying jobs for taking the assignment. Cochran arrived back in Canada on June 16, 1941. Carlisle was eager to get going.

The next morning, as the two pilots and a radio officer made their final preparations, the wives of the two men arrived, ostensibly to bring sandwiches. But the women weren't worried about their husbands' stomachs; they were concerned about the threats made against them. The wives waited in their cars until the bomber took off.

The first leg of the trip to Gander, Newfoundland, was uneventful. But the next morning, the ground roll during the takeoff run was so bumpy it felt like rolling over logs on the runway. Carlisle aborted the takeoff. Suspecting that cold had affected the oleo struts that acted as shock absorbers, he taxied back to the ramp. The crew serviced the struts and off-loaded about six hundred pounds of fuel for good measure. The takeoff was rough, but Carlisle managed to stagger into the air.

With the aircraft safely airborne, Carlisle climbed out of the pilot's seat and Cochran slid in to take the controls. Carlisle headed to the back of the airplane to pass time until a few minutes before landing, when he and Cochran would again perform the change-of-control dance.

Everyone settled in for the eleven-hour flight, mostly above and in the clouds. Cochran saw the aurora borealis for the first time; she found it "weird but entrancing."

Just before daybreak, tracer bullets streaked toward them, breaking the monotony. Carlisle and the radio operator dashed into the cockpit.

The crew didn't know if the bullets were British or German, but there was a way to find out. Carlisle grabbed a signal pistol and ran to the back of the aircraft. He popped open a hatch and fired a signal bullet of a color that indicated they were a friendly aircraft. The bullets from the ground continued, and Cochran worried that maybe the Germans were trying to kill her. But perhaps the cloud cover prevented anyone below from seeing the signal from the Hudson.

The bullets suddenly stopped. When they landed, they found no damage to the bomber. Cochran never learned who fired at them.

For another half-century, women aviators would hear the same arguments the male pilots made in their battle to keep Cochran out of the bomber: they were just in it for glamor, combat flying was too dangerous, and they took jobs from men. Most of all, women were disruptive.

* * *

Four decades after her death, Jacqueline Cochran remains an enigma. One of her biographers, Maryann Bucknum Brinley, summed her up as "an explosive study in contradictions," simultaneously "generous, egotistical, penny-pinching, compassionate, sensitive [and] aggressive." Cochran's two autobiographies contain so much demonstrably false material that it's difficult to know when she was telling the truth.

Cochran claimed to not know when she was born or who her parents were, but she was born in 1906 in Florida's panhandle. Her birth name was Bessie Lee Pittman; she was the youngest of five children in a working-class family. As an adult, she told people she was adopted and wove vivid stories of a childhood filled with gut-wrenching poverty. Another oft-repeated story had her picking the name "Cochran" out of a telephone book in Pensacola. But none of it was true.

The truth was that around 1920, Bessie Pittman married Robert Cochran. They had a son, also Robert, who died in 1925 after setting himself on fire while playing with matches. The Cochrans divorced soon afterwards. Bessie moved to Montgomery, Alabama, to work as a hairdresser and began using the name Jacqueline. As she moved further north, she buried her past along with her son. She never mentioned her first marriage or dead son again, at least in public. And she never had another child.

Cochran arrived in New York City in 1929 and landed a position at a salon in Saks Fifth Avenue. She met Floyd Odlum in 1932, and the two began dating, even though he was still married and had two sons. Odlum was one of the world's most wealthy men. He had founded his own company in the 1920s and thrived during the Depression by snapping up depressed companies and then selling them quickly at a profit, usually 40 or 50 percent. The two made

for an odd couple: Odlum, far from a looker with his horn-rimmed glasses, next to the glamorous Cochran. She claimed she loved him for his mind, and she justified their dating by saying the marriage was over, the divorce just hadn't happened yet.

Odlum sparked Cochran's interest in aviation. She wanted to sell cosmetics on the road; to cover enough territory to make money, he suggested she should fly. Why not get a pilot's license and fly herself?

Cochran liked the idea. The Roosevelt Aviation School on Long Island advertised twenty hours of flight training for $495. Cochran was in a hurry, and Odlum bet her the $495 that she couldn't get her license in six weeks. It was just the sort of challenge she needed.

Cochran started her training on a Saturday and claimed she soloed in a little airplane called a Fleet two days later. During her first solo flight, which involved taking off and landing a few times, the engine quit. Some students would have panicked, but Cochran handled the emergency with aplomb. She glided back to the runway and touched down as if nothing had gone wrong. Three weeks later she had her license, and Odlum paid up.

By 1934, Cochran had earned her commercial pilot's license, meaning she could be paid for her flying. She was also learning how to fly just by looking at instruments inside the cockpit so she could fly in poor weather. By then, she wanted to do more than sell cosmetics: she wanted to enter airplane races. The races, common in the 1930s, garnered front-page coverage in newspapers, and winners often became famous. Cochran's first race attempt—an international route from England to Australia—ended in Bucharest, Romania, after she realized her aircraft, a Gee Bee, wasn't suited to such a long distance.

In 1935, she founded Jacqueline Cochran Cosmetics. Her signature product was Flowing Velvet, a moisturizer she developed to cure her skin problems created by flying, especially at high altitudes. That year, Cochran also set a new target for her racing ambitions: the most prestigious aviation event in the U.S., the Bendix Trophy Race, a transcontinental race founded in 1931 that took place each Labor Day weekend. The National Air Race Committee and Vincent Bendix, who manufactured innovative aircraft parts, each provided half of a $15,000 purse. Cliff Henderson, founder of the National Air Races, hoped the cash prizes would entice

entrants to push the technology bounds of navigation, weather, efficiency, endurance, and speed.

In 1934, Henderson had barred women from the race, saying, "Women have no more place in the National Air Races than on the automobile racetrack at Indianapolis." He didn't have anything against women aviators, of course, but a year earlier twenty-three-year-old Florence Klingensmith had died when a wing fell off her aircraft during a tight pylon turn at a race in Chicago. Male pilots died just about every year during the races, but Henderson apparently couldn't stomach the thought of a woman's death. After Frances Harrell Marsalis died in a crash at the first Women's National Air Meet in August 1934, a writer lamented in *Popular Aviation* magazine, "Just one more victim of the race mania and a desire to feed death-defying thrills to a hungry public." Without any discussion on why he considered a female pilot's death more tragic than a man's, he asked, "Is it worth the price?"

Women pilots thought it was. They railed against Henderson's injunction. Amelia Earhart, the most famous of them all, refused to fly actress Mary Pickford from Los Angeles to Cleveland, where Pickford was scheduled to open the races. Famed aviator Jimmy Doolittle flew Pickford instead.

Henderson relented the next year, and both Earhart and Cochran started the race in Burbank. On August 31, 1935, Amelia Earhart roared down the runway at 12:34 a.m. with two male pilots playing cards in the back of her Lockheed Vega. The trio wasn't interested in winning; they just hoped to come in fifth place to earn $500 to cover their trip expenses. They got their wish.

Fog rolled in after Earhart's takeoff, so Cochran bided time, finally lifting off at 4:22 a.m. A fence at the end of the runway snagged an antenna, leaving her with no radio. After circling her fuel-laden aircraft to gain altitude, she crossed the San Bernardino Mountains. She was in the race.

But the climb had strained her engine, and an ominous vibration rattled her aircraft's tail. As Cochran approached the Grand Canyon at daylight, she knew there were no more airports for hundreds of miles to land in an emergency. Worse, thunderstorms lay ahead. Cochran was bold, but she knew her limits. The race was over for her. She turned around and landed at a nearby airport.

The next year, 1936, the women shone. Louise Thaden became the first woman to win the Bendix race, and women took three of the five prizes. Cochran didn't race, but that year she and Floyd Odlum married.

The 1937 race was a sad time. Earhart had vanished two months earlier during her round-the-globe flight, leaving a giant void in women's aviation. Despite her heavy heart, Cochran placed third. By then, she had honed her long-distance flying skills. To keep her mouth moist, she sipped on a small bottle half-filled with cola—a full bottle fizzed and spilled at high altitudes. Except for a handful of suckers, she didn't eat during a flight and could lose as much as six pounds. After a race, she smiled in front of microphones, grateful that reporters stood too far away to detect the deep lines of fatigue in her face.

In 1938, flying a modified Seversky pursuit aircraft designed for the military, Cochran departed Burbank about two in the morning for her third attempt at the Bendix Trophy. For this race, the pilots pushed higher into the atmosphere, above twenty thousand feet. The high altitude forced them to use oxygen masks.

Cochran flew through the night to the Seversky engine's steady purr. As she crossed the Continental Divide, the engine sputtered and quit. Thinking she had run a fuel tank dry, she switched to another tank. That didn't help. She had plenty of fuel, but it wasn't getting to the engine.

Cochran kicked the rudder pedals back and forth, and the engine started again; the abrupt motion had unseated a blockage. After rocking the wings several times, she found that if she kept the left wing down, the engine kept running. It was a bit awkward, but it worked. She zipped across the country in just eight hours and ten minutes without stopping for fuel, besting nine men for the win. After landing in Cleveland, she refueled, chatted with reporters for a few minutes, and greeted Odlum with "I need some cigarettes! I've been smoking a pipe all the way from Burbank— an oxygen pipe!"

Newspapers, including the *New York Times*, splashed Cochran's win across their front pages, coronating her as queen of U.S. aviation. Even then, some speculated that Cochran hadn't flown the race, that it must have been a male pilot.

* * *

In 1939, Cochran outlined a plan to Eleanor Roosevelt to get U.S. women into the cockpits of military aircraft. If the U.S. joined the war raging in Europe, women pilots could free up men for combat tasks. The plan hadn't gone anywhere, but after ferrying the bomber in 1941, Cochran observed women pilots ferrying aircraft around England. Maybe it was time to revive her idea.

Arriving back in New York from her bomber flight, Cochran planned to sleep until noon. But a call from President Franklin D. Roosevelt woke her at 9:00 a.m. Could she come to Hyde Park at noon? Over lunch, Cochran regaled Roosevelt with tales about the women ferry pilots in England; she hoped American women could do the same thing. The lunch opened doors for meetings with high-ranking War Department officials, including Brigadier General Robert Olds, who was forming a unit to ferry aircraft. He was interested but wanted to hire women on an individual basis, as civil servants or contractors; he would plug them in wherever needed.

Cochran had a much bigger vision: an organization just for women pilots, an organization she would run. She feared a handful of women scattered about the country among tens of thousands of men would "simply go down as a flash in the historical pan."

Cochran's vision languished amid Army bureaucracy for two months. In mid-September, General H. H. "Hap" Arnold, chief of the Army Air Forces, sent her a letter saying, "Not yet." He had a dozen excuses: there weren't enough qualified women pilots, there would be housing and training problems. Cochran was ready with answers. Just as in England, the women could be in an auxiliary corps with military status, separate from the men. Arnold wouldn't budge, but he encouraged Cochran to take some women to England to fly as contractors with the British Air Transport Auxiliary. The "experiment" would prove that such an organization could work in the U.S. To reassure Cochran that Brigadier General Olds would not hire women to ferry aircraft on his own terms while she was gone, Arnold said, "I'll keep Olds away from the women pilots."

Cochran had previously combed through Civil Aviation Authority files to come up with a list of potential women pilots for her planned organization. She sent telegrams to a few dozen, inviting

them to an interview at her New York apartment. Cochran offered to pay all expenses for the trip.

Ann Wood jumped at the offer. When she arrived for her interview, one of the first things she noticed was a glass case crammed full of Cochran's racing memorabilia. She never forgot Cochran's cigarette case, a gift from Floyd Odlum: a gold box encrusted with rubies, emeralds, and diamonds depicting the route of one of her Bendix races.

In October, with Pearl Harbor still more than a month away, Wood went to England. Cochran's women, who eventually totaled twenty-five, had eighteen-month contracts. After initial training, they ferried British aircraft around the country—Hurricanes, Spitfires, trainers, and bombers. Mary Nicholson, the first woman in North Carolina to receive a pilot's license and also Cochran's personal secretary, was the only fatality. She was killed on May 22, 1943, when the propeller flew off the airplane she was flying and she crashed.

Even after Cochran's pilots proved their competence, those in power weren't ready for women pilots in the U.S. It was starting to look like the women would have to find another way into the war.

$$*\quad*\quad*$$

Women pilots weren't the only ones who wanted to support the war. Others clamored to help; many women joined civilian volunteer organizations to train as ambulance drivers or to help defend the East Coast from air attacks. Representative Edith Nourse Rogers, a Republican from Massachusetts, thought the timing was perfect to create a women's Army auxiliary. During World War I, Rogers had served as a volunteer nurse overseas and with the American Red Cross in the U.S. From those experiences, she developed a lifelong passion for veterans' issues. She was also sympathetic to the plight of women volunteers. Men in the armed forces were taken care of if they were injured or became ill overseas, but an injured or ill woman volunteer had to find medical care or a return trip to the U.S. on her own. Rogers wanted to fix that.

In early 1941, Rogers authored a bill to establish the Women's Army Auxiliary Corps (WAAC). The women would work in "air raid warning service, in domestic work for the Army, and as chauffeurs

and mechanics." Rogers wanted women to be full members of the Army, and George C. Marshall, the chief of staff of the Army, agreed. But Marshall was no feminist; his interest was pragmatic. With the war looming, he was concerned about manpower shortages. He also didn't want to waste time training men for things he considered "women's work." But members of his staff, along with many in Congress, pushed back on full military status for women. Rogers instead wrote a compromise bill. The women would have military ranks and benefits similar to men but would not have full overseas protections.

The WAAC bill went nowhere until the attack on Pearl Harbor. With the support of Henry Stimson, the secretary of war, Rogers tweaked her original proposal and resubmitted it. The bill received a warm reception in the House. On January 21, 1942, Frances Bolton, a Republican representative from Ohio, testified at a House Military Affairs Committee that participation in "the organization fighting for freedom" would be a morale booster for women. She scoffed at the notion that women would find the work too arduous. Women did not expect the Army to be a glamorous job. Bolton said, "There is nothing the women of the country will welcome more than to have taken away that word 'glamour.'" An Army brigadier general also testified in favor of the women's corps, and Edgar G. Brown, the director of the National Negro Council, urged committee members to include women of all races.

The bill moved to a House vote on March 17. But first, there was four hours of debate, mostly about whether women would be subject to military discipline, including court-martial (they would). Several representatives also lodged their opposition.

Clare Eugene Hoffman, a Republican from Michigan, claimed that women didn't really want to join the military; he said they wanted to stay home to sew, cook, and do other domestic chores. Andrew Somers, a Democrat from New York, was blunter, calling the bill "the silliest piece of legislation I have ever seen come into this House." Democrat Butler Black Hare, from South Carolina, found the idea of women soldiers mortifying. He raged, "I think it is a reflection upon the courageous manhood of the country to pass a law inviting women to join the armed forces in order to win a battle…. Think of the humiliation! What has become of the manhood of America?"

The bill passed, 249–86. Then it was on to the Senate, where Democratic leaders predicted smooth sailing. But the bill first had to go through the Senate Military Affairs Committee, then be brought to a vote and debated. Even with minimal opposition, it took nearly two more months before the legislation passed on May 12.

<p style="text-align:center">✳ ✳ ✳</p>

One controversy remained, not with the WAAC bill itself, but with the woman the War Department planned to install as the director: Oveta Culp Hobby, who did publicity for the Army and was the wife of former Texas governor William P. Hobby. Edgar G. Brown wrote President Roosevelt, asking him to veto the bill; Brown feared Hobby's Southern background would hurt non-white women who wanted to serve. His fears were well founded: some women's volunteer organizations supporting the war effort had declined to accept Black women. Brown also asked Secretary of War Stimson to avoid selecting a director from the South; he believed such a woman would not inspire confidence that "justice would be meted out to colored women."

However, Eleanor Roosevelt expressed confidence that Executive Order 8802, signed by her husband a year earlier, would ensure Black women got a fair shake. The Executive Order stated, "There shall be no discrimination in the employment of workers in defense industries or government because of race, creed, color, or national origin."

Roosevelt signed the WAAC bill on May 15; Secretary Stimson swore Hobby in as director the next morning. After the ceremony, Hobby announced that the first four hundred recruits would be sent to officer training, that forty of those would be Black, and that at least two of the first companies of women would be Black units. That afternoon, Edgar G. Brown said that, with Hobby's announcement, he was satisfied Black women would be treated fairly.

Hobby said recruiting would begin in a few weeks, but women didn't want to wait. They swarmed or called into recruiting centers asking how to apply. So many women called local newspapers for more information that larger papers had to hire extra telephone operators.

The outpouring of support for the WAAC nudged the other services into using their own "womanpower." By the end of 1942, the Navy had WAVES, which stood for "Women Accepted for Volun-

teer Emergency Service," although some claimed it meant "Women Are Very Essential Sometimes." The Coast Guard had SPARs, which stood for "Semper Paratus—Always Ready." The Marines also had a women's reserve, but a Marine is a Marine. They refused to come up with a cute acronym.

<p style="text-align:center">* * *</p>

Official WAAC recruiting started with a bang. On May 27, ten thousand women poured into recruiting centers across the country. More than one thousand women barged into a center in New York City alone. Some women had been waiting since 5:00 a.m. By 8:30, 250 of them had made it inside. A guard stretched his arms across the entrance to keep more from entering. On the second day, to keep up with the seemingly endless stream of applicants, the Army decided to keep the recruiting center open that Saturday, May 30. The recruiters had Sunday, Memorial Day, off before heading back into the deluge. Finally, on Thursday, the window for initial applicants closed. One bedraggled recruiter said, "If I never see another woman again it will be too soon."

Potential recruits cut across race and class lines. Women sporting fur coats mingled with those wearing inexpensive cotton dresses. A full-blooded Creek Indian woman arrived in traditional Native American dress. She asked reporters, "Don't you think I have more right to join than some of the other women?"

Many women had jobs, and pay phones were kept busy as women called their bosses to let them know they were running late. Some lied, with one admitting she had called in sick for a nonexistent toothache.

As part of their application, women stated in one hundred words or less why they wanted to join the Army. One sounded a lot like many men: "Military life has always fascinated me because of the excitement and adventure it has to offer." Another woman, a naturalized citizen, was more heartfelt: "With my education and previous war experience, I feel partially able to pay for what I have received in this country."

Recruits could be single or married, have a high school diploma, and be aged twenty-one to forty-five years. Women also had to be

of excellent character, in good physical condition, between five-feet and six-feet tall, and weigh at least 105 pounds. A woman was also expected to be "intelligent enough to understand and execute orders and protect herself." And she had to be capable of "transport[ing] herself by marching."

On July 20, 1942, the first 440 women officer candidates reported to Fort Des Moines to begin training. After a whirlwind of paperwork, uniform issue, and indoctrination, the women assembled in the post's theater on July 23. Oveta Culp Hobby, now referred to as Major Hobby, told them, "This is your date with destiny, and a free future will credit your contribution.... You have taken off silk and put on khaki. And all for essentially the same reason—you have a debt and a date. A debt to democracy, a date with destiny. You may be called upon to give your lives."

The women's training was similar to the men's: how to march, how to wear uniforms, and how to live together as a large group. The women "officers" were not commissioned officers, but the enlisted women were expected to salute the officers and address them as "Ma'am." For all practical purposes, the women were in the Army.

The first women graduated on August 29. Only eight had dropped out, three for failing to meet academic standards, one for a physical disability, and the others for administrative reasons. During the graduation ceremony, the women marched with "backs straight and khaki skirts swinging." The two-star general presiding over the ceremony remarked, "Many of our soldiers would do well to emulate them. I am very proud to be a part of this."

Hobby attended the ceremony, along with Representative Rogers, there to see the first products of her bill. During Rogers's commencement speech, she told the women, "You represent a dream which I conceived during the first World War."

After the speech, a captain called out, "Mary Bell Armstrong." Armstrong strode to the front of the bandstand, saluted the general, and shook hands with him. She was now a "third officer." The women were on their way.

* * *

Emma Riley was among the first to apply for a commission that summer. Despite her master's degree, the WAAC rejected her for officer training, so she enlisted. The Army sent her a notice to take a train the last Sunday of August 1942 from St. Joseph, Missouri, to Des Moines. But when she arrived at the train station with her parents, they discovered that the train didn't operate on Sundays.

Her parents drove her sixty miles to Kansas City. Her father, already upset she had enlisted in the Army instead of being an officer, was further irritated by the extra drive. Every few minutes, he turned around and said, "If that outfit can't get someone from Plattsburg to Des Moines, Iowa, I don't know how they think they're ever going to get anywhere in the war!"

Fortunately, the trains in Kansas City operated on Sundays. Riley arrived at Fort Des Moines about seven o'clock Monday morning. The first two weeks were easy. Academics consisted mostly of military history, first aid, a course called "Why We Fight," and a slew of classes on hygiene. Enlisted men cleaned the latrines and pulled KP duty; all the women trainees had to do was make their beds. The fort was an old cavalry base converted into the training center, and the women were housed in a Civil War-era stable transformed into a barracks, with 125 bunks side by side. Riley remembered, "They'd treated the horses very well, I guess, because it was a nice stable." After two weeks, the men left and the trainees did everything, often reporting for KP duty at five in the morning and going to sleep at ten at night.

Riley's worst fear was having to clean a grease trap. Fortunately, she never did, because she was pretty sure if she'd had to, she would not have completed her training. Once she hauled dozens of frozen turkeys with feet and heads attached from a walk-in refrigerator before she cleaned it. When turkey was served the next day, she couldn't eat it.

After basic training, Riley stayed at Fort Des Moines and learned to drive a ton-and-a-half truck. To help the war effort, the Army had removed two of the four rear tires, which made the trucks unstable. Riley was terrified as she drove around town with a load of soldiers, sure she would tip over at any minute.

Riley's truck driving didn't last long; a slot at Officer Candidate School opened. After being commissioned, she and several other women went to a new training center at Fort Oglethorpe, Georgia. The women anticipated donuts and coffee they heard the United Service Organizations (USO) was passing out at a stop in Tennessee. But USO volunteers, expecting male soldiers, refused to give the women donuts. The slight stung.

Fort Oglethorpe was in disarray when Riley arrived. With no uniforms for the fifteen hundred newcomers who poured in each week, the post handed out men's overcoats. Women who had traveled in high heels stumbled about in the ill-fitting coats.

Male soldiers at Fort Oglethorpe didn't hate the women's presence; the men just hated being there because they wanted to be in combat. Riley explained, "They felt that they would have an awful hard time explaining to their grandchildren what grandpappy did in the war."

* * *

The women's status as auxiliaries caused problems for the Army almost from the beginning. Commanders in Europe clamored for women, but because they lacked benefits and protections, the Army limited them to duty in North Africa, which was considered relatively safe. To allow women to serve in Europe, both the House and Senate introduced bills in January 1943 to make the women full Army members.

Not long after the bills were introduced, rumors and innuendo about promiscuity began flying. One story had twenty-six women being sent home from North Africa for pregnancy. A few days later, the number jumped to ninety and then five hundred, an impossible number given that only 262 women had ever been sent to North Africa. Of the three women who had been sent home, two had medical issues. A third woman was married and traveled to North Africa before discovering she was pregnant. Investigators found that only a few dozen women out of tens of thousands became pregnant; most were at a WAAC training center in Daytona Beach, Florida. There was no evidence of rampant promiscuity, but the smear campaign continued.

On June 9, 1943, everything blew up.

John O'Donnell, a columnist with the *New York Daily News*, reported that "contraceptives and prophylactic equipment will be furnished to members of the WAACs, according to a super-secret agreement reached by the high-ranking officers of the War Department and…Hobby…" O'Donnell retracted his claim the next day, but the damage was done.

The same day as the retraction, Secretary of War Stimson minced no words when he denounced O'Donnell's "sinister rumors" as "absolutely and completely false." Singing the praises of the sixty-five thousand women who had released men for front-line duties, the secretary said, "Anything which would interfere with [women's] recruiting or destroy the reputation of this corps and, by so doing, interfere with increase in the combat strength of our Army, would be of value to [the] enemy." Edith Nourse Rogers went a step further, suggesting that those who spread such rumors might be guilty of sedition.

The flap over the allegations died down, and Congress got back to work on the bill to make women full Army members. With Stimson and other Army brass on their side, the bill sailed the rest of the way through Congress. On July 1, Roosevelt signed the bill to establish the Women's Army Corps, or WAC.

Rogers had won her long battle. With the establishment of the WAC, for the first time in U.S. history, women who were not nurses served in the military as full equals to their male counterparts regarding protections, pay, and benefits. The women had not received full equality in other areas, though. They were still restricted largely to administrative specialties, and when the war ended, they would all be dismissed, even if they still desired to serve. But at the time, everyone was happy.

Current Women's Auxiliary Army Corps members had sixty days to reenlist in the WAC. Only about three-quarters of the enlisted women did, although it's not clear how much attrition was related to the vicious rumors. Most women officers moved to the WAC. Emma Riley and other third officers became second lieutenants; Oveta Culp Hobby was elevated to full colonel. The WAC were here to stay, at least for the duration of the war.

* * *

My great-aunt Florence Eighmy was one of the women who joined the WAC and trained at Fort Oglethorpe. Florence enlisted not so much out of patriotism but because she missed her husband, Bob, who was in the Army in Europe. She figured she could ask to be stationed somewhere in Europe, and the couple could meet up on leave.

Born in 1921, Florence had few options after high school. She had good grades and longed to be a nurse, but there was no money for college. Instead, she did some modeling and worked as an accountant in a furniture store.

In 1943, Florence met a handsome young soldier at a local hangout in Portage, Wisconsin. Bob Eighmy was assigned to nearby Fort McCoy, awaiting orders to ship out to Europe. The pair hit it off and married four months later. Bob left shortly afterwards.

Florence enlisted a few months later, on March 29, 1944. She sent Bob a letter telling him she had joined the WAC and left for basic training. She took a train from Chicago to Chattanooga, Tennessee, and then boarded a bus with other enlistees to Fort Oglethorpe, an alien place teeming with cockroaches and mosquitoes that Florence dubbed "the swamps." Southern customs, culture, and food baffled her. She detested watermelon but developed a lifelong affinity for catfish.

The camaraderie among the women and childhoods formed by the Depression helped the enlistees survive boot camp: smallpox and tetanus vaccinations, training in gas masks, and lots of marching and scrubbing floors. Music from local radio stations often filled the barracks, and the women danced whenever they could. In addition to learning the mechanics of being a good soldier, Florence soaked up knowledge about the world through the eyes of women from all over the U.S.

During training, Florence discovered she had made a strategic error: married WAC members weren't allowed to be stationed overseas. The Army assigned her to Romulus Army Airfield in Michigan as an instructor in an airplane simulator called a Link Trainer. Her job involved setting up the trainer for pilots to practice flying in the clouds using their instruments; she also ran equipment that recorded their performance. Florence loved telling the pilots, who all outranked her, what to do.

Some of the pilots were women. They wore uniforms, but they were civilians. They were there because more than a year earlier, Jacqueline Cochran had won her battle to get women into the cockpits of military aircraft.

Figure 1: Women's Army Corps member Florence Eighmy, the author's great-aunt, about 1944. (Courtesy of the Sharon Halford collection)

*　*　*

Getting women into military aircraft had not been easy. And initially, Cochran was furious with how things had turned out. On September 10, 1942, the Army Air Forces announced the formation of the Women's Auxiliary Ferrying Squadron, and Cochran wasn't in charge. She thought her deal with Hap Arnold would ensure no decisions were made until she returned from her job in England.

Instead of Cochran, twenty-eight-year-old Nancy Harkness Love's photo was plastered all over newspapers to announce her as the new organization's "commander." Despite her youth, Love was an accomplished pilot with twelve hundred flying hours. She was rated to fly high-performance aircraft and seaplanes, experienced at flying on instruments, and had ferried military aircraft from factories to the Canadian border, where Atfero pilots picked them up. She was married to Major Robert Love, whose job in Washington, D.C., had introduced Nancy to those who eventually approved her organization.

"Commander" was an honorary title; Love and the women under her were employed as civilians, a decision made to avoid waiting for Congress to pass another bill regarding military women. The women pilots would work for the Air Transport Command, which ferried aircraft from factories to Army airfields in both the U.S. and overseas. Initially, the women would ferry only small airplanes like those they piloted as civilians. There were no plans for them to ferry aircraft overseas.

The women had to be between twenty-one and thirty-five, be high school graduates, hold a commercial pilot's license with privileges to fly airplanes with more than two-hundred-horsepower engines, and have at least five hundred hours of flying time.

Love wasted no time setting up shop. The same day as the announcement, she arrived at New Castle Army Air Base in Delaware to start training the first fifty women. Five women pilots showed up the same day to take ground tests for entry into the program. One of them, Cornelia Fort, had been a flight instructor in Hawaii and was airborne when the Japanese attacked Pearl Harbor. While in the traffic pattern with a student, she almost collided with another

airplane that invaded the pattern. She thought the intruder was a rogue pilot until she spotted the Japanese insignia. She took the controls from her student and landed.

Figure 2: Jacqueline Cochran, about 1943, director of Women Airforce Service Pilots. (Courtesy of U.S. Army Air Force)

Cochran wasted no time either. Hap Arnold knew he had blown it, and he acted quickly to give the famed aviatrix what she wanted. On September 14, he installed her in another civilian position, the director of women's flying training. She would oversee a second organization that focused on training women who had less than five hundred hours of flying time.

Love's women didn't need much training. But there were only about three thousand women pilots in the U.S., and very few of them had more than five hundred hours. Cochran would select women from the larger pool of less-qualified women; they needed only two hundred hours, a requirement lowered in the future. Cochran's women would receive one hundred hours of Army instruction and would fly for Love's unit after they graduated.

Cochran's lower-time pilots needed sixteen weeks of training. The training was at Howard Hughes Airfield (now William P. Hobby Airport), near Houston, Texas. Her trainees were paid $150 per month, rising to $250 after they graduated. The first class in Houston began on Sunday, November 15, 1942.

Arnold wasn't happy with two separate women's organizations; he only agreed to it for expediency. On August 5, 1943, he merged the two groups, creating the Women Airforce Service Pilots, abbreviated WASP. Jacqueline Cochran led the combined organization.

The military had previously used a handful of women pilots as contractors to teach men how to fly small aircraft, but Cochran's and Love's organizations were the first time that women who worked for the government flew military aircraft. The formation of the WASP further cemented their status as military pilots. There was just one problem: the WASP were still government civilians. It was a step above being contractors, but the women were still not in the military.

* * *

Women pilots didn't care about the politics or the names of the women's organizations. They just wanted to serve and fly. Ann Baumgartner was one of them. Her WASP service began in a way similar to other women, but she veered onto a unique path.

Growing up in Plainfield, New Jersey, Baumgartner was a precocious child who took ballet and piano lessons, rode horses, paddled canoes, climbed mountains, and skipped two grades. Her father warned her that smart girls, especially those who liked science, would probably never get married, but Baumgartner ignored his admonitions. During her freshman year at Smith College, she chose zoology and chemistry courses over art and switched her major to pre-med.

After graduating in 1939, Baumgartner traveled to Europe alone and later met up with her mother. Germany's invasion of Poland on September 1 interrupted the sightseeing. The next day, Baumgartner and her mother boarded a U.S.-bound refugee ship in England. After leaving port, a call went out for passengers to help paint the portholes black to reduce the ship's visibility as they passed through now treacherous seas.

Given the uncertain times, Baumgartner put medical school on hold. She landed a job animating medical movies and then conducted research on vitamins. One cloudy day in late 1940, she took a break and climbed to the roof of her office building, where she spotted the silhouette of an aircraft as it prowled across the silvery sky. She imagined doing nothing but piloting that airplane, looking at the world stretching away from her. At that moment, she decided she would learn to fly.

Baumgartner quickly earned her private pilot's license and set her sights on gaining the two hundred hours she needed for a commercial pilot's license. She and another pilot bought a little yellow Piper Cub and flew as much as they could. She also flew with the Civil Air Patrol, conducting patrols, assisting with rescue missions, and taking boys and girls for rides to interest them in aviation.

The war soon crushed Baumgartner's plans. By the summer of 1942, it was virtually impossible to fly a private airplane near the East Coast. But rumors swirled that the Army might start using women pilots.

On September 1, 1942, Baumgartner read Eleanor Roosevelt's "My Day" column, in which the first lady made the case for women pilots. Roosevelt railed against the establishment: "We are in a war and we need to fight it with all our ability and every weapon possible. Women pilots, in this particular case, are a weapon waiting to be used."

Nine days later, Roosevelt got her wish.

Baumgartner was one of twenty-five thousand women who applied for Jacqueline Cochran's training program. After an interview at Cochran's Manhattan apartment, Baumgartner received the best Christmas present ever: orders to report to Houston in January for Army flight training.

The bleak facility that greeted Baumgartner in Houston disappointed. Instead of the rows of shiny military training aircraft with a nearby chow hall and barracks she had imagined, she found dilapidated civilian airplanes and a ramshackle hangar. The trainees stayed in a hotel, two women to a room.

Early training was a slog. The male instructors hated the women. But the women found salvation in Lieutenant Alfred Fleischman, a supply officer on the airfield. He led them through calisthenics, taught them how to march, and turned them into a proud team. Then, finally, some real military trainers—PT-19s and BT-13s—arrived, the same planes the men learned to fly. New instructors with better attitudes arrived as well.

Figure 3: Four members of the Women Airforce Service Pilots (WASP) plan a cross-country flight. (Courtesy of National Archives and Records Administration)

A bout with the measles interrupted Baumgartner's flying dreams for a few months. After she recovered, she joined another class. By now, the women had moved to Avenger Field in Sweetwater, Texas, which was a real Army base, complete with barracks, a chow hall, and a small infirmary.

On August 30, 1943, less than two weeks before graduation, disaster struck Baumgartner's class. Two trainees, Margaret Seip and Helen Severson, along with their instructor, Calvin Atwood, departed on a night cross-country flight in a twin-engine training aircraft. Seip wasn't scheduled for the evening flight; she had volunteered that morning to replace another pilot. Ten miles north of Big Spring, Texas, the trainer suffered a structural failure and crashed. All three pilots were killed.

The accident lay bare one of the problems created for the WASP because they weren't in the military. For civil servants, the government did not pay to return remains and belongings to families. Still in mourning, Baumgartner and her classmates took up a collection to send the women and their possessions home.

Baumgartner and her remaining classmates graduated on September 11, 1943. Of the 127 women who began training, 85 graduated. Jacqueline Cochran awarded wings to each woman. The Big Spring Bombardier School Band provided the music.

After graduation, the women scattered to bases across the U.S. Baumgartner and another WASP, Betty Greene, went to the tow-target squadron at Camp Davis, North Carolina to replace two women who had been killed in accidents.

Baumgartner enjoyed the variety of flying. One day she might fly an A-24 dive bomber at ten thousand feet above the ground while trainees tracked her with radars. The next day she might bounce around at treetop level in a tiny L-5 liaison aircraft while men tracked her with artillery. She also towed cloth targets behind a B-34 bomber and flew radio-controlled drones.

Although the men at Camp Davis did not welcome the women pilots, not all the men they encountered were hostile. One day, Baumgartner and several others landed in a formation of A-25 dive bombers at a Navy base on Manteo Island in North Carolina's Outer Banks. The women taxied to the ramp, shut down their engines, and climbed out. The young linemen sent to greet them stopped

dead when they realized the pilots were women. They shouted, "Girls! What can we do for you ladies?" The linemen confirmed the women had landed on the airfield's short runway used to simulate an aircraft carrier. They proclaimed, "You can consider yourselves carrier pilots now!"

After a few months at Camp Davis, Baumgartner and Betty Greene reported for temporary duty to the Army's Aeromedical Lab at Wright Field near Dayton, Ohio, home to the Wright brothers who had flown the first airplane forty years earlier. Colonel Randy Lovelace, the lab director, wanted to test cold weather flight clothing and study the impacts of high altitude flying and g-forces on women. The women were also asked to design and test something more fundamental: a tube for women to relieve themselves on long flights.

Baumgartner and Greene found the research fascinating. They wanted to transfer to Wright Field to fly the plethora of aircraft that littered the ramp: at least seven different types of fighter aircraft, along with bombers, cargo airplanes, and helicopters. Another bonus: Wright Field attracted aviation royalty. Orville Wright, dressed in his iconic coat and hat, often made the short drive across Dayton to talk "aviation" with the test pilots.

The colonel in charge of the Flight Test Division was open to the idea of employing the WASP. Greene ultimately decided to stay at Camp Davis, but Baumgartner arrived back at Wright Field in March 1944. The male pilots greeted her warmly, with curiosity and interest. Just as I learned four decades later, with a few exceptions, men in the business of testing airplanes had much smaller egos than their counterparts who flew aircraft in daily operations.

Over the next few months, Baumgartner became part of the team, although she kept her distance socially from the men and had a policy of not dating her fellow pilots. But some wives were suspicious. One day Baumgartner overheard a pilot on the phone say to his wife, "Oh, you don't need to worry. She's only interested in flying." She wasn't sure if that was a compliment, but she wasn't concerned about her supposed lack of femininity.

Figure 4: WASP Ann Baumgartner at Wright Field in 1944. (Courtesy of Peter Carl and the Ann Carl Collection)

Baumgartner's first test flight was of a device mounted on the tail of an airplane that would warn a pilot when another aircraft was nearby. Another pilot flew his fighter aircraft slowly while Baumgartner zoomed her dive bomber at his tail from all different angles. The flying sure beat towing a cloth target.

On another mission, Baumgartner flew to an island in Lake Erie to test a new gunsight on a P-51. Her instructions were to aim for a target on the eastern tip of the island and make several high-speed passes while firing the gun. The pilot who briefed her added, "But

first you'll have to clear the fishermen out of the area. Just buzz them and shoot off the guns. They'll get the message. They know they're not supposed to be there."

Sure enough, there were fishermen. She did as she'd been told, wondering what the fishermen would have thought if they knew a woman was shooting over their heads. She was fairly sure she was the only WASP to fire a fighter's guns during the war.

One day, the women's relief tube Baumgartner helped design arrived. It was a small bowl-shaped funnel that could be positioned inside her flight suit and accessed via a crotch zipper or buttons. She chose a dive bomber for the test and was taxiing out when she was called back to the ramp. The lineman told her to take up an enlisted man who needed flying time.

Baumgartner took off and flew around, trying to figure out how she was going to do her test with a corporal in her rear cockpit. Using her rearview mirror, she decided he couldn't see into her cockpit, so she unbuttoned her flight suit and attached the device's long tube to the receptacle used by the men. She looked back at the mirror to see what the corporal was up to. He was looking outside, so Baumgartner placed the device inside her flight suit, careful not to rock the airplane. She managed to relieve herself and didn't feel anything spill, so she figured it must have worked. She put the device away and buttoned up, with the corporal none the wiser.

The device worked, but the Air Force didn't adopt it. Eight decades later, military women who fly high-performance aircraft still have a tough time when nature calls.

Baumgartner's best flight was yet to come. Rumors abounded that there was a secret jet fighter being tested somewhere, and that one might be coming to Wright Field for evaluation. The rumors were true. The XP-59A, powered by two turbo-jet engines, had made its first flight under great secrecy on October 1, 1942, from Muroc Army Air Field, later named Edwards Air Force Base, in Southern California. After initial evaluations, the Army ordered thirteen pre-production aircraft and sent one to Wright Field.

The new colonel in charge of fighter flight test announced who would fly the jet: "certain FFT pilots, and that includes the WASP, who will be the first woman to fly a jet aircraft."

The pilots all flew the jet on the same day: October 14, 1944. The first engine start was memorable: black smoke and red flames shot out the back of the airplane as each of the two engines ignited. The first engine start blew the project's secrecy: everyone on the base could hear the undeniable screech of a jet.

The flights were short; the jet only carried about thirty minutes of fuel. Finally, it was Baumgartner's turn. At the end of the runway, she pushed up the throttles "to a high scream," and the jet lumbered along, its underpowered first-generation engines struggling with every inch. Finally, she was airborne.

With the engine noise behind her instead of up front, the jet was much quieter than a propeller aircraft. As she slid silently through the air, it struck Baumgartner that she was likely in the only jet flying in the United States that day. She certainly was the only woman flying a jet. She had time for just a few maneuvers before she headed back and landed. Given the secrecy of the aircraft, there were no crowds to greet her, just the other pilots. It would be another decade before a second U.S. woman—Jacqueline Cochran—flew a jet.

Figure 5: YP-59A jet aircraft, model flown by Ann Baumgartner in 1944. (Bill Larkins, Wikimedia Commons)

The month that brought the exhilarating jet flight also brought devastating news. The WASP would be disbanded in two months, just before Christmas. Cochran had battled since the first days of her program to get the women military status. But she flatly rejected

suggestions that the WASP be incorporated into the WAC; she even threatened to resign if that happened. She claimed that "women pilots were a very temperamental group, and the administration of the program should be in the hands of one who understood them and their peculiar problems—that is, another pilot." Certainly not Oveta Culp Hobby.

Even with support from Hap Arnold and others, the WASP had an uphill battle. The good news of lower-than-expected combat losses meant there was no shortage of male pilots. There was even a surplus, and men complained that women were stealing their jobs. On June 21, 1944, Congress voted against legislation to give the WASP military status. Women who had expected to enter a class on June 30 were sent home. Existing WASP continued flying, but Arnold realized the women were no longer needed. On October 1, 1944, he ordered Cochran to deactivate the WASP no later than December 20.

Cochran had lost, but she didn't want the women's accomplishments to be forgotten. A month before the disbandment, she praised the WASP during remarks to the National Aviation Conference in Oklahoma City: "I have not the slightest doubt but that these WASPs could have gone, if that were necessary, into combat work, fearlessly and effectively, just as Russian women have done."

In her final report, dated June 1, 1945, Cochran wrote that 1,074 women had graduated from the WASP training, and 900 of them—83.6 percent—remained employed with the program at the time of deactivation. Of the 1,830 women inducted, 58.7 percent finished their training, a completion rate favorable with the men. Thirty-eight women died, either during training or during operational flying, a fatality rate also comparable to men. The women proved they could do a wide variety of flying, from ferrying aircraft and towing targets to instrument instruction and simulated strafing missions. They flew almost every type of aircraft in the Army inventory, from light trainers to the massive B-29 Superfortress bomber, along with fighter aircraft such as the P-51 Mustang.

Cochran also recommended that congressional action be taken to provide veterans' benefits to the WASP who finished the program in good standing. It would take Congress another three decades to act on that recommendation.

<p align="center">✱ ✱ ✱</p>

At the end of the war, the services discharged about 90 percent of those serving. Women were supposed to be discharged within six months of the end of the war, but a few were held back for an orderly transition. Many people, especially military leadership, believed there was a long-term role for women.

The National Security Act of 1947, passed on July 26, overhauled the structure of the armed services and intelligence organizations. The act merged the War Department and Navy Department to create the Department of Defense, with oversight of all the services. The act also spun off the Army Air Forces into a new service, the United States Air Force. Women were not mentioned.

Congress debated the fate of women for nearly another year, even though a bevy of prominent military leadership—James V. Forrestal, Dwight D. Eisenhower, Omar N. Bradley, Chester W. Nimitz, Carl A. "Tooey" Spaatz, Hoyt S. Vandenberg—testified in favor of keeping the women. Finally, on June 2, 1948, Congress passed Public Law 625, the Women's Armed Services Integration Act, which gave women permanent status in the military.

However, Congress and the services did not want women serving in large numbers; they wanted a foundation to build on quickly during an emergency. Thus, the law was far from perfect from a woman's perspective. The number of women was limited to 2 percent of the overall force, only one woman in each corps could be a full colonel, and, with the exception of the Air Force, women were promoted separately from the men, potentially reducing women's promotion opportunities.

But the part of the act having to do with combat would have the largest impact on the future of military women. Almost no one at the time seriously considered that women could be in combat. Quite the opposite: Congress wanted to make sure they stayed away from combat and insisted on writing that into the law. The Army, with the potential for wide-ranging circumstances and areas of operations, could not come up with an easy definition of combat, so they were excused from being included in the law, with the understanding that they would write policies to ensure women didn't engage in combat.

Things were simpler for the Air Force and Navy: just keep women out of cockpits and off ships. The law stated that women "may not be assigned to duty in aircraft while such aircraft are engaged in combat missions" nor "may they be assigned to duty on vessels of the Navy except hospital ships and naval transports."

The language would haunt women for the next five decades.

CHAPTER 2
Cinderella Is Dead! (1950s and 1960s)

In June 1948, the Department of Defense sent Jeanne Holm, a former Army officer, a letter asking if she wanted to rejoin the military. The envelope included a postcard she could return if she was interested. Holm had more than a year of school remaining at Lewis & Clark College in Portland, Oregon. But she believed in keeping her options open. The card had a spot for her to check off which service interested her. Always curious about aviation, she checked the "Air Force" box, mailed the card, and promptly forgot about it. A few weeks later, she received a notice to report to Fort Lewis, Washington, to apply for permanent Army status.

Holm had been in the same Army training class as Emma Riley. Born on June 23, 1921, only ten months after the Nineteenth Amendment to the U.S. Constitution became law, Holm never knew a time when women couldn't vote. She also turned twenty-one just in time to enlist in the first wave of Army women in 1942, leading Lewis and others to nickname her "Junior."

The middle child of John Elza and Marjorie Pearl, Holm preferred playing with boys as she grew up in a comfortable middle-class neighborhood of wooden houses in southeast Portland. Her brothers, John and Dale, were in a small "gang" of neighborhood kids that allowed Jeanne in as the only girl. One day, word arrived that another gang of kids was coming over to fight. Everyone loaded up on ammunition and took up defensive positions. Jeanne climbed

to the roof of the Holm house. When the enemy appeared, she bombarded the boys with water balloons. But Holm wasn't content to be a follower. In addition to the neighborhood gang, she started a club with her brothers dubbed the JDJs, using the siblings' initials. She was clearly the leader.

Holm's father died unexpectedly in 1929. The family moved frequently as her mother scraped together a living working at grocery stores. Sometimes they relied on public assistance. When Holm was fifteen, her mother remarried, and life stabilized.

During high school, Holm took general studies, not college prep courses, but her 1940 senior yearbook photo displayed a glimmer of potential. Next to her photo, the brunette with a broad, toothy smile listed one accomplishment: "Gym Leader."

Holm parlayed high school art classes into a job as an assistant for the only woman silversmith in the United States, who lived in Portland. Holm did some jewelry work but mostly made large silver pieces such as trays and tea sets.

As the U.S. inched closer to war, Holm joined the Oregon Women's Ambulance Corps, a volunteer organization. The ambulance corps operated much like the military: the women had uniforms and did infantry drills. The Portland Fire Department taught them first aid and how to drive trucks. Holm taught a course on how internal combustion engines work.

After the Pearl Harbor attack, Holm desperately wanted to join the military. Her father had been a Marine during World War I, and her brothers were called to active duty in the Navy.

With the Women's Army Auxiliary Corps formation in May 1942, Holm didn't have to wait long. Given her family tradition of sea service, she preferred to join the Navy, but didn't want to wait for them to form a women's organization. Her brothers were less than thrilled with her enlistment, but her mother and grandmother were enthusiastic; they would have joined had they been younger.

In August 1942, Holm took a two-day, un-air-conditioned train ride to Fort Des Moines, Iowa. As she lay in her bunk in the converted stable that night, she stared up into the cavernous ceiling and thought, *My God, what have I done?*

The next morning, the Army dispelled her doubts. A bugle playing reveille woke her, and a woman with a heavy Texas drawl

yelled, "All right everybody, hit the deck!" Holm leaped from her cot. The women felt like pioneers, and it wasn't long before the goddess Hobby herself visited and said they were indeed making history.

After basic training, Holm had three choices: clerk/typist, cook, or truck driver. She had little interest in the first two options, but she knew how to drive a truck. The Army assigned her to the motor pool, and after a few months, she was selected for officer training. After being commissioned, she rode the train with Emma Riley to Fort Oglethorpe. Holm spent the rest of the war training other women. By the time she was discharged, she was a captain and had been a regimental commander, in charge of eighteen basic training companies and hundreds of women. She was not yet twenty-four years old.

Released from active duty in 1946, Holm returned to Portland and attended college using her veteran's benefits from the World War II-era G.I. Bill. Her official major was art; her unofficial major was skiing.

Figure 6: Captain Jeanne Holm at Fort Lee, Virginia, after returning to active duty in the U.S. Air Force, about 1948. (Courtesy of the U.S. Air Force)

* * *

The second letter from the Department of Defense surprised Holm; she wasn't really serious about going back into the military. But she was between semesters at college, and the Army was just asking her to apply to return to active duty, not ordering her back in, so she drove three hours north to Fort Lewis. There she ran into several women she had known in the Army who had already returned to active duty, and they made Holm nostalgic. That night, as the bugle call of *Taps* wafted into her room, she thought, *I just love this*. The next morning, she applied to go back on active duty.

Holm returned to Portland and began her classes that fall. She didn't have the nerve to tell her friends or family what she had done. Her brothers had come to respect her service during the war, but the war was over. Everyone was supposed to get on with their lives. And the Army might not approve her application anyway, so why get anyone riled up?

Within a few weeks, Holm received another envelope: the Army wanted her back. She dropped out of college and drove to a new training center at Fort Lee, Virginia. She was so broke, she slept in her car during the cross-country trek.

Holm was immediately put in charge of a company, but something was amiss. She had applied for a regular appointment in the Army, which came with more rights than a reserve appointment and ensured a military career. But when the list for regular appointments came out, Holm wasn't on it. Her commander called the Pentagon and discovered that the Air Force had claimed Holm, who had forgotten all about that little box she'd checked on the postcard months earlier. The fledgling Air Force refused to let her go.

Holm didn't mind switching; she needed new uniforms anyway. Even better, the Air Force sent her to Erding Air Base, a depot in West Germany. When she arrived, her superior officers had no idea what to do with her, an experienced officer who knew nothing about the Air Force.

A lieutenant colonel suggested Holm train for a supply or maintenance position. If that didn't interest her, how about war plans? "War plans" had a nice ring to it. She dove into the fray of planning the ongoing Berlin Airlift, which continued through September

1949. After the airlift died down, Holm designed plans to defend Erding against an attack by the Soviet Union.

As Holm honed her planning skills, she picked up a mentor, a male colonel who advised her on career possibilities. In 1952, the Air Force promoted her to major, launching her into the "field-grade" ranks, a rung above the company-grade officer ranks of lieutenant or captain. Field-grade officers hold command positions in field units or serve in staff positions at the Pentagon or other headquarters, learning to navigate military bureaucracy.

But before Holm could become part of the bureaucracy, it turned against her. Someone decided she could not be a war plans officer; that was considered an operational job and was too close to a combat job, even though it involved sitting at a desk inside a steel vault. The Air Force stripped Holm of her war plans specialty code and gave her the specialty she dreaded most: administration.

But what should the Air Force do with its new admin officer? Someone decided she should attend the Air Command and Staff College, so off she went to Maxwell Air Force Base in Alabama. The move indicated the potential Holm's superiors thought she had for future promotions, but she was the first woman to attend the school, and not everyone was happy with her presence. Worse, most of the other 499 students were pilots well-versed in the ways of the Air Force. Holm was still catching up. She didn't even know that the nuclear arm of the Air Force was named the Strategic Air Command, usually called SAC. In later years she quipped, "I thought SAC was a paper bag!"

Holm ignored those who didn't like her and became friends with the others, including students from Italy, Turkey, Korea, and Pakistan. One classmate later became the chief of staff for the Italian Air Force.

After graduating from the staff college, Holm transferred to the Pentagon to work for the director of the Women in the Air Force, or WAF. She arrived to a WAF in disarray, a disarray precipitated by the Korean War, but also at least partially caused by someone whose name was well known in aviation circles: Jacqueline Cochran.

*　　*　　*

On June 25, 1950, North Korean forces invaded South Korea. The U.S. again moved into a war footing. Forces poured into South Korea to beat back the offensive. The services recalled former officers to active duty to serve in critical positions. Former WASP were included in the recall; although they had not attained active military status, the Army had placed them in a reserve status when they had been released from their civilian jobs.

In 1951, the Air Force recalled former WASP Yvonne C. Pateman and commissioned her as a first lieutenant. Barred from flying, Pateman became an intelligence officer. But she couldn't go to Korea: other than nurses, military women weren't allowed in the combat zone. Pateman was assigned to Hamilton Air Force Base near San Francisco, where she briefed pilots before they headed to Korea on threats and tactics to expect; she debriefed them when they returned to add their experiences to the Air Force's evolving understanding of the enemy. It wasn't as fun as flying, but Pateman knew the information she passed along could save a pilot's life. Her background as a pilot helped her credibility; the male pilots accepted her more readily than they did the other WAF.

The pilots' wives were a different story. While later stationed in Alaska, Pateman's commander referred to her as "my China watcher" when he introduced her to his wife. The term meant Pateman was his expert on what the Chinese military and political leadership were up to on any given day. His wife's reply reflected a common attitude toward the WAF: "Oh, that's great. It's about time they found a job for women in the service—in the kitchen watching the china."

But the men who worked with Pateman and other WAF didn't think that way, and they agreed on two things: the women did a great job, and they wanted more of them.

At the outbreak of the Korean War, women made up only about fifteen thousand active-duty members, less than 1 percent of the military. Anticipating a flood of women volunteers like that seen during World War II, Congress temporarily removed the 2 percent ceiling they had enacted in 1948. The services picked a lofty goal for July 1952: an additional seventy-two thousand women. The Air Force was expected to contribute a little more than half the increase.

The recruiting job fell to WAF director Colonel Geraldine May. Born in 1895, May had been two years past the Army's age cutoff when she applied for officer training in 1942. Somehow, she slipped through and graduated with the first class of officers.

During the war, May traveled to China, India, and Africa helping to set up new bases. During the fall of 1946, the new Women's Army Corps director, Mary Hallaren, contacted May and said that if the Air Force became a separate service, they wanted her back. Hallaren believed May was the logical choice to be the director of the WAF. May returned to active duty on October 1 and headed to Washington, D.C. She thought women had made a significant contribution during the war and saw no reason why they shouldn't stay in the military.

After the Office of the Director, Women in the Air Force, was established in June of 1948, May was promoted to full colonel and appointed as the first director. When she met General Hoyt Vandenberg, the chief of staff of the Air Force, he said, "You were not my choice as Director of WAF but the military wanted you, so I gave in."

May knew Vandenberg had wanted Jacqueline Cochran.

The era was a time of transition for military women. There was no precedent for establishing and maintaining a small peacetime force of women to build on in a crisis. May and the other women directors had no playbook; they made things up as they went along.

May focused initially on fitting women into the all-male Air Force as much as possible. She did it slowly and carefully; with the women's presence still precarious, she didn't want to make anyone mad.

The biggest problem at first was obtaining new uniforms as the World War II stock dwindled, especially as the spike in recruits depleted uniforms much faster than planned. With uniforms expected to run out by March 1951, May cut the number of enlistees from five hundred in September 1950 to none in December.

May had gotten approval to proceed with a new uniform in August 1950, but the procurement became bogged down by government contracting processes. The contract wasn't even negotiated until December, with delivery of only a summer-weight uniform expected in March 1951; other uniforms were still in the works.

The WAF also faced issues in recalling women to support the buildup. Many of the women recalled now had minor children,

making them ineligible for reenlistment; the women had to be discharged. The problem was particularly acute with former WASP, who had been allowed to serve during World War II even if they had children under eighteen. When the WASP had been given their reserve appointments, no one had checked for children.

May was trying to correct the WAF issues, but her position was buried under layers of Pentagon bureaucracy; she rarely spoke to the Air Force's top brass. She had no idea Vandenberg had any concerns.

In October 1950, Vandenberg asked Jacqueline Cochran to conduct an independent assessment of the WAF to ensure the program provided a "sound basis for expansion in wartime." In addition to an overall review, Vandenberg's memo to Cochran stated: "I am especially interested in Miss Cochran's advise [sic] on our flight nurses, in-flight clothing and equipment, and the functional clothing and equipment of other skilled women specialists."

Cochran spent six weeks on her independent review, focusing on new recruits at Lackland Air Force Base near San Antonio, Texas. Her ten-page report, dated December 6, 1950, set off explosions in the Pentagon. During her time at Lackland, Cochran had encountered an overweight WAF recruit who also had the misfortune of being cross-eyed. Cochran wrote that she was told this particular recruit was not unusual. She recommended the Air Force adopt Navy-style recruiting "to cut down materially the misfits that are now getting into the program…"

After using the "misfits" slur twice in three pages, Cochran continued her attacks. The old stocks of World War II uniforms had led to "the most tattered, bedraggled persons I have ever seen in the services…. The fatigue uniforms…were of at least six different varieties and were exceedingly poor in appearance and unattractive. These WAFs are certainly anything but a credit to the Air Force…"

Some of Cochran's recommendations were almost comical: she suggested the term "fatigue" clothing be changed to "functional" clothing, and she proposed sending one hundred enlisted women to secretarial school. About the only helpful recommendation was that the women's program be strengthened by appointing a permanent special assistant to the chief of staff of the Air Force or the secretary of the Air Force. Some thought this recommendation was

self-serving; it appeared Cochran might be angling for the special assistant job herself.

Cochran failed to back up her allegations with anything beyond anecdotal evidence, and she never addressed the issue Vandenberg had asked about: the special equipment and clothing some women needed. Most military reports devoid of data and analysis are quickly rendered to the dustbin, but the former WASP leader's stature and perhaps some preconceived notions on the part of Air Force leadership gave the report some staying power.

May had been working on fixes to most of the problems the report pointed out, but other Pentagon officers felt the need to do more. Some suggested pulling the WAF out of the integrated Air Force and making them a separate unit like the other services. Although Vandenberg found a separate women's corps acceptable, May objected. She believed women should be as fully integrated as possible, to include a single promotion list for men and women. Even though women might be at a disadvantage when competing with men, May feared a separate list would lead to limits on how many women could be promoted.

By early June, the Air Force had decided to keep an integrated WAF but to get rid of May. They announced she was resigning as WAF director effective June 11 "for personal reasons." This was news to both May and her friends.

The Air Force simultaneously announced May's replacement: Mary Josephine Shelly, who had been a Navy WAVE during World War II. As a civilian, she had held high-level administrative positions at several colleges. Shelly's appointment disheartened some WAF officers who hoped for a promotion from their own ranks. At least it wasn't Cochran. Vandenberg and the secretary of the Air Force, Thomas K. Finletter, may have realized that Cochran was too toxic to be put in charge, or perhaps Cochran didn't want the job.

The press, sensing a scandal behind May's abrupt resignation, began sniffing around. Cochran's report had not been made public, but Drew Pearson, an influential newspaper columnist, dug up a copy. His column, which detailed Cochran's descriptions of "tattered" and "bedraggled" WAF, hit the street about a week after May's resignation. Indignant WAF fought back. Pearson reported

that WAF started calling Cochran "Stonewall Jacky." They also questioned her impartiality as an outsider, given that her husband owned Consolidated Vultee, the contractor that sold B-36 bomber aircraft to the Air Force.

The result of what Air Force leaders considered a "sorority spat" was a mixed bag. The WAF remained integrated with the rest of the Air Force. The WAF director position was strengthened, with a clear set of responsibilities and improved access to the top Air Force leadership. But overall, women gained nothing. And as they nursed their wounds, an even bigger problem caused by the recruiting push was brewing.

<p style="text-align:center">*　　*　　*</p>

As the services tried to bump up recruiting, Anna M. Rosenberg, the assistant secretary of defense for manpower affairs, convinced George C. Marshall to create a committee to advise the armed forces on how to best bring tens of thousands of new women into the military. On August 11, 1951, the duo announced the creation of the Defense Advisory Committee on Women in the Services, abbreviated DACOWITS. The initial committee membership consisted of forty-eight women with varied backgrounds: "education, business, medicine, journalism, radio, stage, civic and social service, dietetics, and personnel management." The women did not have any significant military background, except for Oveta Culp Hobby. Rosenberg expected the women to act as individuals and not represent any organization or faction. In addition to the immediate problem of recruiting, the committee would look at issues such as training, housing, and education.

The women got to work in a hurry. On September 17, they met in Washington, D.C., for a three-day meeting. Senior officials, including Marshall in his last speech as secretary of defense, addressed the women on everything from budgets to overseas housing. Hoyt Vandenberg told them he wanted forty-five thousand more women in the Air Force and promised they would be treated equally with men when it came to promotions.

The next day, the women directors urged caution with the recruiting goals. Army Colonel Mary Hallaren told the committee

that the numbers they wanted to recruit in the next ten months were more than they had recruited during all of World War II. She pointed out that trying to quickly recruit women in times of emergency was not a good strategy; better to have a ready-made flow of women that might even include a draft. Despite the caution, DACOWITS members increased the already lofty goal for new women recruits from 80,000 to nearly 113,000.

On November 11, 1951, after Mary Josephine Shelly had been the WAF director for only five months, President Truman announced the new recruiting push. His Armistice Day speech implored young women: "There is nothing more constructive that young women in the United States can do for themselves and for their country than answer the call to service with our armed forces. This is a way—a real, direct, and positive way—that they can help secure the peace and safeguard freedom in the world."

But women didn't buy it. The patriotism that propelled many to join the fight in World War II didn't translate to a skirmish that didn't threaten the U.S. homeland. Also, low birth rates during the Depression had reduced the supply of younger women, and most of them could make more money as civilians. These problems applied to men as well, but men could be drafted.

One year into the recruiting campaign, Shelly lowered the Air Force's goal from about forty-six thousand enlisted women to about twelve thousand. Six months later, as the fighting on the Korean Peninsula came to a halt, the enlisted force was only about half that, leading the three-star general at the Pentagon in charge of Air Force personnel to question whether it was worth maintaining a women's enlisted force at all. Shelly convinced the general to save the WAF, but the recruiting failure ignited a smoldering, decade-long war against women in the military, especially the Air Force.

The argument against women in the Air Force centered on the draft. As long as the peacetime draft existed, the services believed they could meet all their requirements with men, since the threat of the draft convinced many young men to volunteer for a service other than the Army. Of all the services, the Air Force believed it needed women the least. The Air Force was the most coveted service for those trying to avoid being drafted since, except for aviators and a handful of other positions, most Air Force personnel were unlikely

to experience direct combat. Thus, the Air Force could be pickier about the quality of the men they enlisted. One of the main arguments for women in the military was that they were of higher quality than male recruits, raising the overall quality of enlisted force. But if the Air Force could get all the high-quality men they needed, why did they need women?

The Department of Defense's 1950s strategy of "massive retaliation" rendered the women's programs even more precarious. The Air Force needed only a few crews (all male, of course) to launch nuclear weapons from strategic bombers and missile silos, so why bother with women? Air War College student papers argued against the WAF, and General Curtis LeMay, the gruff bomber pilot who ran the Air Force both as vice chief and then chief in the late 1950s and early 1960s, was reported to be anti-women. It's not clear that LeMay was actually against women, but the air staff behaved as if he was, a case where lower-level personnel may have made assumptions that agreed with their prejudices so they could carry out their own agendas. Within a few months of LeMay's arrival in 1957, Emma Riley, who was now WAF director, was ordered to again reevaluate the WAF program.

Before Riley could finish her study, the women were attacked from yet another direction. In the spring of 1958, with a budget shortfall looming, the Air Force needed to make a small reduction in their 734,000-strong force. Jettisoning the roughly seven thousand WAF was an easy way to meet the goal. Fortunately, Riley's study found that commanders in the field wanted more women, not fewer, especially in nontraditional fields such as statistical analysis and data processing. But Riley, bowing to pressure, conceded that a reduced ceiling of five thousand WAF was feasible.

The women were saved again, but their wings were clipped. The Air Force started removing women from nontraditional fields and limiting the bases where they could be assigned. A woman was transferred from the control tower at Maxwell Air Force Base after some men claimed that women's voices were hard to understand. Not all men agreed; the move outraged many pilots.

The women removed from their jobs were retrained into administrative and clerical positions. The removals impacted only about 4 percent of the enlisted force—about three hundred women—but the

impact on morale across the thousands of WAF was huge. Given their limited roles, the women were increasingly segregated from the rest of the Air Force. It was like relegating the second string on a high school football team to the cheerleading squad: an important role, no doubt, but no longer part of the team.

At one especially low point, Riley briefed General LeMay on where WAF members were stationed throughout Europe. LeMay told her, "I think they should all be brought home because in the event of war they [will] be captured."

Riley pointed out that it would be difficult to bring all the women home at once but said she could do a gradual withdrawal. LeMay asked her to think about it.

As Riley walked back to her office, another general who had been in the meeting asked her, "Why didn't you tell him that they [aren't] in any more danger than the wives and children [who live with service members in Europe]?" The women stayed.

With each staff study, the enlisted women lost a little ground. No one asked about women officers, but Riley was sure that if enlisted women were eliminated, that would also bring the demise of the officers.

In the spring of 1961, a colonel at the Pentagon made yet another run at killing the WAF. But by then, military women had gained an unexpected ally: Carl Vinson, a senator who a decade earlier had insisted that women could not serve on ships. The colonel quietly dropped the idea, but still recommended the WAF be reduced to fifteen hundred women. Secretary of the Air Force Eugene Zuckert stepped in to prevent any further reductions below five thousand, but he did nothing to increase the number. The WAF continued its downward slide until it reached an all-time low of forty-seven hundred in 1965.

Even as bureaucracy tried to kill the WAF again and again, it may have been bureaucracy that saved it. Government programs, especially those enacted by Congress, are almost impossible to kill.

* * *

Claire Griffith listened in disbelief as her father screamed over the phone, "You'll become a whore!"

The twenty-year-old wanted to join the Air Force, but because she wasn't yet twenty-one, one of her parents had to sign her enlistment papers. She couldn't convince her mother, who suggested they wait for her father's call that evening when his ship docked in San Francisco on the way back to Seattle.

Griffith had expected a hearty yes from her father. After all, for years she had heard her father tell her younger brother, "Before you do anything in life, it's your responsibility to serve in the military." Griffith assumed that direction applied to her too. She planned to serve before attending college. Her mother wasn't too keen on college, but she admitted it might be a great place for Griffith to find a husband.

Born a month after the attack on Pearl Harbor, Griffith grew up along the West Coast. Her father, a civilian with the Navy, installed and maintained top secret radio towers around the Pacific. He was gone for months at a time.

In high school, Griffith worked as a nurse's aide. She started nursing school on a scholarship but after a year decided the profession wasn't for her. Plus, she remembered her father's admonition about serving her country. She decided to join the Air Force. If she had been a man, she could have waltzed into a recruiter's office and signed up. As a woman, she was too young, but she didn't think a parent's signature would be an issue.

Apparently, her father believed those old stories from the smear campaign. It was only then that Griffith realized his advice had been meant just for her brother, not her.

Griffith's mother was still reluctant to sign. But Griffith said, "If you don't sign me in tomorrow, you will never see me again." Her mother folded.

While Griffith waited for her final acceptance, she visited the 1962 World's Fair in Seattle. She rode the monorail and took the elevator to the top of the Space Needle. It was heady times: John Glenn had orbited the earth eight months earlier, and almost no one in the U.S. had heard of Vietnam.

Basic training was eight weeks at Lackland Air Force Base. Griffith's nursing skills proved useful at making the right-angle bed corners so coveted in the military. But nursing school also proved a hindrance; the Air Force turned her into a medic, although she

had hoped to do something different. After basic training, she was assigned to the hospital at Amarillo Air Force Base in the Texas Panhandle. Howling winds rushed through the cracks in the uninsulated wooden World War II barracks where she lived.

Figure 7: Airman First Class Claire Griffith, Women in the Air Force member who served 1962–1966. (Courtesy of the Claire Griffith Collection)

The Amarillo hospital had lots of women, mostly nurses, who were all officers, and other enlisted medics like Griffith. But the doctors respected all the women, regardless of rank. Amarillo's primary

mission of training aircraft mechanics wasn't the "real Air Force," which made for a somewhat relaxed atmosphere. But within a year, Griffith married a dental technician and moved to Spangdahlem Air Base in West Germany.

Spangdahlem was nothing like Amarillo. The base had an operational mission: a fighter wing that deployed aircrews to the growing action in Southeast Asia. The clinic's primary mission was to deploy with the fighter wing if needed. She was now in the "real Air Force."

When Griffith arrived in Germany, a senior noncommissioned officer, Master Sergeant Pence, interviewed her. After exchanging a few pleasantries, he said, "You know, Claire, it's good to have you here. But you're not as good as the men. The men are qualified for remote duty." The men could deploy, and she couldn't. Or so he thought.

Griffith blurted out, "Sergeant Pence, I'm a five-oh. I'm qualified for remote duty."

Pence jumped up, snatched her paperwork, threw open the door, and sprinted upstairs. Griffith sat there with no idea what to do. When Pence returned, he said the clinic's commander had confirmed she was indeed qualified for remote duty. Pence wasn't very friendly after that.

A few months later, Griffith and her husband attended a party. Pence was there, drinking along with everyone else. Even though Griffith's husband was at the party, Pence kissed Griffith, and implied his wife was okay with it. Griffith wasn't offended; she was even a little flattered that Pence found her attractive. But she wasn't interested, and she was careful at work when they were alone.

Pence responded to her lack of interest the way a six-year-old might: he punched her on her left arm whenever he saw her. It wasn't unusual for men to greet each other with teasing punches, but Pence hit Griffith so hard at times that she couldn't use her arm until the shock wore off after a few minutes. She didn't know how to make Pence stop. As the only enlisted woman in the clinic, she had no role models or mentors to seek out for advice. The other two women were nurses, who as officers seemed out of reach to a young airman.

But other people were paying attention. One day after Pence punched Griffith, a doctor stormed from his office, pushed Pence against the wall, and said, "I told you to leave her alone." The base commander's wife, who did volunteer work at the clinic, had taken

notice. She told her husband, and the base's legal department started an investigation.

At first, Griffith was happy for the help. But an attorney who interviewed her made her feel as if she were somehow responsible for Pence's behavior. She refused to cooperate further. Even without her testimony, Pence left the Air Force. Griffith never found out what happened, but he likely was allowed to quietly retire.

The base commander's wife crowed, "We did it!" But Griffith was angry about the hell the investigators put her through.

Griffith and her husband left the Air Force in 1966 after completing their four-year enlistments. The couple moved to his hometown and attended Wichita State University using their G.I. Bills. The benefits were great except for one small detail: the World War II and Korean War G.I. Bills paid married female veterans a lower allowance than married male veterans. Men received an additional allowance for their wives, but women did not receive an additional allowance for their husbands.

Claire Griffith didn't know it, but someone was paying attention to the issues she and other women encountered both in and out of the military: the Defense Advisory Committee on Women in the Services. And DACOWITS was becoming more vocal with time.

* * *

For women in the military, the 1950s had been at best a period of benign neglect and at worst a period of outright hostility. That began to change in the early 1960s, with the publication of Betty Friedan's *The Feminine Mystique* and passage of the Civil Rights Act of 1964, which outlawed discrimination based on race and a host of other factors, including sex. A change in doctrine ushered in by the Kennedy administration also played a role. "Massive retaliation" was replaced with "flexible response," which encompassed all types of warfare, from small skirmishes to a nuclear exchange between superpowers. The new doctrine clarified the roles women might play in a non-nuclear war, especially in the Air Force. This clarity, along with vocal support from the Kennedy and Johnson administrations, gave military women hope of a brighter future. However, the number of women continued to decline, even as the

services grew in response to military actions around the world. The services continued to rely on the peacetime draft, and Congress extended the draft again and again with little debate.

The women's movement didn't seem concerned about the plight of military women. It's not clear if this was because movement leaders weren't aware of the women's issues, were aware but didn't like the military, or didn't think it worth their time for only about thirty thousand women. And military women had achieved some of feminism's goals: they received equal pay for equal work and, with a few exceptions regarding dependents, received the same benefits as men. Promotion and career field limitations were likely not high on the list of feminist priorities.

Air Force women, who might have looked to Jacqueline Cochran at one time for help in gaining access to additional career fields, knew that was not likely in the cards after her disastrous engagement a decade earlier. To many, she appeared more interested in making a name for herself than in helping other women.

In the early 1950s, Cochran yearned to fly jets and set speed records. She had become an Air Force reservist like many former WASP, but her stature wouldn't get her into Air Force jets: rules were rules.

Cochran's wealth and connections helped her get around the rules. She worked her way into a Canadian-built F-86 fighter jet to set several speed records at Edwards Air Force Base. Chuck Yeager, the first person to fly faster than the speed of sound, trained her for the flights, which required flying at more than five hundred miles per hour about three hundred feet above the ground, around a tight course marked by pylons. It was exhausting work. In 1961, Northrop hired her to fly a T-38 jet trainer they leased back from the Air Force so she could set a speed record of 844 miles per hour, which she later increased to 1,429 miles per hour, flying in an F-104 fighter as a pilot for Lockheed.

Cochran sneered at former WASP who left aviation to become wives and mothers. She seemed to think all women pilots should have found jobs with the airlines or with aircraft manufacturers; in her opinion, they just didn't want to. It didn't seem to occur to her that after World War II, the airlines hired only white males. A few former WASP worked as flight instructors, and corporations

hired a handful as engineers or test pilots, but most women gave up. They weren't married to billionaire husbands who could buy them anything they wanted.

As the space race heated up, it appeared Cochran wanted women in the space program. She funded a project run by Dr. Randy Lovelace, the researcher Ann Baumgartner had worked with during the war, to see if women could pass the tests given to male astronauts. Cochran found twenty women who wanted to try, a number eventually whittled to thirteen.

Lovelace found that the women were as physically and mentally capable as the military test pilots chosen for the Mercury program; the women were soon dubbed the "Mercury 13." When Congress held hearings in July 1962 to discuss astronaut qualifications, some members questioned why NASA wasn't hiring the women. Perhaps they were being discriminated against? In his opening remarks, the subcommittee chair, Victor L. Anfuso, stated, "We are deeply concerned that all human resources be utilized." It was clear he meant both men and women.

One of the Mercury 13, Jerrie Cobb, testified that women have many advantages over men in spaceflight. They are smaller and consume less food in an environment where extra weight is very expensive during the launch phase. Research had also shown that, compared to men, women were more resistant to radiation, less prone to heart attacks, and less susceptible to uncomfortable environmental conditions such as loneliness, pain, and noise, all traits that would come in handy during long space flights.

But Jacqueline Cochran's testimony threw the women out the window. She didn't believe the women were being discriminated against. She believed that astronaut qualifications should be based entirely on "whether such inclusion will speed up, slow down, make more expensive, or complicate" the planned U.S. launch schedule. And there were plenty of qualified men to serve as astronauts. "It follows that present use of women…cannot be based on present need." She believed women were qualified for spaceflight but injecting them into the space program would be too disruptive.

Cochran's solution was to keep the women separated and conduct additional medical tests. She also believed that a very large group of women would be needed, since there would be attrition

from marriage and childbirth. She claimed the attrition rate from marriage in the WASP was 40 percent, although that contradicted her final report, which said more than 80 percent of the WASP who graduated completed their service commitments. Nevertheless, she claimed women astronauts would have the same "high" attrition rate. "We do not want to slow down our program, and you are going to have to, of necessity, waste a great deal of money when you take a large group of women in, because you lose them through marriage. That is why women are not on airplanes.... Airlines spend $50,000 average to check out a pilot on a 707 or Convair 880. That is expensive if you lose them through marriage."

Anfuso then asked Cochran about the astronaut requirements of being a test pilot and having an engineering background. Cochran went back to the argument of cost; it would be a waste of money to train a woman as a test pilot because after she was trained, she would leave to start a family.

The testimony took a bizarre turn when Cochran tried to reconcile her statements with the purpose of the research program. "I am not against women being in [the space] program. Don't misunderstand. I would not have done what I did to get at least a small group a showing." Anfuso pointed out the obvious: "I don't think your testimony indicates that."

Most of the men on the subcommittee seemed truly interested in having women astronauts. But as in the case of the WASP, Cochran's need for control worked against the other women's interests. It would be twenty more years before NASA selected women astronauts. By then, the Mercury 13 were too old.

* * *

In early August 1964, U.S. and North Vietnamese ships skirmished in the Gulf of Tonkin. What had been a relatively small training and advisory role for U.S. forces in Southeast Asia blossomed into a full-out shooting war. U.S. Marines, soldiers, and aircraft flooded into South Vietnam and Thailand; aircraft carriers headed to the Mediterranean Sea changed course for the South China Sea.

In early 1965, female Army nurses arrived in Vietnam to treat mounting casualties. Air Force flight nurses flew to Saigon to coor-

dinate aeromedical evacuation of patients, while other Air Force nurses worked at bases throughout South Vietnam and Thailand. Twenty-nine Navy nurses served on the hospital ship USS *Repose*, which was stationed off the coast of South Vietnam. Within a year, more than three hundred female nurses served in Southeast Asia.

Only two non-nurses initially went to Vietnam. Two Army women, Major Kathleen Wilkes and Master Sergeant Betty Adams, arrived in Saigon in January 1965 to advise South Vietnam's newly minted Women's Armed Forces Corps. The women didn't regularly endure field conditions during their year-long stay, but the electricity in their hotel only worked every other day the last few months of their tour. Wilkes quipped to *Associated Press* reporter Joy Miller, "You get used to candles and walking five flights. It didn't hurt my hipline."

Vietnam's oppressive heat and humidity made it impossible for Wilkes to maintain the feminine appearance favored by her superiors. By lunchtime every day, perspiration soaked her fatigue uniform, and red dust caked her brown hair. She ignored admonitions against "mannish" styles and cut her hair short so she could wash it daily.

Other miliary women itched to serve in the combat zone, but the services dragged their feet, claiming austere conditions and inadequate housing, although women had served in much worse conditions during World War II. After a female veteran of that war was turned down for a Southeast Asia tour, she howled, "I served in North Africa and Italy—I sure as hell can serve in Vietnam."

Because hundreds of civilian women held government jobs in Vietnam or worked for the Red Cross or USO, the reluctance to send line women to Vietnam was puzzling, and columnist Jack Anderson took the military to task in a January 2, 1966, *Parade* article. A complaint from a Women's Army Corps lieutenant summed up the situation: "What kind of delicate creatures do the brass think we are? There's a war going on in Vietnam, but you have to be a civilian to get assigned there...we aren't allowed to dirty our dainty hands."

Anderson blamed Jacqueline Cochran's obsession with appearance for the shift away from "soldiers in skirts" who did just about everything during World War II. He noted that WAC members didn't mind getting their hair mussed. One woman bemoaned that they no longer received weapons training or learned outdoor

skills: "I know some Girl Scouts who are more rugged than we are." Some WAC spent their own money to take riflery and judo classes, learning skills the Army denied them. And women stationed overseas weren't exactly daring either; Anderson noted that most of them "have been sent to safe, snug countries and have been given nothing more dangerous to handle than a typewriter."

By the time Anderson's article ran, dozens of women had been turned down for service in Vietnam. Wilkes and Adams had been replaced by two other WAC members in early 1966; about ten others wangled desk jobs at the military headquarters in Saigon, even though the official Pentagon position was to "discourage" women from volunteering. Anderson attributed that position to a "fatherly attitude of protection" the women had not asked for and did not want. The other services didn't have any women other than nurses serving in Vietnam.

The handful of WAC members in Vietnam in early 1966 owed their positions to an unexpected source: General William Westmoreland, the commander of all U.S. forces in Vietnam from 1964 until 1968. Westmoreland knew that, like in any war, he had to deal with both "the fighting war and the paper war." Men did the former, but he believed women were exceptionally qualified for the latter, even preferrable over men, who often balked at desk jobs. Within months of arriving in Vietnam, he requested WAC members for his Saigon headquarters.

Air Force women were still stuck in the States. Individual commanders in the field had to request WAF members, and commanders resisted. But in 1966, the WAF had a new director who put up a formidable opposition to the commanders: Jeanne Holm.

Holm had been selected from about a dozen female lieutenant colonels in the Air Force. She was promoted to full colonel and began serving as director in November 1965.

As WAF director, Holm was free to roam, and she had big, even outlandish, ideas. The services soon realized she would not be another women's director who sat back and accepted her lot in life. Holm conceded it was good that military women received equal pay for equal work, but the system still stymied their promotion opportunities and career fields, which put a ceiling on their pay. Women excluded from serving in Vietnam would suffer a double whammy:

they wouldn't receive the extra pay and benefits that come with serving in a hostile area, and their lack of service in a combat zone would be used to pass them over for promotions.

Ironically, another WAF study nudged the Air Force to send women to Vietnam. Published about a year before Holm became director, the new study noted that even if women didn't go to Southeast Asia, they could free up men to deploy there. The study concluded the number of WAF should be doubled. It was the first time since the Korean War recruiting push that a study had recommended an increase in WAF numbers. The study's author, Major General Bertram C. Harrison, was also open to the idea of women serving in the combat zone.

In August 1966, Harrison visited Southeast Asia to see whether women should be assigned there. He concluded the living conditions were adequate. But nothing happened. Low-ranking officers at the Air Force Personnel Center continued to deny WAF requests to serve in Vietnam.

Holm kept agitating. During a December 1966 visit to Eglin Air Force Base, Florida, she told the local newspaper, "I would not approve sending women to Viet Nam just to say they are there, but if they can fill a definite need, and will not be a burden to men who already have enough to worry about, they will be there." Holm was upbeat as she addressed the two hundred WAF members stationed at Eglin, telling them their future was "almost limitless." She believed that in a future national emergency, women could and should be drafted.

A month later, Holm visited bases in Vietnam, Thailand, and Hawaii; she also concluded there was no reason to keep women out of Southeast Asia. General William Momyer, the Air Force commander in Saigon, was rumored to be against women, so she paid him a visit and found him open-minded; he had once requested a WAF secretary and was told it was against policy, so he had hired a civilian instead.

Momyer told Holm that WAF officers could be assigned to some locations in Vietnam immediately; in about six months, when additional housing was available, enlisted women could be assigned as well. Holm reached similar agreements with Air Force commanders in Thailand and Hawaii. In June 1967, the first enlisted WAF arrived in Saigon, along with Lieutenant Colonel June H. Hilton, who was the fourth WAF officer to serve in Vietnam.

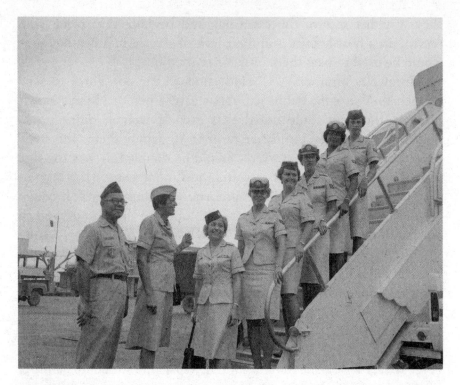

Figure 8: First five enlisted Women in the Air Force (WAF) and fourth WAF Officer assigned to Vietnam arrive at Tan Son Nhut Air Base in June 1967. L to R: Two unidentified, Lieutenant Colonel June H. Hilton, Airman First Class Carol J. Hornick, Airman First Class Rita M. Pitcock, Staff Sergeant Barbara J. Snavely, Airman First Class Shirley J. Brown, and Airman First Class Eva M. Nordstrom. (Courtesy of the U.S. Air Force)

By then, the Pentagon had established one-year rotations for personnel in Vietnam and Thailand to spread the deployments across as many people as possible. Holm advocated to put women into this rotation to reduce the number of men who had to deploy. As the war dragged on, women could also help alleviate pressure on men who might otherwise have to make a second tour. But few others thought of women as a solution, even as commanders in Southeast Asia predicted that some support officers would face involuntary second tours by the end of 1968.

Slowly, the women gained allies. In September 1967, a lieutenant nearly had her orders canceled because someone thought she was too weak to carry equipment for reporters. Brigadier General Robert Dixon, the Air Force Personnel Center's new commander, refused to cancel the orders. He sent a note to the personnel officer in Vietnam:

"I seem to remember some female photographers and reporters who carried their own [cameras and equipment]—don't you?"

*　　*　　*

On January 30, 1968, North Vietnamese forces began a major push into South Vietnam, an attack that became known as the Tet Offensive.

As casualties mounted, a call went out to the 57th Aeromedical Evacuation Squadron at Clark Air Base to evacuate the most seriously wounded. Flight nurse Jane A. Lombardi, a first lieutenant, was assigned to the mission on a C-141, a large four-engine transport aircraft. By the time the aircraft touched down on the runway at Da Nang Air Base, Viet Cong fighters had infiltrated the base.

Lombardi later recalled, "We came under fire at once. It was heavy." The C-141 taxied to a ramp a few hundred yards from Da Nang's hospital. Lombardi dove into a bunker on the ramp and waited for the patients to arrive via ambulance. As soon as the ambulances departed the hospital, guerillas turned their attention from the aircraft to the wounded. As Lombardi said, "They like to hit the wounded and the medics. It's their favorite target." U.S. helicopters flying overhead fired back on the Viet Cong, adding to the chaos.

Twenty-six of the thirty-eight patients could not walk and had to be carried on litters up the cargo ramp in the rear of the aircraft. Lombardi kept her cool amidst the small-arms fire flying around her. Within a few minutes, she got all the patients onboard with no additional casualties. The C-141 crew buttoned up the aircraft and departed back to Clark Air Base. For her role in the mission, Lombardi was awarded a Bronze Star Medal. She was the first woman in the war to earn a combat decoration.

About four hundred miles south of Lombardi, Viet Cong pounded Saigon, where most U.S. military women served. Major Lillian Lewis, an administrative officer, awoke at 4:00 a.m. on Wednesday, January 31, to fire and smoke. From the sky, U.S. aircraft poured return fire on the enemy. Lewis and other women, who were in an unprotected building, dashed to hide behind a row of sandbags surrounding the men's quarters next door.

The initial attack ebbed until early Sunday morning. Then mortar shells slammed into the base.

"Whap! Whap!"

The noise woke June Hilton. For fifteen minutes, more than one hundred rounds crashed around her. The entire base seemed to be on fire. Hilton said, "I've never seen that much fire and it was terrifyingly close."

A nurse recalled, "In the beginning…I was so frightened I could hardly breathe. But you get used to it in a way—to your own fears—and you soon begin to cope and to function—you had to. There was way too much to do most of the time to dwell on it anyway." She thought the women reacted the same as the men: "Anyone who wasn't scared during an attack was either a liar or didn't understand the problem."

After the initial attacks, the Army and Air Force tried to pull women out of Vietnam on the pretext that they required special protection that distracted from the main battle. But the women had received less, not more, protection than the men in many cases. Lillian Lewis's barracks was the only one not surrounded with sandbags, and the women weren't issued flak vests until after the attacks. Determined to stay, the women flooded Jeanne Holm with letters protesting their potential removal. Holm wanted the women to stay too. So did their male counterparts in Saigon. General Dixon stepped in again; the evacuation never took place.

<p style="text-align:center">✳ ✳ ✳</p>

The Tet Offensive petered out in April after the U.S. agreed to halt bombings in the North, and the North Vietnamese agreed to peace talks. The war settled into a simmer mode, especially for those located in Saigon, where Major Norma A. Archer arrived in the summer of 1968 as the operations officer for the 600th Photographic Squadron. Archer was the first WAF in the combat zone to serve in an operational job, something other than nursing or administration. She supervised one hundred men and directed the daily activities of more than six hundred photographers.

Archer was apprehensive when she walked into a conference room to present her first briefing and film footage of recent air

strikes. She was invading a man's world, and she expected the generals sitting around the conference table to toss her out. But that didn't happen.

Eventually, the men didn't just accept her presence. They made her a full part of their team once they realized she was there for the same reason as them: to fight a war. Archer's commander, noticing her compassion in mentoring and assisting the squadron's enlisted men, nominated her for an award from the Veterans of Foreign Wars; he wrote that she "created a spirit of camaraderie and esprit de corps in our organization." Women, it seemed, could be more than pretty faces who typed reports for generals; they were also competent operators and leaders.

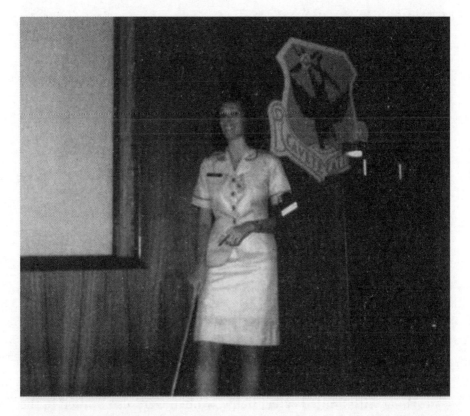

Figure 9: Lieutenant Charlotte Holder Clinger, Women in the Air Force intelligence officer in Southeast Asia, briefs pilots before a mission in 1969. (Courtesy of the Women Veterans Historical Project, University of North Carolina at Greensboro Libraries)

By the time the last helicopter flew refugees and American citizens away from Saigon in April 1975, about seventy-five hundred military women had served in Southeast Asia. About six thousand were nurses and medical specialists. Many were awarded combat medals, including the Purple Heart. Some were wounded, and a few were killed. Seven Army nurses died during aircraft accidents; one Army nurse, First Lieutenant Sharon A. Lane, died after being wounded in a rocket attack. An Air Force nurse, Captain Mary T. Klinker, died on April 4, 1975, when the C-5 cargo airplane she was flying in to evacuate Vietnamese orphans crashed shortly after takeoff.

<p style="text-align:center">*　　*　　*</p>

As military women served in Southeast Asia, Jeanne Holm and the Defense Advisory Committee on Women in the Services kept up the fight back home, pressing for expanded roles and assignments, along with improved promotion opportunities. The only thing Holm couldn't advocate for was getting women into cockpits, since that was forbidden by law. Or was it? Holm believed the language in the law was pretty loose. It didn't say anything about women not flying; it just said women couldn't fly aircraft that engaged the enemy in combat. But the Air Force insisted that meant no women could be trained as pilots. All Air Force pilots were trained the same way and should be able to fly any aircraft in the Air Force's inventory. There would be no limited-duty pilots, which meant no women pilots. And even though the Air Force had noncombat aircraft, such as refueling tankers, they had no problem recruiting enough men to fill those jobs. There was no need for women.

Holm chose her battles wisely. She believed the Air Force was wrong about women aviators, but she knew it wasn't time to fight that battle. She focused instead on things she could change, such as additional career fields, assignments to more bases, improved retention, and better uniforms.

Along with limited career fields, women were also limited in the bases they could be assigned to. Men were assigned to any base with a position in their career field, but women could only be assigned to bases with WAF units. Unless they were nurses, women had few opportunities to serve overseas.

The women also caused some of their own problems. For example, many of them didn't fulfill their initial commitments because they married or became pregnant. Although the Air Force kicked women out if they became pregnant, they did not automatically discharge women for marrying. But the Air Force allowed a woman to leave if she got married, something men could not do. Holm thought it was ridiculous that the military was drafting men who didn't want to serve, while simultaneously letting women volunteers go just because they got married.

Figure 10: A Women in the Air Force member models the uniform of the early 1960s. (Courtesy of the U.S. Air Force)

The easiest issue for Holm to fight was the dreadful state of women's uniforms. The uniforms, Korean War holdovers, were out-of-date fashion-wise and literally rotting on shelves in supply depots. Men bought new uniforms at the base exchange, but women had to rely on what the Air Force issued them. Uniforms might sound trivial, but they were a huge problem. Many potential recruits, especially college students, told Holm they were interested in joining the Air Force but wouldn't consider it because they hated the uniform. *Associated Press* reporter Kelly Smith characterized the long jacket with padded shoulders as something that "looks like it walked out of a 1940 movie."

Updating the uniform was a bureaucratic battle Holm waged for years through her seat on the Air Force's uniform board. The board could take a year of debate to change the shade of blue used in men's shirts; redesigning women's uniforms to keep up with the latest fashions was enough to "give the men on the board ulcers."

Pregnancy and marriage were the hardest issues for Holm, partly because most of the other women directors didn't agree that the rules should change. Only nursing corps leaders favored change—they had huge retention issues during Vietnam. Of the remaining directors, only the Marines were supportive.

Holm crisscrossed the U.S. for the next four years, advocating for increased women's roles. Inevitably described by reporters as "pretty," "petite," and "charming," she attracted attention wherever she went. Media coverage often implied that Holm's biggest concern was better uniforms, even though she spent two-thirds of her time on other issues.

Holm dribbled a few changes here and there, but the Defense Advisory Committee on Women in the Services helped take a giant leap in 1967. For years, the group had fought against the part of the 1948 law that restricted promotion opportunities for women. The grade ceiling wasn't just unfair; it meant the military couldn't retain its best women. Women promoted to lieutenant colonel had only a miniscule chance of becoming a full colonel every four years when the director position turned over. Once they reached twenty years of service, they had little motivation to remain in the military, and most retired. Even more unfair was what happened to the women

directors. At the end of their four-year tour, they had to either retire or revert to being lieutenant colonels if they wanted to continue serving. Male colonels could serve for thirty years in valuable staff and leadership roles, but women were simply cut loose.

DACOWITS wasn't the only one up in arms. President Lyndon B. Johnson's personal secretary, Juanita Roberts, was a WAC reserve lieutenant colonel; Johnson wanted to promote her but was stymied by the law. He said, minus his typical colorful language, that if he couldn't promote someone to colonel, he didn't know why he was president of the United States.

After much pressure from DACOWITS, the Department of Defense drafted legislation to lift the grade restrictions on women and eliminate the 2 percent ceiling on their numbers. On November 8, 1967, Johnson signed the resulting bill into law. But changing the law didn't automatically result in women generals or admirals. That would still take a few years.

<p style="text-align:center">* * *</p>

As the 1960s drew to a close, an unusual issue of the normally stuffy *Defense Management Journal* offered a glimmer of hope for change. Every article in the Winter 1970 issue was authored by a woman in a high-level government position.

Jeanne Holm wrote that pressures for equality fomented a "quiet revolution" working to overcome "barriers of discrimination, of ignorance, of myth, of stereotypes, and of woman's own sense of inadequacy." People didn't like to talk about "discrimination"—the word evoked images of "feminism," and feminism had somehow become a four-letter word, a word so negative that those who fought for feminist causes often found themselves claiming they weren't feminists.

Holm believed the federal government could play a role in advancing equality, "But in the past 21 years, military women have generally fallen into the same patterns of employment that prevail in the private sector…that is, a concentration in the jobs traditionally classified as 'women's work' and in the lower skill/grade levels…. Most of the military services still designate jobs as 'his' and 'hers,' even though this practice is not permitted in other employment sectors…" She conceded the concept might be valid regarding combat positions

but not for support positions.

Finally: "One of the most formidable barriers to women's full participation in the many professional, creative, managerial, and technical career fields is their own lack of confidence in themselves, collectively as well as individually.... It is high time we stop telling children that girls don't have the aptitudes for mathematics, engineering, science, etc.... We raise a little boy to believe that plans for his life's work are his number 1 priority when he grows up. Boys are forced to face up to this reality at an early age. Most girls, on the other hand, are still raised with a romantic image of life—school, marriage, family—and they lived happily ever after. *But Cinderella is dead!*"

CHAPTER 3
Uncorking the Genie (1970–1975)

As Claire Griffith left the Air Force in 1966, another young woman joined the Army. Unlike Griffith, Carolyn Becraft didn't give any thought to joining the military as she grew up in North Dakota. The only thing she knew about the military was that her father had been a colonel in the Army reserves, someone who went off to the local armory one weekend each month.

A chance to join the Army fell into Becraft's lap her senior year at the University of North Dakota. Her major, dietetics, required an internship after graduation, and a family friend said the Army's internship was the best. Becraft joined a program for medical personnel and was commissioned as a second lieutenant after graduation. After her internship in Denver, she was assigned to Fort Lewis in Washington State and then to Fort Devens in Massachusetts. There she met her husband, another Army officer.

Becraft did not consider herself a feminist; she barely paid attention to the women's movement. But her marriage to another Army member soon enlightened her on women's issues.

A few days after she married, Becraft arrived at the personnel office to change her name. The name change was no problem, but the Army also took away her quarters allowance, several hundred tax-free dollars that she earned each month to pay for housing. When a man got married, his quarters allowance went up, since he now had a wife. If an Army woman married a civilian, she could keep her

housing allowance but did not receive the higher rate that a married man did unless she could prove her husband was dependent on her. Married men did not have to prove their wives to be dependent—a wife was automatically granted that status, even if she was an heiress to millions of dollars. Becraft's situation was the worst of all: her husband wasn't anything to her, as far as the Army was concerned.

The couple moved to Fort Knox a few months later and went to the housing office to apply to live on base. Base houses are allotted by rank—the higher the rank, the better the house. Becraft outranked her new husband by a few months; it wasn't much, but it was enough that it might make a difference. It didn't matter. The housing office only cared about her husband's rank. It was as if Becraft had ceased to exist.

At Fort Knox, Becraft was the head dietician at a one-thou-sand-bed hospital. Still in her mid-twenties, she was the youngest Army officer to have a position at such a large hospital. She was also the only captain; other dieticians at large hospitals were majors, one rank higher than her.

None of that mattered two years later when she became pregnant. It was 1971, and pregnant women were still not allowed in the military, even though the rules were likely to change soon in the wake of a lawsuit. The Army made Becraft an offer: she could stay in if she gave up total custody of her child to her husband or her parents.

Becraft said no. The Army had given her three strikes in her five years on their team. She was out. She began following her husband around, going from "being a member of the firm to having no rights whatsoever."

It would take a few years, but Becraft would parlay her negative experiences into a formidable weapon to help both women officers and military wives.

<p style="text-align:center">*　*　*</p>

The 1967 legislation lifted promotion restrictions but didn't guarantee women would be promoted beyond the rank of lieutenant colonel. They still had to meet a promotion board. For the Air Force, that meant a faceless group of men who sat around a table reviewing the records of each officer eligible for promotion. Board members

scored the records on quality, then ranked the scores highest to lowest and drew a line at the number of promotions available. Officers who scored above the line were promoted; those who fell below were not. The other services had separate promotion boards for women, but WAF officers competed toe-to-toe with the men. In theory, WAF members had the same promotion opportunities as the men, but they were consistently promoted at lower rates.

In 1969, only 30 percent of eligible WAF had been promoted to major compared to 60 percent of all eligible captains. Jeanne Holm noted that some of the disparity was likely due to issues with the quality of female officer recruits in the late 1950s, but even allowing for quality differences, anecdotal evidence indicated the system was biased. WAF performance reports contained statements such as "I have never agreed with the concept of female officers and/or airmen. Capt XXXX, regardless of gender, is however, an asset to the Air Force and her effectiveness has overshadowed her sex to the extent that I can rate her an outstanding officer in the best of conscience." Holm argued, "Such statements raise serious doubts as to the rating officer's capacity for objectivity in supervising and rating women. It is not inconceivable that people like this serve on promotion boards, even as chairman."

The WAF promotion issue emboldened Holm to advocate for opening Reserve Officer Training Corps (ROTC) programs to women. The U.S. military has three ways to commission line officers: the service academies, where cadets receive full-time training and education for four years; ROTC programs on civilian college or university campuses, where students receive part-time military training; and officer training schools, which people attend after they have graduated from college. Students at the service academies essentially receive a full four-year scholarship; ROTC students may also receive scholarships. Until the late 1960s, women had only the third option, which meant women officer candidates paid for their own college unless they received a separate scholarship.

There was no law banning women from ROTC; it was simply policy. The ROTC Vitalization Act passed in August 1964 used masculine language throughout but did not explicitly bar women.

On February 20, 1969, Air Force officials ordered the Air University at Maxwell Air Force Base to develop a plan to enroll women in

a test ROTC program. The Air Force envisioned few changes to the existing program except for adding specialized training in areas such as personal grooming and hygiene. However, some language in the letter indicated that the Air Force wasn't exactly welcoming women into ROTC with open arms: "The Air Force recognizes that the enrollment of women in AFROTC is not essential to national security—not a military requirement—and that the numerical requirements for WAF officers are being met by OTS [Officer Training School].... However, we are prepared to support the national objective of equal opportunity by initiating this pilot program..."

The commander of Air University, Lieutenant General Albert P. Clark, who oversaw all commissioning sources in the Air Force, was against women in ROTC. With men still burning draft cards, he had enough trouble recruiting men, let alone adding women to the mix. He and other leaders thought women would be disruptive. Clark finally consented to the trial run.

Holm sent Captain Nancy Buzard to Maxwell Air Force Base to kick off the women's ROTC program. Seven women entered four Air Force ROTC units in 1969. That summer, the women attended a six-week training camp at Myrtle Beach Air Force Base in South Carolina alongside their male counterparts. The cadets marched in the hot sun and practiced simulated parachute drops. The women's training also included modeling and applying makeup. That fall, one of the women dropped out for low grades, leaving six women spread across Auburn, Ohio State, Drake, and East Carolina universities. Like the men, the women cadets earned fifty dollars each month, tax-free. Unlike the men, the women's program was only two years long compared to four years; women had to wait until their junior year to enter.

Instead of being disruptive, the women improved the perception of ROTC on college campuses and helped solve the shortfall of men. The women's presence made more men want to join because ROTC now seemed like a more normal environment. The Air Force, pleased with the early results, pledged to open ROTC to women on 125 campuses by 1971.

But flying was still a bridge too far for the Air Force, even for many women advocates. In a December 1969 interview with Jon Nordheimer, a *New York Times* News Service reporter, Nancy Buzard

said, "There's no doubt in my mind that women could do the job of a pilot, but I don't think they have the desire to do it."

At least one of the first ROTC cadets disagreed. Jane Leslie Farr, who later went by Leslie Farr Kenne, had transferred to Auburn specifically to enter the ROTC program. She learned to fly while at Auburn, hoping the Air Force would open pilot training to women by the time she graduated. She also switched her major to aeronautical engineering.

Interviewed for the same article as Buzard, Kenne tapped her long fingernails on the table of a soda shop booth and said, "Personally, I'd love to be able to fly, but I wouldn't want anyone shooting at me." She continued, "I'm not doing this because I feel women should be in everything that men are. I'm not a champion of women's rights—I'm not that type. But I don't think I should have to suffer because I'm a female, that I should receive lower pay in private industry because of my sex."

On March 17, 1971, Kenne became the first woman commissioned as a second lieutenant from ROTC. The Air Force had yet to open pilot training, so she became a maintenance officer.

* * *

In mid-1970, Jeanne Holm was ready to call it quits. The Air Force had extended her past the normal four-year WAF director tour, but she was exhausted from fighting to open more doors for women. Then Robert Dixon, her old ally in getting women to Southeast Asia, called from Vietnam. He was about get his third star and would be assigned to the Pentagon as the new chief of personnel.

His reputation for eating staff officers for breakfast had earned him the nickname "the alligator," and Dixon asked Holm, "Is anybody jumping out of the windows over there yet?"

Holm wasn't about to jump out of any windows. She knew if anyone was going to make changes, it would be him. But Holm wouldn't be a part of those changes. She had put in her retirement papers and would be leaving a few weeks after Dixon arrived at the Pentagon in August.

Dixon knew the Air Force needed Holm's talents; a few days into his new job, he tried to change her mind. First, he tried pleading,

throwing in a little teasing for good measure: "You've been trying to get a lot of things changed. I need you. I wish you wouldn't retire. If you do, I'm going to have to be the director of WAF. Would you go tell the secretary that you want to withdraw your papers?"

Holm wasn't convinced. She'd heard plenty of promises in the past few years about getting rid of policies that held women back. She wanted action, not talk.

Dixon called a meeting with his staff of generals and colonels to discuss the nonsensical policy that kicked women with minor children out of the military, even if they married a man who already had children. Dixon invited Holm to the meeting, although he knew his staff would be unhappy with her presence. Holm didn't have to say anything; Dixon knew her talking points by heart.

"The alligator" rebutted each point his shell-shocked staff made for retaining the current policy. He asked one colonel, "Do you really want to open that can of worms right now or do you want to quit while you're ahead?"

Two generals squirmed. Finally, a colonel ended the torture by saying he would change the policy. He picked up his stack of charts and left.

Dixon turned to Holm and asked, "Colonel, is that enough action for you?"

Holm stayed. Dixon became her mentor, the general who looked out for her and recommended she be promoted to brigadier general.

But the Army beat the Air Force in pinning stars on a woman. Two women, actually. On June 11, 1970, General Westmoreland, now the Army chief of staff, pinned stars on Colonels Anna Mae Hays, the chief of the Army Nurse Corps, and Elizabeth P. Hoisington, the WAC director. Westmoreland pinned a star on each of Hays's shoulders. He then declared "a new protocol for congratulating lady generals" and kissed her on the cheek. He did the same a few minutes later for Hoisington.

Holm waited another year. On July 16, 1971, she finally received her silver stars. The little tomboy from Portland said, "I never expected this in my wildest dreams. The publicity associated with the promotion of a woman to this rank will help people realize there are women in the armed forces. And it will prove to women that they may now aspire to the higher ranks."

Figure 11: Major General (2-star) Jeanne Holm in 1973. In 1971, Holm became the first woman promoted to brigadier general (1-star) in the U.S. Air Force. (Courtesy of the U.S. Air Force)

Holm's pinning didn't receive as much publicity as the Army ceremony a year earlier, but the press made up for that as Holm traveled the U.S. as a one-woman recruiting poster. In late July 1971, columnist Bob Considine wrote of his meeting with the general in New York, "The star on each trim shoulder matched her own sparkling personality at lunch" as Holm plugged the

Air Force for giving female college graduates more equality with men. "The business world and, to a degree, the other branches of the armed services first ask the applicant if she can type. If she has the identical qualifications of a young man applying for the same job in business, the job goes to a man." Holm then rattled off a list of jobs that WAF could have, everything from mathematicians and computer programmers to air traffic controllers and psychologists. But she admitted there were still no pilots or navigators. "And the only reason we're not represented there is because, in time of war, all pilots and navigators are subject to combat service." Ever pragmatic, Holm knew it wasn't yet time to push the pilot issue, especially when other issues impacting all women still persisted.

But a younger generation of women was tired of waiting on those other issues. They started taking matters into their own hands.

<p style="text-align: center;">*　*　*</p>

In early 1970, First Lieutenant Sharron A. Frontiero, a physical therapist at Maxwell Air Force Base, eagerly awaited her paycheck, anticipating a small raise in her housing allowance after getting married. But when she opened her pay statement, there was no raise. She thought it was a simple administrative error, but base officials told her she wasn't eligible for the increased pay. The Air Force's logic? Her husband, Joseph, received $205 each month in veterans' benefits, and Frontiero didn't pay more than half of his expenses; therefore, he wasn't a "dependent."

Her marriage also didn't make her eligible to live in a house on base; only male service members with dependents had that privilege. And Joseph was ineligible for the health care that wives received automatically upon marriage.

Proving a husband was dependent—something men did not have to do for their wives—was elusive. In 1959, an Army nurse had argued that her husband, involuntarily separated from the Air Force because he was too old at fifty-seven, was a dependent because he would be unable to find a job. The Department of Defense comptroller had ruled against her claim, stating that a husband had to show he was disabled and unable to work to be a dependent. The

lengths the department took to deny women money that flowed automatically to men went beyond mind-boggling; it bordered on a mean-spiritedness that saved the government a few thousand dollars a year but resulted in much ill will. Given their precarious position, few women protested.

Frontiero, though, wanted her money. As a younger woman, she embraced feminism and had no qualms calling out something she saw as clear discrimination. She sought out other women on the base to see if they were interested in joining her in a lawsuit. They all declined.

Frontiero's duty station, next to Montgomery, proved fortuitous. She hired Joseph J. Levin Jr. as her lawyer; a year later, Levin became one of the cofounders of the Southern Poverty Law Center.

On December 23, 1970, Frontiero filed suit in federal court in Montgomery. On April 6, 1971, the court decided against her with a 2–1 vote. The court's reasoning was that Congress had written the statute with the understanding that it would be onerous for the services to demand more than one million male service members prove their wives were dependent. Collecting the information from women carried no similar burden, since there were so few of them. The court agreed that some men with wives who had outside income likely received "windfall" benefits they didn't deserve, but the onus was still on women service members, who weren't "unreasonably burden[ed]." The judges didn't deem the law unconstitutional, but they seemed sympathetic to Frontiero. They nudged Congress to relook at the law.

The "let's pick on them because they're women" logic didn't sit well with Frontiero or Levin. He appealed to the Supreme Court.

As Levin prepared for the Supreme Court case, Ruth Bader Ginsburg, who had recently become the founding director of the ACLU's Women's Rights Project, reached out to him and asked if the WRP might join in the appeal. In October 1972, before the appeal made it before the court, Frontiero separated from the Air Force when her four-year commitment ended. But the lawsuit continued.

On May 14, 1973, the Supreme Court ruled, 8–1, that female service members were entitled to the same benefits as their male counterparts. The only dissenting justice was William H. Rehnquist.

With Frontiero's appeal pending before the Supreme Court, other inequities also fell. One day in 1973, Claire Griffith, now a struggling single mother with no child support, arrived home in Everett, Washington, to find a legal-sized envelope from the VA. She could hardly believe the contents: an official government check for several thousand dollars. The accompanying letter said it was payment for the G.I. Bill dependent benefits she had been denied while going to school.

In 1972, Congresswoman Margaret Heckler, a Republican from Massachusetts, had introduced an amendment to correct the wrong. When Public Law 92-540 was enacted, more than a half-million women veterans could claim the new benefit, including Griffith. The disparity, although only about forty dollars a month, had added up during her time as a student. The windfall put her back on her feet.

The biggest fight in the early 1970s, and one that took the longest to resolve, involved pregnancy. In the summer of 1970, Air Force Captain Susan Struck, an unmarried nurse, discovered she was pregnant while serving in Vietnam. The Air Force evacuated her from the combat zone to McChord Air Force Base outside Tacoma, Washington. On October 16, a board recommended she be honorably discharged "with the least practical delay." Ten days later, the secretary of the Air Force agreed with the recommendation. Officials at McChord set her discharge date for October 28.

Struck decided to fight. She enlisted the help of the ACLU, and through a series of stays and other delays, she remained in the Air Force and gave birth to a daughter on December 3. Struck was no longer pregnant, but the Air Force still wanted to kick her out—even with Dixon's push a year earlier, the policy on women with dependent children had not yet changed. Struck gave the baby up for adoption.

Like Frontiero's, Struck's case had broader implications for women. And pregnant service members were no longer shy about fighting: lawyers for a half-dozen other pregnant women contacted Struck's lawyer for advice on their cases.

On December 7, Struck lost in the district court in Western Washington, but ten days later, Supreme Court Justice William O. Douglas stayed her discharge. On February 1, 1971, the Western

Washington court again denied her claim, saying that the Air Force regulation on discharge was "reasonable and constitutional." Further appeal to the Ninth Circuit Court in San Francisco also ended in favor of the Air Force.

Struck's ACLU lawyers began preparing for their Supreme Court run. Ruth Bader Ginsburg stepped in to help for a second time. The case had three arguments: equal protection, fundamental rights, and freedom of religion. Under equal protection, Struck argued that pregnancy was the only temporary condition for which the Air Force discharged members. If she had broken her leg skiing, she would not be discharged. And since only women could become pregnant, the rule was unfair.

Struck also argued for her "fundamental right to control her own reproductive and procreative decisions." The Air Force had no compelling reason to discharge pregnant women since other personnel could cover a pregnant woman's duties when needed. In fact, it should be easier to cover for pregnant women than for injured or ill service members, since delivery dates are known in advance.

Finally, Struck argued on the basis of freedom of religion. The Air Force revoked a discharge if a pregnancy was terminated, whether through miscarriage or abortion. Few legal options for abortion were available in 1970; Washington State voters approved an initiative to make abortion legal in the fall of 1970, but that was too late for Struck. Access to abortion was irrelevant for Struck anyway: she was Roman Catholic. Staying in the Air Force would have required an abortion against her religion, thus violating her constitutional right to freedom of religion.

With the case still ongoing, the Air Force moved Struck to Minot Air Force Base in North Dakota. It might have been a normal rotation, but with its remote location and harsh winters, Minot can also be a place to send troublemakers.

On December 1, 1972, Struck's troubles abruptly ended: the Air Force gave her a waiver to remain on active duty indefinitely. In the meantime, the service had quietly updated their rules regarding pregnancy. A pregnant woman still had to leave the Air Force if she wanted to have her baby, but she could apply to come back on active duty within a year of giving birth. Within a few more years, pregnant women didn't have to leave the Air Force at all.

* * *

As lawsuits eliminated unfair practices for military women, other movements helped increase their numbers and opened career fields. By the 1960s, the peacetime draft was becoming increasingly unpopular. Except for the Civil War and World War I, U.S. tradition had long been an all-volunteer force, until World War II, when conscription of able-bodied men was nearly universal; professional baseball players and movie actors served alongside small-town barbers, and exemptions were rare. At war's end, the draft went away briefly, but the Cold War brought it back. After Korea, the draft became less universal. The peacetime army needed fewer people and the huge baby-boomer population meant a low percentage of men had to serve. By 1962, there were so many exemptions—students, fathers, even married men—that just about anyone could avoid the draft if they wanted to. The unpopular Vietnam War dealt the last blow to the increasingly irrelevant and unfair draft.

The Pentagon began studying whether to eliminate the draft in 1963, but the idea didn't gain traction until 1968, when Richard M. Nixon pledged during his election campaign to eliminate selective service. After he became president, he set up the Gates Commission to figure out how to transition to an all-volunteer force. In 1971, Congress passed Public Law 92-129 to abolish the draft, and on September 28, Nixon signed the bill, which extended the draft until July 1, 1973, to allow for an orderly transition.

The Gates Commission recommended that civilians replace some military personnel but was strangely silent about women. Six months later, another piece of legislation pushed the issue of women to the forefront.

On March 22, 1972, the Senate passed a joint resolution, by a vote of 84–8, that put forth the Equal Rights Amendment. The language in the proposed amendment to the U.S. Constitution was simple: "Equality of rights under the law shall not be denied or abridged by the United States or by any State on account of sex." The passage ended a forty-nine-year fight by feminists, many of whom erupted from the gallery in applause and loud cheers. There were even a few cowbells.

But the fight wasn't finished. Three-quarters of the states—thirty-eight of them—had to ratify the amendment within seven years before it became part of the constitution. It appeared that would happen; only thirty-two minutes after the vote, Hawaii became the first state to ratify the amendment.

Not everyone believed the ERA would be ratified, but it spooked the military into making room for more women. The Army and Navy set goals to double the number of women in their ranks; the Air Force went higher still, to triple the number. The Marines agreed to a more modest 20 percent increase.

Although scheduled to end July 1, 1973, the draft was eliminated six months early. Between January and May 1973, Army enlistments declined from about eighteen thousand to nine thousand each month. Military officials called for a reinstatement of the draft; to them, it was clear the All-Volunteer Force, or AVF, wouldn't work. Raising a signing bonus from $1,500 to $2,500 didn't help; enlistments still fell short of goals. Some recruiters tried to make up for the shortfall through nefarious means such as faking a high school diploma. Experts (all of them men) bemoaned the shortage of men; few thought, publicly anyway, women might be the answer.

The ERA set in motion other gains for military women. The chief of naval operations, Admiral Elmo R. Zumwalt, saw women as playing an important role in the Navy's future. In general, he wanted to improve quality of life for sailors, thinking that would increase the Navy's dwindling reenlistment rates. Women could also help the shortfall.

On August 7, 1972, Zumwalt issued Z-Gram 116, titled "Equal Rights and Opportunities for Women." The Z-Gram did not explicitly state that women would become naval aviators, but that was the result.

On November 7, 1972, the Navy announced they were looking for eight women to volunteer to be trained as pilots. The women could be Navy officers or officer candidates. After training, the women would be assigned to noncombat aircraft, such as "transports, search planes, and helicopters."

On February 22, 1974, the world of military pilots ceased to be an all-male domain when Lieutenant (Junior Grade) Barbara Allen received her Navy "wings of gold" at Corpus Christi Naval

Air Station in Texas. Her father, a retired Navy commander, pinned on her wings.

After graduation, Allen went to Naval Air Station Alameda in California to fly the C-1, a small propeller cargo aircraft used to deliver people, spare parts, and mail to aircraft carriers. There was just one hitch: the Navy's interpretation of the combat exclusion laws meant that Allen couldn't be on an aircraft carrier, even if all she did was land and take off again a few minutes later after delivering her cargo. She was instead limited to flying to bases and airports on land.

Two of the original eight women dropped out of pilot training, but the other five graduated not long after Allen did. One was Rosemary Mariner, who had wanted to fly since she was a small child. Her parents had both been in the military, her mother as a nurse and her father as an Air Force pilot. Even though her father was killed in an airplane crash when she was three, Mariner longed to fly the Navy airplanes she saw soaring above the family's home in the San Diego area.

Figure 12: U.S. Navy Ensign Rosemary Conatser (later Mariner) at the controls of an S-2 anti-submarine aircraft at Naval Air Station Oceana, Virginia, January 9, 1975. (Courtesy of National Archives and Records Administration)

Mariner started her pilot training in a way typical of many teenagers: she went to her local airport and got a job washing airplanes. When she had saved enough money, she started flying lessons. After high school, she attended Purdue University, graduating just in time to join the Navy's first class of women pilots.

After earning her wings in June 1974, Mariner headed to Naval Air Station Oceana near Virginia Beach to fly the S-2, a propeller aircraft used for training missions. The squadron she was assigned to also flew A-4s, small attack jets that had seen extensive service during Vietnam. Mariner had her eye on the A-4s; the jets at Oceana were used for training, not combat, so maybe she could fly one.

Her squadron commander was open-minded about her arrival, telling reporters that women pilots were "long overdue." He added that the male pilots seemed to accept Mariner. "The only thing that bothers them is that she can wear her hair longer."

The Army also moved forward on women pilots. Second Lieutenant Sally Murphy became the first Army aviator on June 4, 1974, when she graduated from the Army Aviation Center at Fort Rucker, Alabama. She was qualified as a helicopter pilot.

But the Air Force still had no room for women pilots.

<div align="center">✳ ✳ ✳</div>

In 1973, Leslie Kenne applied to attend the Air Force's Test Pilot School, which had recently begun training engineers and navigators alongside pilots. The curriculum was similar for all students, with engineers and navigators flying in the rear seat or back of an airplane or sitting in a control room on the ground monitoring a mission as the pilot flew.

Kenne's application apparently caused little consternation with the selection board. She met all the qualifications for entry, and there was no rule against women flying in the back seat of airplanes used for testing. The board selected her, and she arrived at Edwards Air Force Base in the summer of 1974 to begin her training.

One of her classmates, Jeff Peer, an Israeli pilot, told me he didn't think anything about "Les," as they called her, being in his class, although he initially had a hard time understanding her Southern accent. He was used to working with women in the Israeli Air Force,

who did pretty much everything except be pilots. Besides, he wasn't one to talk about qualifications; he had somehow gotten into the class without a college degree.

The only "issue" Peer recalled was Kenne's bouffant hairstyle, common for the time. Peer wondered how the volume of teased hair would fit under the helmet she wore when flying in an ejection-seat aircraft. When he flew with her the first time, he found out: the bouffant was a wig. She removed the wig and revealed a short, tight haircut that easily fit. After the flight, she pulled off her helmet and popped the wig back on.

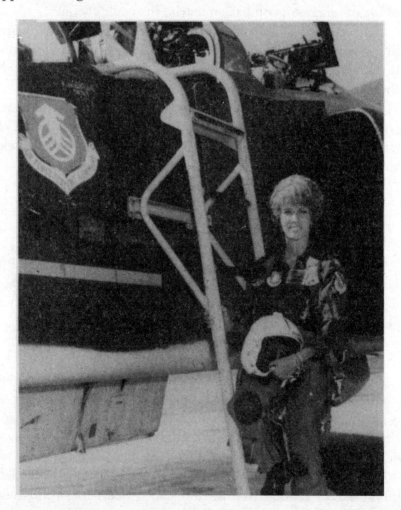

Figure 13: Captain Leslie Holley (later Kenne), first woman to graduate from the U.S. Air Force Test Pilot School flight test engineer course, 1975. Pictured with an F-4 aircraft. (Courtesy of the U.S. Air Force)

Roy Martin, another of Kenne's classmates, confirmed there were no issues. The only accommodation he remembered was a special parachute made for her five-foot-two, ninety-nine-pound frame. He enjoyed flying with her; she tolerated his singing in the cockpit. She was, he told me, "part of the team without being one of the guys." As Baumgartner experienced thirty years earlier, pilots from the test and evaluation community graciously accepted women into their fold.

On July 2, 1975, Kenne became the first woman to graduate from the USAF Test Pilot School. The *Bakersfield Californian* ran an article along with a photo of Kenne standing in front of an F-4 fighter, decked out in her flight suit and poofy wig, cradling her helmet in her arms. She told the paper, "I am grateful the school staff has neither favored me nor inhibited me in any way because I am a woman. From the beginning I wanted to be sure whatever I accomplished in this course, I accomplished on my own. I only hope I have done well enough so other women will be welcome here."

The Air Force had let a woman fly in a fighter airplane, but not as a pilot or navigator. Those career fields were still off-limits, despite now being open to Navy and Army women. But the Air Force is the only service whose primary mission is to fly; aircraft in the other services play support roles, and pilots and other aviators are not lionized as they are in the Air Force.

The thought of women pilots made many Air Force men uncomfortable. If a mere woman could be a military pilot, maybe being a pilot wasn't so special after all. It was an idea that took a while for senior Air Force leadership to embrace.

$$* \quad * \quad *$$

Other than a vague awareness of the ERA, I was oblivious to the changes in the military as I attended high school in the early 1970s. I was the second of four girls, and I grew up loving sports, math, and science in a family that spent more money on books than on television and movies. Even though I was occasionally frustrated that boys got to do things that girls couldn't—I longed to play Little League Baseball—the first time I felt the sting of sexism was in the ninth grade in Florida, where all boys had to take science and all girls had to take home economics. To take a science class, I had to use one of

my electives. I opted for biology and German. I really did want to learn how to sew, but it irked me that it was forced on me. On the other hand, I don't remember anyone actively discouraging me from taking math and science classes.

Born in 1957, I was just a little too old to reap the benefits of Title IX, the civil rights law passed in 1972 that forbade discrimination in federally funded education programs, including athletics. I enjoyed running but had no girls' track team to join. Girls born a few years after me found more sports teams at public schools and universities. And Florida jettisoned the home ec requirement some years ago.

Despite living near several large military bases and having a father in the Air Force, I was largely ignorant of the doors opening to women in the military. Only a handful of girls participated in my high school's Junior ROTC program. Most students thought ROTC girls were weird; they certainly weren't part of the in crowd and, even though my love of math and science meant I wasn't part of that crowd either, I also found the ROTC girls weird. Especially their uniforms. Our school district had recently loosened the dress code to allow girls to wear pants instead of dresses, so why would anyone want to wear a uniform when you could finally wear jeans and a peasant shirt?

Besides the uniform, I wondered why anyone, boy or girl, would join the military. As I filled out college applications my senior year, my father suggested I apply for an ROTC scholarship. I don't recall my exact response, but it was something along the lines of "Why would I do that?"

A lot of girls had the same attitude as me, but others hoped for military careers, perhaps to be generals someday. However, another obstacle blocked their path. Even though ROTC doors were open, the doors to the service academies were still closed.

<p style="text-align:center">*　*　*</p>

Once the court battles over pregnancy and dependents finished, the battle over the service academies began in the halls of Congress. The three academies—Air Force Academy, Naval Academy, and West Point—each graduated about one thousand new second lieutenants each year, all men. With all expenses paid by the government and a four-year immersion into all things military, the schools were viewed as the best path to those wanting a military career.

The ERA passage emboldened women to apply for the academies through their representatives and senators, who had the ability to nominate constituents. A few nominated highly qualified women, who the schools dutifully rejected. One returned Air Force Academy application suggested the woman apply for ROTC.

In September 1973, two congressmen filed separate lawsuits, one against the Air Force Academy and one against the Naval Academy. Not waiting for the courts, during late 1973 and early 1974, legislators introduced six separate bills in the House to eliminate discrimination by sex in academy admissions. On May 29, 1974, as I was getting ready to graduate from high school, a subcommittee of the House Armed Services Committee began hearing testimony on the proposed legislation, testimony that continued into August. Dozens of people testified, including Jacqueline Cochran, but Jeanne Holm was conspicuously absent. Apparently, the Air Force did not want anyone to hear her contrarian views.

The first entry into the official record, a written statement from William P. Clements, the deputy secretary of defense, set the tone for the military's testimony. After first stating that the purpose of the academies was to "train men for duty at sea...[and] produce male officers to fill combat billets," he pointed to the Air Force and Navy combat exclusion laws and the Army's policy that prohibited women in combat. Since the academies were restricted by both laws and facilities in the number of people admitted each year, each woman would reduce the number of male officers that graduated. Clements concluded that women attending the academies "would work serious harm to fleet and combat units and other activities which have an increasing demand for Academy graduates." He pointed out that women could receive commissions through other sources, including the recently opened ROTC programs. In other words, women should be happy with what they had.

Patricia Schroeder, the first to testify and the co-sponsor of one of the bills being debated, pounced on the arguments against women. The issue was partly personal for the freshman representative from Colorado. Born into a military family, Schroeder had wanted to go into the Air Force ROTC unit at the University of Minnesota. But it was 1957, and the Air Force flatly turned her down. Instead, she earned a pilot's license on her own and ran a small flying operation to help pay her tuition.

Schroeder noted that, with passage of the ERA, "the eventuality of the admission of women to the service academies is clear. My question is, why, then, is the Department of Defense so vehemently fighting the inevitable?" And why would the academies want to automatically eliminate more than half of their potential applicants just because they were women?

Schroeder displayed a chart, prepared by the Department of Defense, showing that as officers advanced in rank, the percentage of academy graduates also went up; the difference was especially dramatic at the higher grades. Academy graduates made up less than 15 percent of second lieutenants or ensigns, but they made up about half of all generals and admirals. Without access to the academies, women would struggle to achieve the highest levels. The other commissioning sources were just a bone tossed to women.

Schroeder, who saw nothing wrong with women becoming fighter pilots, was in favor of repealing the combat exclusion laws, saying that would be the easiest path to admitting women. But she didn't believe the repeal was necessary. Even in the Army, 85 percent of officer positions did not involve direct combat; there were many jobs for women academy graduates.

Another representative pushed back against concerns over the potential cost of facilities to accommodate women; he thought the costs would be relatively low and funds readily available. His comments prompted Schroeder to recall her own experience as a trailblazer: "I am very sensitive to [the issue of facilities]. I went to Harvard after they let women in, and I got so tired of the dean saying how many volumes he could have bought for the library if they had not had to build a women's restroom."

To a suggestion that women cadets would have to have a different training regimen from the men, Schroeder replied, "I don't think women want to be treated differently. They don't want to be carried on a sedan chair." One congressman thought men would need time to adjust psychologically to the women, but Schroeder shot back, "I think most of these gentlemen have been exposed to women. As I understand it, they all had mothers…"

Schroeder and others pounded the academies on the number of male graduates who did not go into combat positions. The Air Force Academy was especially vulnerable; about one-quarter of

its graduates did not go on to fly airplanes or occupy positions considered combat.

Representative Samuel Stratton from New York expressed frustration that he had warned the academies three years earlier not to oppose the inevitable. Stratton drove a stake into the heart of the excuse that the academies only trained combat personnel. He called the excuse "unmitigated nonsense.... These are primarily engineering schools, and I think most experts would regard them as second-rate engineering schools."

Stratton had no issues with women being in combat. He had served in three combat landings during World War II, dug foxholes, and ducked falling bombs, yet he had never fired a shot in anger. He said, "I try to convince my children I was some kind of war hero, but I have often wondered privately—including during some of those moments in the foxholes—how much of my job could probably have been performed just as well by a qualified woman. Almost all of it, I'm afraid."

On June 5, the military returned fire, and Department of Defense lawyers stood their ground. They again argued that the exclusion of women from the academies had a rational basis and did not constitute discrimination. It was the "will of the American people" that women should not serve in combat leadership roles; therefore, they should not attend the service academies. And yes, ROTC had opened to women, but women would "change the essential nature of the academies." An education in combat leadership, which cost about $70,000 at an academy versus $10,000 for ROTC, would be wasted on them. Supporters of the women pointed out that they attended staff and war colleges, which provided education for combat leadership. Why not the academies?

The service secretaries, service chiefs, and superintendents of the service academies all testified and repeated the arguments the lawyers had made.

Jacqueline Cochran testified on July 18. The bottom line for her: "It is my firm very considered opinion that women should not be permitted to enroll in the Air Force Academy." Cochran claimed she "was privileged to reorganize the WAFs under General Vandenberg, got it back on the track. They are pretty difficult, women are; I know, I have dealt with them my whole life." Cochran vastly overstated her role in the minor WAF restructuring in the early 1950s and said

nothing of the turmoil she caused. She continued, "The basic reason why I hold this opinion is that the Academies are for the purpose of teaching combat to their students." She might as well have photocopied the testimony of the parade of generals, admirals, and high-ranking Department of Defense civilians.

Cochran wrongly stated that the WASP attrition rate after training was 36 percent and said most left to marry. "There are sound biological reasons why a woman should not be trained for and used in combat." Women, in her opinion, would not be able to pay back the twenty or thirty years expected of academy graduates. "Strangely enough, practically none of [the WASP] did much with their flying after the war was over." Cochran did not mention the discrimination the women faced. She also believed—with no evidence—that women who attended medical or law school did not "carry on for long in the practice of their profession." She was firmly against women in combat: "I haven't adequate vocabulary to express my indignation over women who want to go into combat." This, despite telling people nearly thirty years earlier that the WASP would have made capable combat pilots had they been needed.

Fortunately, Lieutenant Colonel Grace King, an Army reservist, had rebutted many of Cochran's comments in previous testimony. She submitted a "Summary of the WASP Controversy" in a folder to each subcommittee member and said, "In short, this 'highly qualified' group of 800 was forced out by the Army Air Force which had by then built up its male complement and by congressional action which abolished the WASP in December 1944. Given the alternative of joining the WAC with the knowledge that they would not be assigned as pilots nor allowed flying duty of any sort, they did indeed choose to melt away, but only after waging and losing a bitter battle for survival."

Representative Barbara Jordan from Texas summed things up best: "Women want to go to the service academies for the same reasons men do—they are interested in a military career. We should not automatically relegate their desires to a second-class military career. We do not tolerate second class lawyers or doctors. Those women who wish to pursue a military career should be given the opportunity to qualify for a first-class military career, to go first class and be admitted to the service academy of their choice."

* * *

The proponents prevailed, and President Gerald Ford signed Public Law 94-106 on October 7, 1975, ordering the three service academies to admit women in the summer of 1976. Despite their opposition, the schools had been planning for the inevitable for years. But the Air Force was still not ready for women as aviators: they announced that any women admitted to their academy would not be eligible for flight training, since there were no women pilots or navigators in the Air Force.

John L. McLucas, the secretary of the Air Force, was frustrated that his service still discriminated against women. Years of listening to arguments from people who supported women's rights, including his daughter, had convinced him that women needed career paths equal to men. During his swearing-in ceremony in 1973, he had pledged to work for more equality for both minorities and women. He'd made progress on some fronts, including bringing in more women and expanding ROTC opportunities, but the goal of women pilots he and Jeanne Holm cherished still seemed out of reach.

McLucas sometimes found himself operating in opposition to his own beliefs. He, like the other service secretaries, had testified against admitting women to the service academies, even though he personally thought the Air Force Academy should admit them. He found the argument that the academies trained only combat officers unconvincing. He was also not convinced of the argument that all Air Force pilots had to be combat pilots. In April 1975, he'd asked the Air Force to take a look at a two-track training system similar to the Navy's: one track would be for fighters and the other for bombers, transports, and refueling tankers.

In May 1975, McLucas and Holm both spoke at a Defense Advisory Committee on Women in the Services meeting. Holm, who was about to retire, lamented about her "unfinished business." She "favored admitting women to the academies, into aircraft cockpits, and aboard ships." She was also in favor of women serving in at least some combat jobs.

On October 7, one of Holm's wishes came true when Ford signed the legislation to admit women to the academies. A week later, he nominated McLucas to lead the Federal Aviation Administration.

The study on the two-track pilot system was nowhere near complete, but rather than leave his own unfinished business, McLucas decided to speed things up. He couldn't ask the air staff to go faster; the colonels would give him a hundred reasons why that wouldn't work.

Then McLucas saw an opening. Secretary of Defense James R. Schlesinger was scheduled to preside over McLucas's farewell ceremony, set for November 7. A few days prior to the ceremony, Ford announced he was removing Schlesinger, effective November 19. With Schlesinger's imminent departure likely to attract much more press than a normal farewell ceremony, McLucas planned his move.

As predicted, the press arrived at the ceremony in droves. Schlesinger first gave a rousing speech on the need for a strong defense. The reporters lapped it up. McLucas blandly reviewed the years he had spent with the Air Force. People fidgeted in their seats or yawned and glanced furtively at their watches. Then McLucas mentioned his push for more opportunities for women and said, "We will soon open limited pilot duty to our women, who, while prohibited from participation in combat, can still serve us in transport activities and others."

Jeanne Holm, now retired, turned to those sitting next to her and asked, "Did I just hear him correctly?"

She had. Holm was thrilled. The air staff officers who thought they had months or years to complete their study were not. Air Force public-affairs officials were also beside themselves. Something this big would normally be preceded by weeks of crafting carefully worded messages to be revealed at a press conference set up just for the announcement. McLucas had just upended all that, like a gorilla tossing furniture about in their Pentagon offices.

With the hoopla surrounding Schlesinger, most reporters either missed McLucas's comment or decided it didn't warrant reporting. And for almost two weeks, the official Air Force position remained that they were still studying the issue of women pilots. Then on November 20, the chief of staff of the Air Force, General David C. Jones, sent a message to commanders in the field: "Rather than delay further the introduction of women into pilot training, I believe it is prudent now to announce that we are embarking on a carefully structured test program for the training and utilization of women." With a test program, the Air Force still hadn't given away the farm.

After all, they knew from the WASP experience in World War II that women could be trained to fly military aircraft. The test program seemed to be about "utilization," to figure out how to use pilots who would not be flying combat missions.

A week later, more than thirteen hundred miles away from the Pentagon, a college senior and ROTC cadet at the University of Oklahoma spotted an *Air Force Times* article titled "Women Soon to Train as Noncombat Pilots." It was the moment Kathy Rambo had been waiting for since 1962. She was determined to be one of those first women pilots.

CHAPTER 4
The First Women (1970s)

Air Force Second Lieutenant Kathy Rambo peered through the windscreen of her C-141 cargo airplane. The runway was several miles away. Ensconced in the right seat of the one-hundred-ton aircraft, her right hand clutched the control yoke, while her left hand grasped the four throttles on the console beside her. A gusty wind buffeted the massive airframe as she guided it through the turbulent approach.

Someone on duty in her training squadron had woken Rambo at 4:00 a.m. that fall day in 1977. As the wind rattled the windows in her room at Altus Air Force Base, Oklahoma, she wondered why he was calling: a copilot in training like herself wouldn't be flying in such conditions. But some senior officers had other ideas.

When she arrived at the training squadron her flight instructor, Lieutenant Colonel George Drake, said, "Kath, they want to see if you can handle the airplane in more than fifteen knots."

Landing with more than fifteen knots of crosswind was a difficult maneuver, one only performed by experienced pilots. Like all new copilots, Rambo's limit was fifteen knots. But Drake told her the senior officers had waived the limit for her that day.

That's not fair, Rambo thought. The male trainees didn't have to make landings in out-of-limit crosswinds. However, she was the first woman pilot to fly the C-141 cargo aircraft, and some were skeptical of her capabilities.

But Drake was on her side, literally and figuratively. He would be in the left seat as she flew the aircraft, and he assured her: "I'll talk you through it. They just want to see you do it once."

Drake and Rambo were joined by three flight examiners, seasoned pilots whose sole job was to give check rides—flights dedicated to evaluating other pilots to ensure they met Air Force standards. The number of examiners was crazy; usually only one or two at most were on board for a training mission. There weren't enough seats on the flight deck for all of them, so two stood behind her during the short flight.

The wind howled across the runway at twenty-five knots as Rambo took off. That was the easy part. She maneuvered the aircraft around the base in a giant rectangle and arrived back on the final approach a few minutes later. The wind forced the airplane to the right, so she turned the nose left to keep her ground track straight toward the runway. As the wind constantly shifted during the descent, she made minor corrections to keep the plane tracking straight. Drake provided occasional suggestions. So far, not too bad. But the hardest part lay ahead.

Fifty feet above the runway, Rambo gradually pulled the aircraft's nose up to reduce her speed. Simultaneously, she pushed on the right rudder pedal to swing the nose straight while she turned the yoke to the left to keep from drifting sideways. She focused intently on keeping the nose as straight as possible. Everything moved: her feet danced on the rudder pedals, her right hand pulled and twisted the yoke, her left hand nudged the throttles. Drake calmly coached her: "A little more aileron, a little less rudder, throttles idle, you got it…"

The left tire hit the pavement with a satisfying *thunk*, followed a second later by the right tire. Rambo slammed the nosewheel onto the runway, while keeping the yoke turned all the way to the left. They sped down the runway at more than one hundred miles per hour for a few seconds until she yanked the throttles into reverse thrust and mashed the brakes with her toes. The airplane lurched from side to side and bumped up and down like a four-wheeler over rough terrain. Finally, she slowed enough to turn onto the taxiway at the end of the runway.

She relaxed with a mixture of relief and triumph.

After she taxied back to the ramp, the maintenance crew discovered a crack in the nose gear strut. But that wasn't Rambo's problem: trainees broke airplanes all the time. If anyone got blamed for this damage, it would be the examiners who thought it was a good idea to make her land in the horrible wind.

* * *

Kathy Rambo grew up in a military family, learning early in life to adapt to change. She was born in France in 1955; a younger brother followed fifteen months later in Germany. Her mother, Helga, was German, and Kathy's father was a U.S. Army supply sergeant. The family moved back to the U.S. in 1959, and Helga used a forged birth certificate to enter Kathy into kindergarten at age four. When the Army sent Kathy's father to Korea, Helga divorced him and married a U.S. Marine; a half-sister was born a few years later.

On February 20, 1962, Rambo watched John Glenn's historic launch on television, and the launch inspired her to become a pilot. Not just any pilot, but an Air Force pilot. No one told her that, as a girl, perhaps flying professionally was a goal out of reach. Her parents told her she could do anything if she worked hard. As she later found out, a little luck didn't hurt either.

When Rambo was ten, she went to live with her grandparents in Germany for four years. She became fluent in German and played the flute in her school's classical orchestra. Returning to high school in Texarkana, Texas, she was shocked that the school band was all about marching and football games. Her inability to march relegated her to the last flute chair, but a year later, she moved up to first chair.

Except for the band, Rambo found high school excruciating. Her relative youth put her at a disadvantage in navigating the Texas high school scene. She felt awkward, never sure what to say or do. Making matters worse, just before her senior year, her stepfather was reassigned to Quantico, Virginia, where she attended a small school that housed seventh through twelfth grades. She wasn't surprised when no one asked her to the senior prom.

The move to Quantico wasn't all bad. The school's music director transformed his tiny army of sixteen kids from a pathetic marching band into a jazz band. Rambo transitioned to the saxophone. She

was good enough that her teacher said he could get her a music scholarship to Louisiana State University. But she had no desire to major in music—she still wanted to be a pilot. And with ROTC now open to women, that was starting to look like a possibility. In 1972, the military wasn't yet training women to fly, but Rambo was optimistic. When they changed, she planned to be ready.

Rambo chose the University of Oklahoma. Her stepfather was an alumnus, and the school met her requirements: it had an Air Force ROTC program and a band. Her parents were upset that she didn't take the LSU scholarship, but they didn't force the issue. She was accepted into the ROTC program and slated to become a maintenance officer.

As a non-scholarship ROTC student, Rambo's finances were tight, but she breezed through her classes and had time to play in Oklahoma's band. She majored in German with a minor in math. She might have switched the major/minor order except for long hours worked in pizza parlors and an occasional midnight to 6:00 a.m. shift at Dunkin' Donuts. During the summer before her sophomore year, she mopped floors and made Jell-O at the Quantico Officer Candidate School's mess. After tuition, her earnings left only enough money for a bicycle. A car remained out of reach until graduation.

During Rambo's freshman year, she'd watched the door to her dreams crack open when the Navy and Army began training women pilots. In late 1975, her senior year, she read the *Air Force Times* article that said the Air Force was planning to send twenty women to pilot training as an experiment. She called a personnel office to get more information, but when she mentioned she was an ROTC cadet, she was told, "Sorry, honey, we're not accepting any second lieutenants." Rambo thought, *Are you kidding?* Why would the Air Force only want older women who were already on active duty when the standard male pilot trainee was a twenty-two-year-old second lieutenant?

A few weeks later, another *Air Force Times* article said that two of the twenty slots available were for non-active-duty officers: one with the Air Force Reserves and one with the Air National Guard. Rambo knew nothing about the Air National Guard, but she had some knowledge of the reserves. With the post-Vietnam drawdown

still happening in 1976, ROTC cadets could choose a commission in the reserves instead of going on active duty. Rambo wasn't really interested in the reserves; she wanted to make the Air Force her career. But if she could get a pilot training slot as a reservist? That beat out being a maintenance officer on active duty.

Rambo called another office; the person who answered suggested she go to the nearest Air Force base with a reserve unit to apply for the pilot position. That wasn't hard: Tinker Air Force Base was only twenty miles away. Rambo figured her application was low risk. If she didn't become a pilot in the reserves, she could still be a maintenance officer on active duty. She would keep applying for pilot training until she was accepted.

Rambo knew she was likely ahead of other women who applied for the reserve spot. She was lucky the Air Force had opened pilot training to coincide with her graduation, but she had also done everything she could to take advantage of that luck. She had taken the pilot qualifying tests her sophomore year of college and had already passed the flight physical during a weekend trip to Tinker a few months earlier.

In May 1976, now Second Lieutenant Rambo returned to Virginia to wait for the Air Force's verdict: maintenance school or pilot training. One day, she went to nearby Andrews Air Force Base in Maryland to fill out some paperwork. The base buzzed with excitement: The French president would be landing in the Concorde. It was the supersonic aircraft's first visit to the U.S. Rambo rushed to the flight line and watched the sleek airplane approach and land. A few weeks later, the phone rang; a voice on the other end congratulated her on being accepted for pilot training. In a few months, she would be piloting her own supersonic airplane through the Arizona skies.

There was just one catch. Since Rambo lived near the Pentagon, the chief of the Air Force Reserves, a three-star general, wanted to meet her. Rambo was taken aback. Did he want to make sure she was polished enough to represent the reserves? A few days later, a colonel whose burly size matched his last name of Bear met her at a Pentagon entrance and escorted her to the general's office, where she and the general talked for about twenty minutes. If it was a test, she must have passed. The general's staff told her to report to her post-

pilot training base, McGuire, in New Jersey, to pick up her orders for pilot training. After training, she would fly one of McGuire's aircraft models, the C-141 cargo airplane.

Rambo zipped to McGuire in her new red-and-white Mustang and then raced to Lackland Air Force Base for the first phase of her training. Her first night there, she met the other nine women in her class. At twenty-one, Rambo was the youngest. Connie Engel, the oldest at twenty-seven, had been a nurse and had her private pilot's license; she was married to an Air Force pilot, Rich, who was finishing his master's degree at Arizona State University.

Rich had encouraged Connie to apply for pilot training, although he had initially been skeptical about the experiment. He doubted the Air Force could find ten qualified women. If they did, he thought the women's legs wouldn't be strong enough to hold the brakes on the T-38 training aircraft. He told Connie, "I can just see all ten getting pregnant within a year or two. Goodbye to all those taxpayer dollars poured into their training."

Connie retorted, "At the rate young pilots are leaving the Air Force, that would hardly be a change."

* * *

At Lackland, the women spent several weeks in the Flight Screening Program, flying little propeller-driven airplanes at the municipal airport in nearby Hondo. The purpose of the program was to ensure that potential student pilots had basic air sense before sending them into jet aircraft.

The first week was spent on administrative details. The first thing the women learned was that the Air Force was ill-prepared for them. Flight suits were designed for men, and it was impossible to find a good fit. A flight suit that fit a woman's hips was baggy in the shoulders, and the crotch drooped halfway to her knees. The flight boots were too wide for most of the women's heels. The Air Force agreed to make some adjustments, but the women spent their own money and time on other alterations. Even so, the flight suits never fit right.

The women quickly bonded over their shared problems. When the flight surgeon told them they would not be allowed to fly while on their period, the women decided they wouldn't tell anyone when

they were menstruating. As far as the men knew, they were the only ten women in the world to collectively go without a period for ten months without being pregnant. Regarding pregnancy, the flight surgeon said if they became pregnant, they would be immediately grounded. But if they wanted to go on birth control pills to prevent pregnancy, they would be grounded for sixty days to ensure the pills had no side effects.

The final indignity was restrictions on the women's appearance. Women Air Force members were allowed to wear long hair in a bun, but the pilot trainees had to cut their hair to above the bottom of their collar and above their eyebrows. They couldn't use hairpins or rubber bands that might come loose and jam an airplane's controls. Makeup was also forbidden; oils in the makeup might catch fire in their oxygen masks. The women weren't happy, but they spent the weekend getting their locks sheared at hair salons in San Antonio.

Rambo and the other women expected extra scrutiny during their training, but they were unprepared for the attention the media showered on them beginning their first official day at Lackland. At 8:00 a.m. sharp, John W. Roberts, the four-star general who headed up Air Training Command, greeted them along with several reporters in an auditorium. The women had yet to fly a single flight, but the headline the next day in the *San Antonio Express* read, "They'll fly by the seats of their skirts," a play on an old saying about pilots "flying by the seat of their pants." What about combat? Connie Engel was ready: "We all believe in the Air Force. If I am needed to protect the country, I would not hesitate to enter combat."

General Roberts acknowledged the obvious: many people would be watching the women's progress. He said they would be treated the same as their male classmates, but given the media interest, that seemed unlikely. A week later, reporters and photographers besieged the women when they piled onto a bus to Hondo for their first flights. One reporter trailed Engel through all her preflight activities; she finally escaped the cameras after she lifted off the runway and climbed away.

After completing the Flight Screening Program, the ten women headed to Williams Air Force Base in Arizona, nicknamed "Willie," to meet their forty male classmates and begin pilot training on September 29. Introductions to the men were awkward. Nearly

all the men were recent Air Force Academy graduates, and since all the women except Rambo had been on active duty for a while, they outranked the male students. Connie Engel, already a captain, became the class leader. She couldn't imagine being thrust into a worse situation.

Being the youngest and a reservist helped Rambo fit in. She was the same rank as the guys and, at twenty-one, a little younger. Most important, as a reservist she knew she would be flying a C-141 cargo aircraft, so the men didn't view her as competition for an airplane one of them wanted. She became a regular attendee at the officers' club on Friday evenings, downing her share of beer and stumbling back to the bachelor officer's quarters.

After a few weeks of pilot training, Engel was pleased that the women were doing well. They were earning the men's respect. But she sensed the class wasn't pulling together. The men weren't overtly hostile, but some resented the photographers and reporters who followed the women everywhere. On the other hand, some men, like Dave Clary, welcomed the attention the women got—he liked flying under the radar. No one cared if Dave Clary got a "fair"—the equivalent of a C-minus—doing departure stalls during a flight, but all the senior leadership at Williams knew when one of the women did. And Clary wasn't concerned about being part of a close-knit team. He was just happy to be at pilot training after four years at the Air Force Academy, finally free from the school's oppressive atmosphere, living on his own in an apartment and seeing women regularly for the first time in four years.

Bruce Deane agreed. He and most of his male classmates were ready to party, while the women were more serious. One Friday, a woman asked the men if they wanted to join them to study on the weekend. Deane said, "No, we're going tubing!"

But Engel longed for camaraderie. She wanted her classmates to laugh and tease each other at their Friday class meetings the way the instructor pilots and other classes did. She mentioned her worries to her husband, who was still finishing his degree in Phoenix.

Once a bachelor student pilot himself, Rich suggested that Connie bake brownies for the next Friday class meeting. She thought it was worth a try. But that Thursday, she was exhausted and fell asleep on the couch before dinner. On waking the next

morning, she found a pan of brownies Rich had baked. The food worked: the men started to kid around, and one said, "Hey, Mom Engel, you're all right."

A few weeks later, the students voted on a "prize" called the Horse's Award for the student who did the dumbest thing during any given week. The award was given in fun, but it was also a way for the students to learn from each other's mistakes.

Dave Clary first nominated Mary Livingston. After flying back to the base, her instructor had told her to land in the center of the runway. He meant she should land on the centerline, instead of either on the right side or left side, as was common practice. But Livingston thought the instructor meant for her to land halfway down the runway. She added power and pulled up her nose to stretch out the landing. The instructor grabbed the stick and yelled, "What are you doing?" Livingston replied, "I was going to land in the middle!"

Another student told a story about Connie Engel. Students were not allowed to fly in clouds unless they had an instructor in the airplane, but she had accidentally entered some clouds in the training area while flying solo. After finishing the story, the student said, "I nominate Mom Engel for the Horse's Award."

The students voted. Mom Engel won by a landslide.

She was thrilled at the hooting and hollering as she accepted the award. The women were part of the team.

* * *

Pilot training proceeded at a furious pace. Flying often started at 4:00 a.m. with a T-37 or simulator ride, kept going with academic instruction or exams, and finished late at night with studying. After flying the T-37 primary trainer for several months, Rambo and her classmates moved up to the supersonic T-38. As Rich Engel had predicted, some women struggled to hold the T-38's brakes during the initial engine run-up. A few trips to the gym solved the problem.

As they progressed, the women kept their word about not telling anyone when they were menstruating. Only once did Rambo regret doing so. She woke up with horrible cramps but

decided to fly. Her flight involved flying on instruments alone, as though she were in the clouds. She normally had no problems with such a flight, but that day one of the key instruments was acting up. Between the balky instrument and her cramps, she meandered about the sky.

After a few minutes, her instructor asked, "What's the matter with you today?"

Rambo thought her instructor was tough, but fair. Still, not wanting to admit her problem, she said through clenched teeth, "Why don't you ask your wife what's the matter with me?"

"Oh." The instructor paused as Rambo's words sank in. "Do you want to incomplete the ride?" In other words, did she want to land now? Yes.

They went back up the next day and finished the flight. It was the only time in training Rambo asked for special treatment, and her instructor didn't hold it against her. Most students have an occasional bad day, male or female.

There were a few differences between the men and women. Bruce Deane recalled that Rambo knitted during class and flight briefings, which raised some eyebrows. One day, Deane commented on the knitting, and Rambo said, "I'm listening." Deane knew she was listening; he just thought it looked bad, as if she wasn't paying full attention. It also seemed to Deane that there was sometimes a double standard. He once watched one of the women touch down a little short of the runway during a check ride. It wasn't dangerous—the concrete underrun was stressed to handle such a mistake. But if it had been him, he would have busted the check ride. The woman passed, although with a low grade.

But overall, the women did well. The only major difference noted during the year-long training was that the women tended to express their frustrations in tears. The flying wing commander, Colonel Carl Bailey, flew with all the women, and he believed some were good enough to pilot combat aircraft.

Soon it was time for the students to list the airplanes they wanted to fly after graduation. Student desires played a role in aircraft assignment, but so did class rank. Higher-ranked students were more likely to get the aircraft they asked for. Only the highest-ranked students could expect a fighter.

Rambo's class rank didn't matter; if she graduated, a C-141 cargo plane awaited her at McGuire. It did matter for the other women, even though they were only allowed to request tankers, cargo or passenger aircraft, or trainers. Engel was selected to stay at Willie as an instructor pilot flying the T-38 trainer. It was the closest a woman could get to flying a fighter, with some of the same performance characteristics and the ability to fly in close formation and do aerobatic maneuvers such as loops. Christine Schott wanted to fly fighters but settled for a C-9 aeromedical evacuation aircraft.

The class graduated on September 2, 1977. Connie Engel was one of three distinguished graduates; she also received the Commander's Trophy, which is given to the top student. Mary Donahue, a math whiz who had previously taught at the Air Force Academy, received the Academic Award; she had missed only one of nearly 400 questions during a year of exams.

After graduation, the women scattered across the U.S. to their new assignments. They were on their own to make their way with their new units. They would not see each other again for many years.

Figure 14: The first ten women to graduate from U.S. Air Force pilot training, 1977. Kathy Rambo is second from right. (Courtesy of National Archives and Records Administration)

* * *

As the women pilots made history, the generation that preceded them made their own mark. Prior to disbanding, the WASP had created an organization, the Order of Fifinella, named for the WASP mascot, a gremlin cartoon character designed by Walt Disney. Former WASP used the Order of Fifinella to remain in touch, organize reunions, and advocate for the benefits denied to them. With the military's renewed interest in women pilots, the WASP doubled down on their advocacy, and, as with many women's issues, found an ally in an unexpected place. Barry Goldwater, a conservative Republican senator from Arizona and one of the eight senators who voted against the ERA, took up the WASP's case in 1976 and introduced a bill to provide military recognition.

One might have thought that by the 1970s, it would be obvious the women deserved recognition. There was plenty of evidence that the WASP had been a military organization except in name. The long hours, the highly classified missions such as Ann Baumgartner's jet flight, the uniforms, and the extensive training programs similar to the men's made it clear the women had not just been another civilian support organization. Also, Colonel Bruce Arnold, son of Hap Arnold, knew his father had wanted to militarize the WASP. Unfortunately, the elder Arnold had died in 1950 before he had a chance to do anything about it.

A surprising number of factions opposed recognition, including the Veterans Administration, who worried that giving benefits to the small number of WASP would open the floodgates for anyone who had served in a quasi-military organization such as the Civil Air Patrol. Bruce Arnold pointed out that the WASP had much more dangerous jobs than those other organizations. Didn't the WASP deserve the same benefits as an Army private with an office job whose biggest worry was a paper cut?

Finally, in the fall of 1977, Congress agreed. Both the House and Senate passed a bill to provide veterans' benefits to the WASP. President Jimmy Carter signed the bill into law on November 23, 1977.

* * *

A few months after the first women arrived at Williams for pilot training, the Air Force announced a new test program for women navigators. Officials at the navigator training wing at Mather Air Force Base, California, obsessed over making sure there would be few, if any, problems. They even sent a woman, Second Lieutenant Veronica Long, through a brief "test" program for, of course, the test program. Long kept up with men in physical training and operated the equipment required on the aircraft used to train navigators, the T-43, a military version of a Boeing 737.

The colonel who oversaw flying operations at Mather still wasn't happy; about a month before the women arrived for training, he claimed they created several "issues" and directed his staff to prepare papers to address the alleged problems.

The staff dutifully wrote up seven "issue papers" on bachelor quarters, physical training, parachutes, counseling of women, dress and appearance standards, medical care, and publicity. The authors found nothing that would prevent women from completing the training. But the combat exclusion came up. One author wrote, "If women are only assigned to 'good deal' aircraft such as airlift, weather, research, flight test or special air missions, friction may develop between male and female navigators as males will have to crew all the combat aircraft." It was an odd position for an officer to take, given that most men preferred to fly combat aircraft.

One of the more interesting papers addressed men counseling women on their performance; the author feared a woman might use a male counselor's concerns about their tears and "emotional fragility" to gain an advantage in the relationship. However, the author noted that professional counselors did not consider this to be a problem. The paper concluded that women should be counseled in the same way as men. Instructor pilots had already come to that conclusion. Roger Brady, who was an instructor at Reese Air Force Base in Texas when the second set of women pilots came through, recalled a meeting where another instructor asked what to do if a woman started crying during a debriefing. A crusty old instructor sitting in the back row piped up: "The same thing you do when one of the men starts to cry. You tell them to suck it up."

The student navigators came from a variety of backgrounds. Florence Parker, a munitions maintenance officer, was so excited at the prospect of flying that she sang all the way during her drive from Texas to Mather. Captain Bettye Payne had been a maintenance officer; one of the F-4 fighter pilots she worked with encouraged her to apply. At Mather, she found that "everyone wasn't as friendly as they could be…. They thought it was an Air Force publicity stunt." Another woman was told, "My buddy didn't make nav training because of you." One poor instructor had to call an office in the Pentagon every Friday at 4:00 a.m. to report how the women were doing.

The women did fine; in some areas, they outperformed their twelve male classmates and in other areas underperformed the men. In October 1977, one of the women graduated at the top of the class; another woman was a distinguished graduate.

The navigator program broke a second barrier: Bettye Payne became the first Black female rated officer in the Air Force. She told a United Press International reporter, "Give me a sextant, and I can take you anywhere in the world." But the combat exclusion law meant Payne could only navigate anywhere in the world on a cargo airplane or refueling tanker. She said, "Personally, I have no qualms about going into combat. But until Congress changes the law, there's no chance." She was assigned to fly C-141 cargo aircraft at Travis Air Force Base, California.

The women navigators had opened another door, but it wasn't yet clear if any other women would come through behind them. There were no plans to admit other women to navigator training until the women's performance was evaluated under operational conditions. But at least one man was convinced the women were here to stay, even if he wasn't sure where to put them all, given the combat limitation. Colonel Attilio Pedroli, a combat veteran of both the Korean and Vietnam wars, and the women's wing commander, proclaimed: "[The] results speak for themselves. Two out of the six women were named Distinguished Graduates. I think they've proved there's a place for women in navigation."

* * *

After graduating from pilot training, Kathy Rambo headed to Altus Air Force Base to learn to fly the C-141. The cargo aircraft was ten times the size of the T-38 trainer she flew at pilot training. In some ways, it was like driving a sports car in the Indianapolis 500 one day and jumping into a semi-truck the next, but she found the transition straightforward. Most of the training was done in a simulator and involved learning procedures and running checklists. The only time she flew in the airplane was to practice takeoffs and landings, including the day she landed in the twenty-five-knot crosswind.

Rambo finished her training on a Friday, then drove to the Oklahoma City airport and hopped on a commercial flight to Phoenix. She had one more mission to accomplish before reporting to McGuire: getting married.

Rambo had met Bob Cosand during pilot training. He was in a class behind hers and hadn't yet graduated. He picked her up at the Phoenix airport, and they were married at the Willie chapel on Saturday. On Sunday, she flew back to Oklahoma City, grabbed her car, and started driving. She reported to her squadron at McGuire on Monday.

That same day, Bob visited his squadron commander's office. The commander had previously hinted that Bob would be staying at Willie as a T-38 instructor. Normally, that would be music to a student's ears; a T-38 at Willie meant that in a few years, the student was likely to be flying fighters, if the student was a man anyway.

Bob had other ideas. He slid his fresh marriage certificate across the commander's desk and said, "Sir, that's a C-141 to McGuire Air Force Base."

Shocked, the commander said, "You can't get married without my approval."

"Well, I did."

The commander had a hard time believing Cosand wanted to follow Rambo to McGuire. Women were supposed to follow their husbands, not the other way around. For decades, with women largely in administrative and nursing positions, that formula had worked. Not anymore. Bob Cosand joined his wife, now Kathy Cosand, at McGuire.

Another pilot couple was also bending gender norms. Rich Engel was about to graduate from the Air Force's Test Pilot School. He also wanted to join his wife. He normally would have been assigned to Edwards or to Eglin Air Force Base in Florida; career-wise, those were his best options. But the Air Force had a position for a test pilot in a research lab at Willie. Rich, now accustomed to being referred to as "Connie Engel's husband," requested the Willie assignment. His superior officers agreed.

* * *

It didn't take long for the combat restrictions to cause problems for the Air Force's women pilots. In May of 1978, Kathy Cosand had been flying around Europe for five months when her aircraft commander, Major Hepburn, approached her.

"Hey, Kath, we're going to go do some stuff down in Zaire. Do you want to go?"

Cosand's eyes lit up. "Yeah!"

"Get your gear, go out to the airplane, and go hide."

In the wake of an uprising, Zaire was a hostile area. Cosand's legal ability to fly a military aircraft into the country wasn't clear. But American aircraft weren't flying in the area of the immediate conflict. Her C-141 cargo aircraft couldn't shoot anyone or drop any bombs. But did flying combat troops into a hostile area constitute a combat mission? If an enemy on the ground tried to shoot down her aircraft, did that mean she was on a combat mission? The law's language left a gray area large enough to fly a cargo aircraft through.

Cosand crawled into a part of the aircraft used for resting during long flights while Hepburn recruited other crewmembers. He wrote Cosand's name on the flight orders, but since she was the only woman east of the Mississippi flying C-141s, no one who reviewed the orders thought to check for a woman's name.

The crew stopped to pick up some French Foreign Legion soldiers, deposited them in Liberia, and then flew to Kinshasa in Zaire. Cosand flew several missions around Zaire, shuttling French and Belgian troops and moving U.S. support personnel into locations outside the conflict area near Kolwezi.

The flying was adventurous, but the living conditions were even more so. In Zaire, everyone seemed to be armed, and the aircrew carried only small .38 caliber pistols. When the C-141 landed for the first evening's rest, Cosand decided she didn't want to be by herself. She asked Hepburn, "Can I have a roommate?"

Hepburn surveyed the aircrew standing on the ramp and said, "Pick one."

Cosand chose the other copilot. He was six-foot-two and lugged around a Bible and a picture of his wife and kids. She figured they would be safe from each other.

"Hey, what do you think? Separate beds and all that?"

It worked. Nothing happened.

After about a week, Air Force higher-ups realized a woman was flying in Africa. They weren't pleased. They ordered the crew back to the U.S., but when Cosand and the others arrived, her superiors didn't seem to mind what had happened. Neither did Bob nor the copilot's wife. One of the first things they did was introduce their spouses to each other. The shared quarters were not an issue.

The Air Force gave each crewmember in the Africa operation an Air Medal, which is awarded for "single acts of heroism or meritorious achievement while participating in aerial flight." At first, they contemplated not giving one to Cosand as she wasn't supposed to be on the flights. But someone decided that how she got to Zaire was irrelevant. A handful of female nurses had previously been awarded Air Medals, but Cosand was the first woman pilot to earn one.

* * *

With no role models to guide her and no other women pilots at McGuire, Cosand was on her own to figure out how to fit in with her male counterparts. Understanding that she was intruding on the men's domain, she tried not to draw undue attention to herself. She never insisted the men make changes to accommodate her. Instead, she struck a balance between accepting much of the men's culture while drawing the line when something made her uncomfortable.

Like pornography. Most of the men, including Bob, carried porn magazines on the airplane; they perused them to pass the

time after leveling off at cruising altitude. Cosand disliked the porn, but the men were usually discreet, so she tolerated it. She knitted to pass the time. But then someone complained, and her squadron commander asked her to stop. She objected. There was no safety issue: she knitted without looking at her needles. She could easily monitor the aircraft instruments and look outside. She told her commander that if she couldn't knit, she didn't want porn in the cockpit. She got to keep knitting.

The men crossed Cosand's line on one trip, sharing details over the aircraft intercom about the naked women they were viewing. Another woman was on the trip, so during a layover, the two bought a *Playgirl* magazine. The next day, they laid Mr. August out on the center console and began discussing his attributes over the intercom. The guys got the message.

Despite Cosand's desire to avoid attention, the combat exclusion sometimes made that impossible. In the late 1970s, the Air Force modified the C-141s that Cosand flew so the aircraft could be refueled in flight to extend their range. But not every pilot became qualified to do aerial refueling. The tricky maneuver, performed only tens of feet away from another huge aircraft, a KC-135, required special training. In January 1979, Cosand headed back to Altus for training to upgrade to aircraft commander, which would allow her to fly from the left seat. One of her superiors, confident in her capabilities, requested she take a second course on aerial refueling. But an even higher-level superior considered aerial refueling a combat-related mission; he canceled Cosand's attendance at the second course. If she'd taken the training, she could have trained male pilots on how to conduct aerial refueling, but the superior said she shouldn't even be doing that. She settled for flying aerial refueling missions as a copilot. She ran checklists, monitored the pilot in the left seat who flew the actual maneuver, and trained to do an emergency breakaway if ever needed. Despite its dramatic name, the breakaway involved no actual skill: just push the nose of the airplane down and turn away. Any pilot could do it.

Twenty years later, her unit offered to train her on aerial refueling. Her response: "I put up my middle finger."

*　　*　　*

In late June 1976, Margie Clark from Gainesville, Florida, was one of 157 women who arrived at the Air Force Academy campus in Colorado Springs to begin Basic Cadet Training, also called "Beast." In the fall of 1975, Clark's father had showed her a newspaper article about the academy accepting women, and she'd sent off for a catalog. When Clark read in the catalog that at least 65 percent of academy graduates attended pilot training every year, she was hooked. She didn't realize the catalog was from the previous year when only male cadets were at the academy. She pressed ahead with her application. As a gymnast with high academic scores and other extracurricular activities, she was easily admitted. During Beast, she impressed both men and women with her ability to do pullups.

Anne Martin of Albuquerque had a rockier path to admission. Unlike Clark, she had read the fine print and realized from the start she was gambling on the Air Force to open pilot training to women before she graduated. She had good grades and SAT scores, but not quite high enough to qualify academically as a non-pilot applicant. The academy was only taking women as non-pilot applicants since they weren't expected to go to pilot training. And while one might think pilot candidates would have higher academic scores, the reverse was true. Because so many applicants couldn't qualify as pilots, primarily because of poor eyesight, competition for the non-pilot spots was fierce and the academic standards for admission much higher. But there are other ways to get into a service academy. A family friend introduced Martin to an academy coach who recruited her as a swimmer. When the coach saw her swim after arriving in Colorado Springs, he sent her to the cross-country running team instead. But she was in.

During Beast, some upperclassmen harassed the male cadets more than usual because the presence of women supposedly resulted in an easier program. But the women quickly put some men in their place. Classmate James M. Dunn III, who hadn't expected the women to last a week, later told United Press International reporter Deborah Frazier: "But there they were—girls who had long curly hair the week before doing things I did as well or better. The real clincher was the obstacle and assault course. It was the toughest

thing I had ever done. And the girls did it. My theories about women were disproved before my very eyes."

<p style="text-align:center">*　　*　　*</p>

The academy women were shocked when they learned they wouldn't be fully integrated with the rest of the cadets. Fearful that men would not accept the women, academy leadership housed the female cadets in a dormitory far away. Women were also assigned to only half the forty cadet squadrons; academy leadership worried that spreading 150 or so women across forty squadrons would result in too few women per squadron. Six or seven women in each of the twenty squadrons would apparently achieve some sort of critical mass.

The women participated in all squadron activities such as marching and other military training, but it was soon obvious that being isolated in the evenings and on weekends hurt their acceptance by the male cadets. This was especially true for the upperclassmen, many of whom were openly hostile to the women.

One advantage to keeping the women together was that they formed a tight-knit group that remains together to this day. But they were still relieved when academy leadership moved them in with the rest of the cadets in early 1977. They were also integrated into all forty squadrons, which caused some initial consternation from male cadets who thought they had escaped having to deal with women. But most men were supportive; their classmates even helped the women shuttle belongings across the campus into the new dormitory areas. The women initially lived on a separate floor but after another year were mixed throughout the dorms. The only rule was that roommates had to be the same gender.

The Air Force decided the pilot and navigator training experiments had succeeded. Aspiring pilots in the academy class of 1980, including Margie Clark and Anne Martin, were allowed to train in a small Cessna aircraft a year before they graduated.

As the women proved themselves, the men in the class ahead of them, 1979, made a last jab at the indignity they believed they suffered from the women's presence. The class dubbed themselves the "Last Class with Balls" and ordered class rings engraved with the

initials L.C.W.B. When Brigadier General Thomas Richards, who took over as commandant of cadets in March of 1978, learned of the inscription, he canceled the order.

On February 21, 1979, just a few months before graduation, cadets were greeted by a giant banner hanging on the side of one of the cadet dormitories. The banner bore a caricature of Richards dressed in a king's robe, adorned with a crown, and an erect penis in place of his nose. Words above the crown made the offenders clear: "King Richard—You can be as hard as you want to, but not for long."

The next day, Richards assembled the senior class and asked those responsible to come forward. When no one did, he grounded the entire class, all 907 of them. They could not leave their quarters until someone claimed responsibility. Late that same evening, the guilty parties confessed.

Once the 1979 class graduated, the academy had only cadets who had worked with women from their first day of training. The change was apparent one day when the class of 1980 assembled prior to lunch on the quadrangle outside the dining hall. On some days, one or more aircraft from the local area or on a cross-country flight from another base flew over the formation of cadets, a treat timed to excite and motivate them about their future Air Force careers. On this day, a single T-38 training aircraft swooped toward the cadets, leveled off a few hundred feet above the quadrangle, and flicked onto its side as it swept by with engines screaming in a thunderous roar. The cadets jerked their heads skyward and cheered before entering the dining hall.

Inside, the cadets listened to a few administrative notes before eating. Then the announcer said, "And finally, the pilot of that T-38 was Lieutenant Eileen Collins from Vance Air Force Base!"

It took a second for the pilot's gender to sink in. Then the cadets broke into applause and cheers, with female cadets yelling the loudest. In a few short months, they too could be flying that T-38.

Fifteen years later, Eileen Collins, now a lieutenant colonel, became the first woman to pilot a Space Shuttle. In 1999, she became the first woman commander of a Space Shuttle.

* * *

On May 28, 1980, the first class of women graduated from the Air Force Academy. Ninety-seven of the original 157 had survived the four-year program, along with 790 of their male classmates. The top woman graduate, Kathleen M. Conley, was ranked eighth in the class with a 3.82 GPA. She didn't appreciate the extra attention the press showered on the women. When a reporter asked June A. Van Horn, who graduated three spots behind Conley, what was the hardest part about attending the academy, she replied, "Putting up with the press." Several of her male classmates chorused, "Right on!" Some of the men still resented the continued media presence, while others realized the attention wasn't the women's fault. One of the men said, "In a few years, people will say it's no big deal."

Peggy Carnahan had seen much progress in male attitudes during the four years: "When we came, there were a few diehards who really didn't want us at all and thought maybe they could make us leave. Now, they accept us as people. They don't see us as an intrusion into their private world."

Figure 15: The first women to graduate from the U.S. Air Force Academy, May 1980. Margie Clark is in the second row, fourth from right. (Courtesy of the U.S. Air Force, Margie Varuska Collection)

* * *

My father retired from the Air Force in 1974, right after I graduated from high school, and our family moved to Seattle. I enrolled at the University of Washington in January 1975. After starting out in aeronautical engineering, I switched to computer science.

In college, I became accustomed to being the only woman or one of a handful in my technical classes. No one seemed to mind my presence. But it bothered some people, as I learned one day when I met up with a school friend for lunch. She often brought along other friends of hers to our lunches, and one day, one of the young men asked me what I was majoring in. His eyes narrowed when I told him computer science.

"What are you majoring in that for? You're wasting your time, and you're taking away a slot from a guy who should be getting that degree. You're just going to get married and have babies."

I stared at him for a few seconds, not believing what I had just heard.

"I am not just going to get married and have babies. I'm going to have a career."

"No, you won't. I bet five years from now you're just going to have a bunch of babies."

"No, I'm not. I'll show you."

No one stood up for me, and I saw there was no point in arguing. I stopped having lunch with my friend, and I never saw my antagonist again. I have occasionally wondered what it would be like to run into him and say, "See, see! I didn't just get married and have kids." Although I imagine he would launch into another tirade about how I had wasted my life by not ever having kids.

This young man's attitude wasn't unusual for the 1970s. The women's liberation movement had helped open doors, but going through the doors was still perilous. You never knew what sort of attitude you might collide with on the other side, as I learned again and again.

The summer between my junior and senior years, I landed a coveted paid internship with Boeing. Along with other interns, I worked in the flight test department. Like most interns, I toiled over grunt work, such as data entry on keypunch machines, but

we were supposed to fly on a few test missions as well. These were relatively mundane flights, such as checking out the cabin air flow provided by a new environmental control system, not the sort of risky flights popularized by Tom Wolfe's *The Right Stuff*. Nevertheless, the idea of going on a test flight appealed to my sense of adventure.

On the day of my first test flight, I boarded the aircraft, a 727, with several other interns, all of them male. We fastened our seat belts and waited for the engine start and takeoff.

One of the pilots entered the cabin and came over to me.

"I'm sorry, you have to get off."

I looked at him, shocked.

"Why?"

"I took my secretary for a flight last week and I got in a lot of trouble."

"I'm not a secretary. I'm an intern."

"I'm sorry. I can't risk it."

None of the male interns stood up for me.

I was furious, but I had no idea what to do. I got off the plane, walked back into the office where I worked, and sat down.

One of the women who helped with data entry spotted me and walked over. "I thought you were flying."

"Apparently I'm the wrong sex."

After I told her the story, she dragged me into the office of our immediate supervisor, who was one of the first women ever promoted to a significant supervisory position at Boeing. She listened to my story in disbelief and said she would take care of it.

She did. A few days later, I flew on a photo flight with Boeing's chief pilot, Lew Wallick. The pilot who kicked me off the airplane never apologized, but no one at Boeing hassled me about flying again.

* * *

As the 1980s began, military women had made significant progress. Women were no longer dismissed for pregnancy or dependents, their spouses were full dependents, they could be commissioned through ROTC or attend a service academy, and more career fields, including aviation, were open to them.

Even with all the progress, Carolyn Becraft, the dietician who had left the Army a decade earlier to follow her husband, knew there was much more work to be done. And she wanted to help. She had earned a master's degree in education while her family was stationed in Germany. Acutely aware of women's issues after her own experiences, she wrote her thesis on the effects of the women's movement on officers' wives. Viewed by the military as critical to their husbands' careers, the women were expected to throw great parties in spotless houses and keep a stiff upper lip when stationed in locations such as the swamps of Georgia. Becraft's research was easy: she knew all the wives. Her topic clearly hit a nerve: she got an unprecedented 75 percent return rate on the questionnaires she sent out. The results weren't a surprise: the women's movement had made the wives aware that they could be more than just an appendage of their husbands, and the women hated their circumstances. Their living situation was too restrictive, and they wanted to work, to do something meaningful.

Becraft wasn't sure what to do next, but she knew she wouldn't be going back into dietetics. After she finished her thesis, her family moved to Fort Myer in the Washington, D.C., area. The Army officers' wives club was hosting a seminar on Army families, and she thought perhaps she could be part of it. It wouldn't be a paid gig, but it could lead to something.

Becraft called the woman organizing the seminar and told her she'd like to volunteer. After the organizer asked a few questions, she said, "Why don't you be a facilitator? You've done that before."

"Of course," said Becraft. After she hung up, she grabbed her dictionary and looked up "facilitator." She figured she could do the job.

Being a facilitator involved working with retired generals' wives who saw Becraft's passion for family and women's issues. After the seminar, she chaired the after-action committee that developed six recommendations for the chief of staff of the Army; he accepted them all. None of them were earth-shattering. The women knew it was best to start small. One suggestion was to establish a liaison office for family issues, another to establish an office to disseminate information to families.

Becraft's volunteer work began to take off. Another year and symposium later, she was volunteering fifty hours each week. She

designed a new Army process, the Family Action Planning Process, on her kitchen table. The process allowed commanders at all levels to solve problems within their purview; for example, if families wanted the post's veterinary clinic to stay open on Saturdays, the post commander could make that decision. Issues that impacted multiple Army posts or the other services would make their way up the chain until reaching someone with the authority to make a decision. A few issues required congressional legislation to solve, and in the process of working those issues, Becraft began to fill her Rolodex with people she met in other Washington agencies.

One person Becraft met steered her to a paid position with the Women's Equity Action League, or WEAL, founded in 1968 as a conservative alternative to the National Organization for Women, or NOW. In 1982, WEAL was looking for a director of their Women in the Military Project. Becraft read the job description and thought, *I wouldn't even have to lie to get the job*, unlike her volunteer gig at Fort Myer.

Jeanne Holm was on WEAL's advisory committee, and she liked that Becraft had military experience and plenty of Washington contacts. The other applicants were academics, and Becraft got the job. Her Rolodex continued to expand. And in politics, a Rolodex can be a lethal weapon.

CHAPTER 5
Part of the Team, Not One of the Guys (1980-1985)

It was a Friday night at Holloman Air Force Base, New Mexico, in 1983. My flight had landed late, and I didn't have time to go home and change into civilian clothes before I headed to the officers' club. I tried to stroll nonchalantly into the bar, but my path might as well have been marked with orange cones and a flashing yellow sign that screamed, "Danger, danger, female in flight suit approaching!" I grabbed a beer and walked toward my usual crowd.

A tall, blond F-15 pilot with a history of excess fighter pilot bravado stepped into my path and stared at me. He was also a lieutenant.

"What's up with the flight suit?"

"Usually I go home and change, but I flew late today."

"I think that's usually a good idea."

My brain exploded with so many bells, buzzers, crashes, and clanks that I thought I might spontaneously combust. I felt obligated to defend my honor and the honor of every female aviator. But not a single word formed in the cognitive dissonance that ping-ponged off every nerve in my body. My throat was clamped shut.

After several seconds of uncomfortable silence, I mumbled something about using the restroom and slinked away.

Just three years earlier, me dressed in a flight suit and dealing with fighter pilot machismo was not a scene I would have imagined possible.

A couple of weeks before the first class of women graduated from the Air Force Academy, I raised my right hand and enlisted in the Air Force. Two days later, I left Seattle to attend Officer Training School in Texas. Mount St. Helens erupted that same day.

The ash cloud from the volcano delayed my flight for several hours, and I arrived in San Antonio about two in the morning. Thirty minutes later, I sat in a car with an officer trainee sent to retrieve me. Despite the hour, he wore a crisp blue uniform. He said he had been in training for six weeks.

As he drove to the base, he warned about what lay ahead.

"You have to take tests, give briefings, write papers, march, and do sports. Everything is graded. If you get three busts, they'll kick you out. I've got two busts already and I'm not sure I'm going to make it."

Despite my grogginess, he had my full attention. Three busts? What chance did I have?

He continued, "They have this thing called 'drill performance review,' where you have to march your flight around. I busted that twice."

I was wide awake now. It hadn't occurred to me that, as an officer, part of leading would mean giving the marching orders, not just taking them.

"That sounds awful," was all I could manage.

I was pretty sure I was doomed.

After a couple hours of sleep in a spare room and no breakfast, another upperclassman gave me a one-inch-thick book of regulations and showed me to my room.

"Hi, I'm Jo Ellen," my new roommate said. "I got here on Friday, so I've kind of got things figured out."

Oh, good, I thought. *Maybe I'm not doomed after all.*

After some chit-chat, Jo Ellen showed me the ropes. First, the regulation way to roll up a pair of socks: Lay the socks flat on top of each other and roll them from the toes to the top, keeping the roll as tight as possible. Then take the outside sock and fold it back onto itself, tucking the roll inside. When you turn it around, the socks now look like a smiley face without eyes or a nose.

I managed a passable smile.

Opening a dresser drawer, Jo Ellen pointed to a formation of socks that looked ready to march into battle and said, "Just line them up, all touching, and make sure they're smiling."

Sure enough, there were no frowning socks in Jo Ellen's drawer.

I thought about my laundry basket back home, the one I often used as my sock drawer because I was too lazy to put my socks away.

I was now certain that I was doomed.

* * *

I took a computer programming job after graduating from college but grew bored after about six months. I began to see computer programs as tools—a means to an end, not the end itself—and I wanted to use the tools, not just build them. As part of my search for a new job, I signed up for an interview with Boeing and, on a whim, the Air Force, at the University of Washington placement center.

The military had changed dramatically since I had graduated from high school, and my attitude had softened as well. My closest male friend in college was now a Navy pilot, and I didn't consider him weird, as I had the high school Junior ROTC students.

I had planned to just talk to the Air Force recruiter, but the next thing I knew, I was filling out forms and scheduling an appointment to take aptitude tests and a physical examination. Within a few months, the Air Force had accepted me for officer training. But they didn't want my computer science degree. They were short on engineers and wanted to send me back to school for eighteen months to get a second bachelor's degree in aeronautical engineering at the Air Force Institute of Technology at Wright-Patterson Air Force Base in Ohio. The program was designed for people like me, who had lots of college-level math and science courses but had earned degrees other than engineering.

I figured out how to roll my socks and survived the marching drill. My classmates learned that, although we received individual grades as leaders, we all performed better if we acted as a team. If the person leading the formation accidentally called a left turn when we knew the next turn was supposed to be to the right, the person at the head of the formation turned to the right anyway. When the flight leader called for us to halt and make facing maneuvers, we subtly

shuffled ourselves to correct minor alignment errors. The instructors praised us for our teamwork.

After everyone in my flight passed the drill test, my confidence soared. I no longer had any doubts about my ability to graduate. And for the first time in my life, I truly felt part of a team.

But not everyone at officer training felt as if they were on the team. A woman in a different flight from me was harassed by her flight commander. During an inspection, he asked her to open her personal drawer—a drawer in our room where we kept items such as prescription drugs or valuables. The personal drawer was fair game during an inspection, but only to be sure it contained no contraband. When the trainee opened her drawer, he asked, "Is that where you keep your birth control pills?"

The trainee was horrified. It wasn't the first time the flight commander had said such a thing, and she was tired of him. She submitted her resignation.

I didn't know the woman well; I heard about her situation from one of my female flight mates. But I was incensed.

I told my flight mate, "That's just wrong. She should say something to someone higher up the chain of command like they tell us to do."

"She's sick of it. She just wants to leave."

"Shouldn't we say something?"

"I doubt it would do any good at this point."

I thought, how could one person in charge ruin another person's career, especially when the person in charge was the one at fault? I felt powerless. It wouldn't be the last time.

* * *

After a couple months of officer training, it dawned on me that if I was going to be an Air Force officer, I probably ought to be flying. I couldn't be a pilot; my nearsightedness prevented that. But I could clear the eyesight bar required for navigator training. I consulted someone on the staff about changing career fields, but he thought it was too late. He suggested I complete the engineering program and then apply for navigator school.

After getting my commission on August 15, 1980, I headed to Ohio, but my real goal was now navigator training. Still, I had doubts. As a navigator, I would probably fly in either C-141 transports or KC-135 refueling tankers. It irritated me that I wouldn't get to fly in more exotic aircraft like the F-15, the Air Force's hottest new fighter.

Then a casual conversation changed everything. A first lieutenant I met in a chance encounter told me he had been a flight test engineer at a base called Holloman, near a town named Alamogordo in New Mexico. He had flown in the back of C-141s and F-4s, testing something called inertial navigation systems.

I had no idea what an inertial navigation system was, but I knew that an F-4 was a fighter, even if it was an older Vietnam-era aircraft. Was it possible I could fly in the F-4?

The lieutenant explained that since this F-4 was used for testing, it wasn't a combat airplane. He knew of several women flight test engineers who had flown in fighters. In fact, one was going through Test Pilot School at that very moment.

That engineers could go through Test Pilot School was another revelation. The lieutenant said there was a regulation that explained it all, a regulation I found and devoured a few days later.

I had one more question: "How do I get a job at Holloman?"

The lieutenant said he would get me some phone numbers.

I abandoned all thoughts of navigator training. Why would I do that when I could fly in fighters instead? It wouldn't be a combat aircraft, but like a handful of other Air Force and Navy women, I had found a loophole that would at least get me into the cockpit of one of those coveted beasts.

But first, I had to get through the engineering program. The pace was unrelenting, six quarters of nothing but engineering classes, three or four at a time. Two students in my class of thirty dropped out before we even started. Three more were dismissed during the program. The only way most of us survived was to study together as much as we could.

My first study group got off to a rocky start. There were eight women in my class, an astonishing number given that women made up less than 10 percent of technical degrees in the U.S. at the time. The number may have been a coincidence, but the Carter administration's push for more women likely played a factor. Five

of the eight women met regularly with our study group, which had an equal number of men. But the men were seldom prepared, and they'd waste at least a half hour talking about football. The women agreed: the men had to go. We didn't kick them out; we just stopped inviting them. Our study group's productivity soared, along with our grades.

A few months later, three graduate students—all captains—joined one of our most difficult classes: heat transfer. They hadn't taken the course as undergraduates at the Air Force Academy. The trio huddled together in the back of the classroom, as if intimidated by twenty-five second lieutenants.

One day after class, the captains approached me. They looked desperate.

The spokesman said, "We've been out of school for too long, and we're dying. We were wondering if we could join your study group. We promise we won't say a word. We'll just sit in the back and watch."

They seemed sincere. Plus, they were all pilots, and it might be a good chance to learn about flying in the real Air Force.

"I'll have to ask the others, okay?"

I made their case, and we let them in. The pilots kept their word. As the quarter wore on, they occasionally asked questions or contributed to the discussion. Then they starting hanging around after our session, and we picked their brains about military flying. We all passed the course.

*　　*　　*

In November 1980, Ronald Reagan was elected president. A few months into his presidency, it appeared to me that a war on women in the military had begun. The next class of undergraduate students that summer seemed to confirm my suspicions: the class had only one woman. How could we have gone from eight women to one? Something sinister seemed afoot, and I blamed the administration.

But it wasn't Reagan's fault. He opposed women in combat roles, but his administration favored continued increases in women. So why the apparent war?

The services were to blame. Reagan's election had emboldened them. They recommended that the transition team minimize the number of women brought in until they could do additional studies.

The services must have thought their recommendation was a brilliant ploy. They had lost the ability to ask, "Why should women serve?" So they shifted their strategy to ask, "What impact do women have on readiness?" The March 30, 1981, *Air Force Times* reported that Pentagon officials were planning to study the issues that women brought along as they flowed into nontraditional career fields: "pregnancy rates, married service couples, dependent care, and single parents." Surely, the services believed, those factors must have a negative impact on readiness. The motivation was obvious: if a study showed that women hurt readiness, the services could scale back on their numbers. With fewer women, the services would be unlikely to meet recruiting goals. The ensuing manpower shortage would force a return to the draft, which is what the services wanted.

A year into the administration, Reagan officials fought back. Defense Secretary Caspar W. Weinberger wanted "the fullest use of military women." Although he did not suggest a repeal of the combat exclusion laws, he believed women were essential to maintaining the numbers needed for a ready force. Turning the tables on the services, he asked them to identify barriers in their personnel policies that reduced recruiting or career opportunities for women.

Lawrence J. Korb, in charge of manpower for the Department of Defense, piled on. He thought the services weren't doing enough to recognize the contributions of women. Not only did he seek to elevate women, he believed the new studies did great harm. When he visited military bases, women told him the studies implied their presence had a negative impact on readiness.

The studies continued, but others also questioned their relevance. Testifying before the Subcommittee on Military Personnel and Compensation of the House Armed Services Committee in November 1983, Carolyn Becraft quoted Senator William Proxmire's exasperation: "Every study indicates that qualified women can serve in any capacity. But each time the Pentagon receives a report confirming this conclusion it…simply commissions another study."

It was time to stop viewing women as a social experiment. Becraft testified that instead, "they should be viewed as full members

of the defense team.... It is not the utilization of women that poses a threat to military readiness and national security, but rather the lack of commitment to women in the military."

Becraft further decried the inconsistent interpretations of the combat exclusion laws and policies across the services. She called out the Army for closing twenty-three specialties to women in 1982 and closing additional units to women in 1983, even after some women had been selected for assignment to those units. After much criticism, the Army backtracked, but Becraft urged Congress to "not overlook that the Army's study of women and shifting policies have had a devastating effect on the morale of Army women." Becraft finished her testimony with an admonishment: "Continuous studies measuring the 'effect of women on military readiness' sends signals to women that their presence is neither appreciated nor respected and may be tenuous.... Military readiness and unit performance can only improve when women are assured of a permanent role for themselves in the military."

I followed the politics du jour regarding the shifting stances of the services. As an engineer, I wasn't directly impacted by the combat exclusion policy, but every time I saw an attack on a group of women or an individual woman, I had to wonder when someone might come after me.

* * *

I earned my bachelor's degree in aeronautical engineering in March 1982 and arrived at Holloman a few weeks later. I had landed a flight test engineer job, so I spent the first six weeks filling out paperwork and rushing around the base to get a flight physical and pick up the equipment I needed: Nomex flight suits, gloves, official long underwear, prescription aviator glasses, helmet and oxygen mask (for emergency use only, since I'd initially be flying in cargo aircraft), and miscellaneous gear such as an official Air Force aviator's watch that I never wore because it was too big. Then it was off to Reese Air Force Base for three days to train in the altitude chamber—a pressurized cylinder that simulated flight at high altitudes. We practiced taking off our masks to become hypoxic so we'd know what our symptoms were if it happened in real life. There was also

a rapid decompression so we'd recognize one—a bang with a thick spray of mist and rush of cold air. A flight surgeon had warned me before my training that women were more prone to get the bends—decompression sickness—after their chamber rides, but I didn't have any problems.

When I returned to Holloman, my supervisor, a captain, pushed to finish my paperwork to put me on flying status. I was excited to start flying, but he was doing it for himself, not me. On a recent long-duration flight that required an overnight stay at a base in Georgia, the airplane had broken, and the crew wound up staying in Georgia for several days. His wife was upset and didn't want him to fly on the next long flight; he needed me to replace him. The captain was lazy about getting most things done, but he pushed my paperwork through in time for the flight.

I was soon flying regularly in the back of a C-141 cargo aircraft. The airplane didn't belong to my unit; it and the crew had come down from a test wing at Wright-Patterson. We loaded our inertial navigation systems onto cargo pallets and pushed them onto the aircraft, along with another pallet that contained a reference system—a highly accurate navigation system we used as our "truth source" to see how well the systems under test were performing. A couple of other pallets with seats for the crews running the navigation systems rounded out our equipment.

After a couple of flights, my boss decided I was proficient enough to be a "mission commander," meaning I was in charge of running the tests in the back of the airplane. As mission commander, I coordinated with the pilots on routes and turn points, made decisions on whether to continue a test if there were problems, and kept an eye on everyone in the back of the airplane: a mix of enlisted system operators and equipment technicians, plus a couple of officers who ran the reference system and analyzed the data.

It was heady stuff for a twenty-four-year-old second lieutenant, and I was pretty clueless at first. But the enlisted members I worked with were old pros, especially a technical sergeant I often flew with. If I wasn't sure about something, I'd solicit his advice. He'd say, "Captain so-and-so would usually do this." I'd say, "Okay," and then I'd do "this." After a few flights, I gained enough confidence to make my own decisions.

I loved the flying but, like other women aviators, my biggest problem was relieving myself in flight. The C-141, designed to carry passengers, had an airline-style lavatory on board, but it was replaced a couple of months later with a C-130, a smaller propeller airplane used for more tactical missions. For that reason, the aircraft had been built to accommodate only men. The "facilities" consisted of a relief tube connected to a funnel and a "honey bucket," a large can with a toilet seat attached. I didn't trust the flimsy privacy curtain around the can; I could see myself crashing to the floor with the slightest turbulence. I vowed I would never use the honey bucket, even on six-hour missions.

Our flights almost always took off early in the morning, so I limited my fluid intake before we took off. I carried a single can of soda, which I drank about an hour before we landed. One of the enlisted technicians was a woman, and at the end of the longer flights, we raced each other to the single women's restroom in our building. If we were both desperate, the loser pounded on the door of the men's room to clear it out.

A few months after I arrived at Holloman, I learned how to navigate the fighter pilot culture at the officers' club on Friday nights, obnoxious lieutenants notwithstanding. Holloman was home to two fighter wings in addition to the test group I was assigned to. One wing flew F-15s. The other wing's mission was Lead-In Fighter Training, where pilots learned how to fly basic fighter maneuvers in an advanced version of the T-38 they'd flown at pilot training. On Friday nights, the bar was jam-packed with fighter pilots and fighter pilots-to-be, all decked out in flight suits with bright unit patches and colorful scarves that indicated which wing and squadron they belonged to.

Since Holloman had only fighter aircraft, there weren't any women pilots. Most of the women officers on the base were in administrative jobs. I wore my uniform the first few times I went to the club, but most of the other women officers wore civilian clothes. I started doing that as well. No need to make myself a target.

I quickly made friends with some of the pilots, especially those who flew the advanced version of the T-38 trainer. The humbling experience of being sent to fly a lowly training aircraft again seemed to dampen their egos compared to the F-15 pilots.

I learned to play "crud," the national pastime for fighter pilots. Although the goal was to knock your opponent's ball into a pocket using the cue ball, the game consisted mostly of chasing each other around a pool table. There were no cue sticks involved—legend had it that Canadian officers had developed the game after breaking all their cue sticks during an alcohol-fueled evening. The game became very physical at times; I often woke up on Saturday mornings with bruises. One time an opponent ran into me, and we both crashed into the wall next to the pool table. I watched, fascinated, as several drinks jumped off the windowsill and smashed into smithereens on the floor. The club's management didn't mind. They handed us a broom to clean up the mess, and everyone bought new drinks. You have to expect a few casualties in a game of crud.

The women officers at Holloman had individual ways of dealing with the base culture. Some hated the bar scene and didn't go to the club at all. I respected their decision, but I thought they missed out on a lot of camaraderie; I learned a lot about flying fighters from the pilots I partied with, and they learned about flight testing from me. Other women went the opposite direction, matching the men drink for drink and with four-letter words.

I took a middle road. I enjoyed the culture, but I knew I couldn't keep up with the drinking. I regulated my alcohol intake, sipping on two or three Miller Lites throughout the evening. Although I occasionally overindulged and spent the night on someone's couch, the approach seemed to work. At a leadership course for lieutenants and captains that I attended later, my instructor told me in a feedback session, "You're part of the team without being one of the guys." I thought it was one of the highest compliments I could get.

<p style="text-align:center">*　*　*</p>

In 1984, I was selected to attend the U.S. Air Force Test Pilot School as a flight test engineer. During my time at Holloman, we never tested our systems in a fighter aircraft, so I had yet to fly in the back seat of an F-4. I would finally get my chance at Edwards.

I'd loved the flying at Holloman, but the F-4 and T-38 at Edwards took things to a whole new level of exhilaration. I only vaguely remember my first flight in the rear cockpit of the F-4, but I

remember the thump on my back as the afterburners kicked in during the takeoff roll and the dizzying speed as we accelerated quickly past three hundred knots, still only a few hundred feet above the ground. The aging F-4 was a sturdy, honest airplane, and I couldn't wait to go back up again. Even after flying in more than a dozen different fighters, the F-4 remains my favorite.

Even though Air Force women had been flying high-performance jets for almost ten years when I arrived at Edwards, poorly fitting equipment was still an issue. The life support shop that maintained our flight gear issued us custom-fitted helmets and oxygen masks, but I had a hard time with my mask. It had two openings, one on either side of the nose, for something called a Valsalva maneuver used to clear my ears during altitude changes if they didn't clear on their own. Doing a Valsalva without an oxygen mask is easy: pinch your nostrils shut and blow. But the openings in the mask didn't align with my nostrils, so I usually dropped my mask, performed the Valsalva, and popped my mask back on. It only took a few seconds, but it could be a hassle if I was trying to record data or talk to the pilot at the same time. And dropping my mask at a high altitude, even briefly, could have been dangerous. Fortunately, I never had to do that.

I didn't complain about my mask, which I considered just an annoyance; like Kathy Cosand and other women, I didn't want to draw attention to myself. Instead, to prove myself, I never turned down a flight at Test Pilot School. I loved flying, but I also didn't want to be viewed as a "weak sister." If I could be counted on more than some of the guys, I figured it would gain me more respect.

But one day, my eagerness to fly could have ended my flying career. I had a cold, along with several others in my class, which meant we were all grounded from flight. The scheduler was having trouble filling a seat in an A-37 attack aircraft the next day. Could I do the flight?

I was happy to help, and I figured it would bolster my reputation for always being willing to fly. Plus, the A-37 was a souped-up version of the T-37 used for primary training, and I hadn't flown in it before. I was eager to try it out.

With the cold lingering a bit, I pinched my nose and blew. My ears popped, albeit a little slowly. Good enough. I told the scheduler I could fly.

The next morning, I stopped by the flight surgeon's office to get a quick sign-off. My ears were still a little slow to pop open, but the flight surgeon, who was new, cleared me to fly. Perhaps he was as eager to please me as I was to please the scheduler. The flight was a blast, and I forgot about my ears. I relaxed as the pilot demonstrated various maneuvers, and I flew quite a bit as well. The view was great: in the A-37, the seats were side by side like a car instead of tandem like the F-4 and T-38. The pilot had flown F-15s before, and when he spotted an F-15 in the area, he rolled in on him. We chased our prey around the skies for a few minutes, and then it was time for some dive-bombing practice.

Starting from about twenty thousand feet, we screamed toward the ground, pointed at an imaginary target. It was like an extended downhill on a roller coaster. Passing through about fifteen thousand feet, my right ear blocked. It felt like I'd been knifed in the ear. I immediately dropped my mask and did the Valsalva.

The pilot yelled, "Are you getting sick?"

I popped my mask back on.

"No, no, I just had an ear block. I'm okay."

"Why did you drop your mask?"

"I'll tell you later."

The A-37 was unpressurized; the cockpit was at the same altitude as the ambient air, which meant the full five-thousand foot drop had assaulted my ears instead of the one-thousand feet of change I might have had in a pressurized aircraft. I hadn't considered how the lack of pressurization might impact my slow-to-clear ears.

We landed, and I told the pilot what had happened with my ill-fitting mask. I didn't mention my cold. He didn't seem too concerned. Sitting in class an hour later, my right ear closed back up. I cleared it, but a few minutes later, it closed again. This went on all afternoon. I was terrified. Had I blown out an eardrum during the rapid descent? I didn't pay much attention to the lectures the rest of the day as my imagination ran wild with all the horrible things I might have done to my ear—things that might ruin my flying career.

I mentioned my problem to one of my classmates; he thought some fluid might be trapped in my ear. That evening, I lay down on my couch on my right side. After about fifteen minutes, my

ear opened, followed by what felt like fluid draining. To be on the safe side, I waited a few minutes before I sat up. I was fine. But I never let my eagerness to please cut my safety margin after a cold again.

Flight gloves were another problem. The fingers were too long, and the extra material sometimes made it hard to grab the myriad knobs and switches in the cockpits. I often yanked my right glove off to do something and then pulled it back on. That wasn't too much of an issue, but more seriously, the extra material interfered with my ability to quickly release the harness I wore in the F-4 fighter, which required two steps: first, insert index fingers into the bottom of the latches and push up; then, pull down on separate latches to release the fitting from the ejection seat. At the end of a flight, I normally took my gloves off before I did the flick-flick motion to release myself from the seat. But the fittings also held the parachute; during a water survival exercise, I was dragged behind a boat to simulate landing in the water in a parachute, and I couldn't get my fingers into the bottom of the latches. I finally did it, but only after swallowing what felt like a gallon of water.

* * *

During Test Pilot School, I gained an appreciation for what women aviators in the Navy endured. My class spent two days on the USS *Constellation* to observe aircraft carrier operations, and I discovered I could do something a female naval aviator couldn't: spend the night on the carrier.

A few Navy women could land on ships for missions such as carrying supplies and mail via a small cargo aircraft. But the Navy's interpretation of the combat exclusion law meant the women couldn't stay overnight, even though female contractors and other visitors, like me, could.

The twisted interpretation was especially odd given that, in some ways, the Navy was ahead of the Air Force in letting women fly in combat aircraft. Rosemary Mariner had qualified to fly an A-4 attack aircraft in the 1970s, and women routinely flew electronic combat aircraft to train male Navy pilots. A few women pilots had even been trained in flying air combat maneuvers. And the Naval Test Pilot

School graduated their first woman test pilot, Colleen Nevius, in 1983, six years before the Air Force had their first female test pilot.

During Test Pilot School, I flew with a female Navy pilot stationed at Point Mugu, a Navy test base near Edwards. As part of our course, we flew in lots of aircraft to gain an appreciation for how different aircraft flew, how different systems worked, and how design choices made an aircraft easier or harder to fly. The Navy sent a two-seat version of the A-4 attack aircraft over to Edwards for a few days, along with a woman pilot. I was excited to fly with her, but it was just another flight, and I was expected to take copious notes to share with a classmate who had to write a report on the aircraft.

We briefed the test points we'd be flying and walked up to the operations desk to complete our paperwork before heading to the airplane. The instructor running the ops desk scowled at us as we approached and said, "I'm not sure this is safe."

I hesitated. Was he kidding? He was a nice guy and a good instructor. But he wasn't laughing.

I gave him the benefit of the doubt. The Navy pilot said nothing. I managed a wan smile and small chuckle. It was a great flight.

In addition to airplanes coming to Edwards for us to fly, we flew to other bases to try things out. As my class neared graduation, we piled into a KC-135 tanker and flew to Castle Air Force Base near Merced to fly a simulator for the B-52 bomber. During the downtime after our simulator rides, a group of us visited the base exchange, which was much better stocked than our tiny store at Edwards. I zipped around looking at enticing things to buy and settled on some kitchen towels.

We toted our bags back to the flight line where the tanker awaited. As we boarded, one of my classmates asked me what I'd bought. I proudly showed off my new towels.

About a week later, my classmate said, "You know, I never thought of you as being different from us guys. But at Castle, you were so excited, I thought you'd bought a drill or something. And it was towels. Towels! And then I realized that you *are* different." We both laughed.

Yes, different. But still part of the team.

Figure 16: Author with F-4 aircraft at Edwards Air Force Base, about 1988. (Courtesy of the author)

* * *

Although I struggled with some of the same sexism, equipment, and physical issues as other women aviators, I at least had no limits on my career. I was theoretically equal to a male flight test engineer. Women aviators on the operational side did not have that equality; the combat exclusion laws got in their way.

As I had embarked on my Air Force career in 1980, the "eighties ladies" from the Air Force Academy had launched theirs as well. Margie Clark went to pilot training at Laughlin Air Force Base in Del Rio, Texas, while Anne Martin went to Reese Air Force Base.

Some sexist barriers still existed. Clark had always been interested in flying transport aircraft, so she wasn't disappointed when it came time to select her aircraft, the C-141 cargo airplane. But Martin wanted to fly fighters, and she held out hope that the rules would change. If she wanted to fly fighters someday, it would be best to stay at Reese as a T-38 instructor. But to be a T-38 instructor, she had to be FAR-qualified. FAR stood for "fighter-attack-reconnaissance" and was reserved for the best pilots in the class. Connie Engel had been FAR-qualified years earlier, which allowed her to be a T-38 instructor, even if she couldn't fly fighters like the F-15. Martin thought she flew well enough to be FAR-qualified, but her

flight commander said, "Anne, I'm not going to waste a FAR slot on you." His idea of taking care of her was to get her a C-141 while a less-accomplished male pilot became FAR-qualified and took the T-38 or fighter that was rightfully hers.

Figure 17: A KC-10 tanker aircraft refuels a C-141 transport aircraft in the early 1980s; these were two of the few models of aircraft U.S. Air Force women were allowed to fly. (Courtesy of the National Archives and Records Administration)

As more women became pilots, commanders dealt with how to remain within the confines of the combat exclusion. As with Kathy Cosand in 1978, the rules were far from clear—even absurd, as demonstrated by several events in the 1980s.

On October 23, 1983, suicide truck bombers destroyed two barracks in Beirut, Lebanon, that housed members of a multinational peacekeeping force. More than three hundred people died, including 241 U.S. personnel, most of them Marines.

Margie Clark, now a first lieutenant flying C-141s at Charleston Air Force Base, had recently upgraded to aircraft commander, allowing her to fly in the left seat of the aircraft. The day after the Beirut bombing, she was scheduled to fly to Lebanon as part of the recovery operation. With Beirut still a hot zone, her male copilot suggested they make an "airdrop penetration," a series of maneuvers designed to keep transport aircraft safe from small-arms fire from the ground. Clark had never flown such a maneuver: she wasn't

allowed to train for airdrop missions, which were considered combat flights. She readily agreed to let the copilot hop into the left seat to fly the maneuver; safety was more important than squabbling about who got to fly the airplane.

Clark and her crew first landed in Germany, where they picked up flak vests and pistols, a strange set of equipment for someone who supposedly couldn't fly in combat. From Germany, they flew a load of Army troops to Beirut. The copilot made the airdrop penetration; they landed, off-loaded the troops as fast as possible, and took off again.

Two days after the Beirut bombing, U.S. forces invaded the Caribbean island of Grenada after the overthrow of the incumbent communist government. In addition to dispatching combat troops to help stabilize the situation, the U.S. planned to evacuate more than six hundred U.S. citizens attending medical school on the island. C-141s carrying troops and supplies headed to Grenada, where ground forces and Navy and Marine Corps attack aircraft pummeled targets. The island was clearly a combat zone. That didn't prevent Clark from flying three missions to Grenada after she returned from Beirut. The squadron scheduler didn't think anything of it: he put her name on the flight schedule and no one noticed until later. Women pilots at Norton Air Force Base in California weren't so lucky; their commander decided Grenada was too "hot" and replaced women already on the schedule with men. Once again, the ability of women to fully participate was subject to the whims of their commanders, not any well-thought-out policies or rules on the part of the Air Force.

The aircrews from Charleston received commendation medals for their flights into Grenada. The medal citations mentioned the crews had performed in a combat zone. Some of the wing leadership expressed doubts about awarding a medal to Clark. How could she get a medal for being in a combat zone if she wasn't supposed to be in combat? After some discussion, Clark got her medal.

Figure 18: U.S. Air Force Captain Margie Varuska (formerly Clark), wearing a maternity uniform, receives a commendation medal for flying a C-141 in combat support flights during Grenada operations in 1983. (Courtesy of the Margie Varuska Collection)

About 170 Army women also served in Grenada, mostly in military police units. A few women flew helicopters, and others served in roles such as driving trucks and interrogating POWs. At the start of the invasion, some women were sent back to the U.S. over concerns that they were too close to combat. The women were furious, and their units needed them. Major General Edward Trobaugh, the commander of the 82nd Airborne Division, agreed; he ordered the women back to Grenada.

The Grenada invasion highlighted the increasing role of women in the military and made it clear that it would be impossible in future conflicts to keep women completely away from combat. Now that they were fully integrated into their units, the military could no longer go to war without them. The women were part of the team.

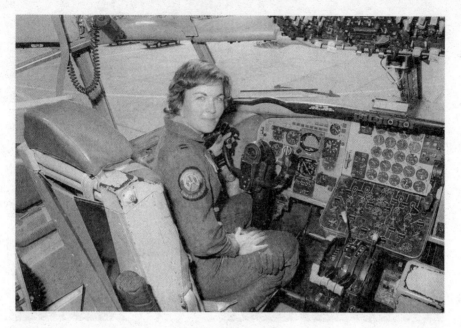

Figure 19: Captain Linda Phillips, the first female instructor pilot in the U.S. Air Force's Strategic Air Command, in the cockpit of her aircraft, about 1984. (Courtesy of the National Archives and Records Administration)

CHAPTER 6
You're in Combat When You Get to Shoot Back (1986-1989)

In November 1985, Lawrence Korb, now the former assistant secretary of defense in charge of manpower, told *Newsweek*, "A woman cannot fly a fighter or a bomber, but she can fly a tanker to refuel them. Now let's have an intellectual exercise: You are a Soviet fighter pilot and you've got one missile. What do you shoot down? You get the tanker, you got the bombers." Women aviators agreed: The combat exclusion kept them from shooting at the enemy, but it didn't keep the enemy from shooting at them. They coined an expression: "You're flying a combat aircraft if you can shoot back!"

A few months later, the importance of the tankers the women flew would become apparent.

In the early evening on April 14, 1986, twenty-four U.S. Air Force F-111 fighter aircraft and five EF-111 electronic warfare aircraft departed bases in the United Kingdom to begin a flight to Libya. They planned to bomb targets in Tripoli before returning to the U.K. To complete the mission, dubbed Operation El Dorado Canyon, the aircraft would refuel multiple times from aerial refueling tankers.

For months, the Air Force had planned a response to Libya's escalating state-sponsorship of terrorism, and recent attacks that killed six Americans in Germany prompted President Reagan to green-light El Dorado Canyon. Navy aircraft on carriers in the

Mediterranean would also strike targets in Benghazi and provide additional support aircraft.

Air Force Captain Gail Wojtowicz, who went by "Wojo," was one of four officers who planned the refueling tanker details of the highly classified combat mission. They worked in a small office at Mildenhall, a Royal Air Force base in the U.K.

Graduating second in her navigator class in 1981, Wojo had her pick of aircraft, as long as it wasn't a fighter or bomber, of course. She had heard about an aerial refueling tanker that carried special jet fuel required by the SR-71, a reconnaissance aircraft that flew at high altitudes and reached speeds above Mach 3. The special tankers were called KC-135Qs, shortened to "Q." Wojo was attracted to the connection with the SR-71 mission, but she also liked that Q crews deployed often, unlike other tanker crews, who spent most of their time sitting on alert status with strategic bombers at frigid northern bases.

Although Wojo was stationed with the Qs at Beale Air Force Base in Northern California, she spent almost half her time on temporary duty at Mildenhall to support SR-71 flights. While there, she also worked with regular tanker planners. In early 1986, when it was time for her next assignment, she thought, how about Mildenhall? The major in charge of Q ops agreed she was a perfect fit. But he didn't want to wait for the normal summer rotation; he wanted her there as soon as possible.

Arriving at Mildenhall the third week of March, Wojo discovered the reason for the urgency: the Libya raid. She didn't even unpack her bags before she started working with the planners.

A couple weeks later, the mission was set for April 14. The Friday before, Wojo boarded a small Navy aircraft with another planner and flew to Fairford, a base that held another set of tankers. When the two planners arrived, they revealed the highly classified plan to the Fairford leadership and told them their tankers would refuel the five EF-111 electronic jamming aircraft during the seven-hour flight. The Fairford staff started coordinating with the EF-111 crews, and Wojo and the other planner returned to Mildenhall.

Saturday morning, the planners received terrible news: France wouldn't let the U.S. aircraft fly over their country. Instead, the strike package would have to make a wide sweep to the west over the

Atlantic Ocean before entering the Mediterranean Sea by Gibraltar. The length of the mission doubled, to thirteen hours. The number of tankers required tripled, to twenty-eight.

The Mildenhall tanker wing commander, Colonel Lynn Berringer, didn't miss a beat. He grabbed a brown paper grocery sack and sketched out a new game plan. "We've gotta make some changes here. We're gonna need this many tankers here…"

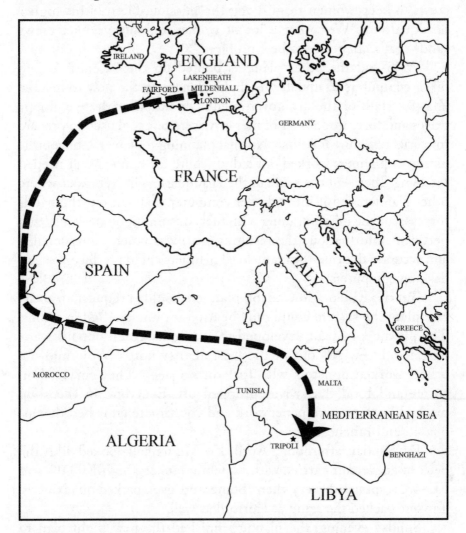

Figure 20: Route taken by aircraft during Operation El Dorado Canyon, 1986. (Courtesy of Mary Skomerza)

With the new route, the KC-10, a new tanker based on the commercial DC-10 aircraft, became indispensable. The KC-10 was much larger than the older KC-135s, carried more fuel, and flew longer distances because it could also be refueled in flight. A call went out to bring every flyable KC-10 in the Air Force to England. And Berringer didn't care about the gender of those tanker crews. Early in the planning process, he made it clear he would not juggle crews to keep women from flying the mission. He told his higher headquarters, "We've got a lot of women on those tanker crews [and] that's not going to be a problem."

Wojo and the other planners booted up their Zenith Z-248 office computers to update the flight plans with the new route. The Z-248s, state-of-the-art government computers with two floppy drives and forty megabytes of memory, were one tool used to prepare for aerial refueling missions. Normal planning took weeks of coordination as planners worked out a draft route for fighters that needed refueling. They sent the route to the headquarters in Nebraska, where other planners fed it into a larger computer that spit out the winds forecast for the mission, along with fuel consumption rates and other pertinent information. The resulting plan was much more detailed and accurate than anything the local planners could produce on their desktop computers.

But the El Dorado Canyon planners couldn't request an accurate plan; the system could only be used for unclassified missions. The planners instead developed the route based on default standard winds—winds out of the west at fifty knots. Wojo and the others worked nonstop, with little or no sleep. They survived on coffee and food that wives dropped off. Everyone in the shop pitched in to prepare paperwork and coordinate crew bed downs, busses, and lunches.

By Sunday afternoon, April 13, Mildenhall looked like the deck of an aircraft carrier, with refueling tankers, both KC-10s and KC-135s, sprawled everywhere. Some were even parked on taxiways. Tankers packed the ramp at Fairford as well.

Sunday evening, the planners finished the new flight plan to fly around France. Wojo and another planner hand-carried the new plan back to Fairford and returned to Mildenhall to get ready for the Monday launch.

There was one last detail to take care of: a combat communications package. It held special radio codes and phraseology for the crews to use to ensure that an enemy listening in wouldn't figure out what was going on. The tanker planners and aircrews weren't used to the complexity of combat comm requirements; they normally just took off, navigated to a point where they met up with receiver aircraft, off-loaded their fuel, and went home. The combat communications package made it clear to the tanker crews that this mission was the real deal; they would be flying right up to the edge of combat. Things got even more real when the tanker crews were told to sterilize their flight suits: remove all patches and other identifying information, in case something went terribly wrong and they were captured by an enemy.

The communications package was finally finished at the last minute. Wojo grabbed a copy and dashed to the flightline, where a KC-10 tanker waited with its engines running. She scrambled up the stairs, and the door closed behind her with a dull *thock*. The only sound was the whine of the engines. She clutched the comm package and glanced around. She was the only passenger on the gigantic airplane. She hadn't slept in three days.

The KC-10 landed a few minutes later at Fairford, and the bright lights of the wing commander's car greeted her on the ramp. Wojo jumped into the car, and they sped off to hand the comm plans to the tanker crews, who finished their preflight briefings and readied their aircraft. Wojo was designated the Fairford mission coordinator for the tankers refueling the EF-111 jamming aircraft. Because she had detailed knowledge of the plan, she would answer any questions the crews in the tanker or EF-111s had about the overall mission.

Operation El Dorado Canyon began about five that afternoon. Operating under radio silence, the aircraft launched in three waves and headed for Land's End, the southwestern tip of England. From there, the gaggle of aircraft turned south. In addition to Wojo, the tankers held six other women: one pilot, four copilots, and one boom operator.

Figure 21: EF-111 similar to those refueled by U.S. Air Force Captain Gail Wojtowicz's KC-10 tanker during Operation El Dorado Canyon. (Courtesy of the U.S. Air Force)

About two hours after taking off, the KC-135s drained their fuel into the KC-10s, giving them enough fuel to fly the entire mission and refuel the fighters as well. After off-loading, most of the KC-135s headed back to England; a few KC-135s that carried more fuel pressed further south to do additional refuelings.

The tankers led the way to Libya, with each tanker acting as a "mother ship" to several fighter or jamming aircraft. The tight formation reduced the workload for the fighter crews so they would be sharper when they attacked their targets. It also made it easier to conduct the eight to twelve refuelings required during the mission. Another benefit was security. The smaller aircraft flew so close to the tankers that air traffic controllers only saw a pack of tankers streaking across the ocean, not the combat aircraft.

The refuelings were done at night and in radio silence, a first for some of the crews. Some F-111 pilots had never refueled from the newer KC-10 aircraft at all, let alone at night and without radios. The wake from the larger aircraft pushed the fighters around more than a KC-135 did, and it took some getting used to.

Early in the trip across the ocean, the inaccuracies of the manual flight plan became obvious. Headwinds soon slowed the flock. Once

the tanker crews realized they were behind schedule, everyone added power to fly faster. The extra power burned more fuel, which meant more refuelings at higher airspeeds that made it even harder to refuel.

Over the Mediterranean Sea, Wojo's KC-10 prepared for its first fuel off-load. She went to the back to sit with the boom operator as he refueled. The KC-10 had sprung a hydraulic leak, and the thick fluid oozed onto his window. He needed to plug the refueling boom—a fifty-foot-long tube with a nozzle on the end—into the receiver's receptacle, but he could barely see the EF-111 jamming aircraft as it approached. Nozzles occasionally bang into the side or top of an aircraft being refueled; the collision usually only scrapes off some paint. But the jamming aircraft resembled porcupines; special radio antennae jutted from everywhere. Crashing the nozzle into the aircraft could knock off an antenna, and that might take the aircraft out of the fight.

The boom operator hesitated. Should he try to plug the EF-111? To his left, Wojo had a clear view through her window. She guided the operator: "Move the boom one foot left, one foot left…" until the boom slid into the receptacle. They completed the refueling, but the boom operator was too worried to try the next EF-111. In tears, he sent the pilot to another tanker.

But Wojo's tanker wasn't done yet. After some discussion with another KC-10, they decided to off-load their fuel to the other tanker while the fighters made their bombing runs. The KC-10 was much easier to refuel than the EF-111. The huge tanker had a bright blue triangle painted on its nose that was easily visible through the boom operator's partially obscured window. They off-loaded their fuel, and Wojo's tanker turned back to Fairford.

The attack on the Libyan targets succeeded, but one F-111 coming off its target went down in the water. The crews of the surviving aircraft spent the next hour trying to locate the downed crew. With fuel running low, the mission commander reluctantly conceded that the crew had likely not survived. The remaining aircraft headed for four spare KC-10 tankers that Berringer's grocery sack plan had, luckily or brilliantly, placed in an orbit above Malta. After refueling, all the aircraft returned to the U.K.

Two days later, Chief of Staff of the Air Force Charles Gabriel said he was proud of the raid and was struck by the number of

women who participated. Senator John Warner, long an advocate for increasing roles for women in the military, put out a press release to draw attention to the unnamed women.

Reactions were mixed.

Carolyn Becraft was pleased. "The women participated in all aspects of the mission. It shows that America owes much and can expect much from the women in uniform."

NOW found Warner's release "patronizing" and outdated. "For many years we were going through 'first woman' this and 'first woman' that, and we think it is time that America forgot about a person's sex and started concentrating on the job that person does."

The NOW spokesperson had a point but didn't seem to understand how far women still had to go in the military. Yes, just as in the 1960s, military women had equality of pay for the same jobs, but they were still barred from the jobs they needed to reach the highest ranks. Their glass ceiling was still real.

Warner defended the release to an *Air Force Times* reporter: "I thought that the participation of women deserved special notice to show people the range and type of positions women hold in the Air Force today."

Becraft declined to get in the middle of the squabble with NOW, saying: "I don't want to take on Senator Warner. I'm sure his motives for the release were well-intentioned."

I don't recall the kerfuffle over Warner's release, but the incident reflected the attitude of many women in my generation. We just wanted to keep our heads down and do our jobs; we didn't need to shine a light on our accomplishments. But if we never took credit for the things we did, how would other people know how well women in the military were doing?

$$* \quad * \quad *$$

After I graduated from Test Pilot School, I was assigned to the unit at Edwards that tested the F-16 fighter aircraft. My boss, a civilian, sat in a building several miles away from me, and I rarely saw him. A few weeks into my new job, a couple of women I worked with warned me about my boss. He had been an officer in the Air Force who had been involuntarily separated during the drawdown after

Vietnam. One of the women said, "He doesn't like officers, he doesn't like women, and he doesn't like TPS grads. And you're all three."

Great, I thought. But I figured as long as I did a good job, he'd have a hard time justifying a poor performance report. The Test Pilot School grads I worked with would keep the guy from hurting me. One of the grads was Rich Engel, now a lieutenant colonel in charge of my unit. Connie Engel was also a lieutenant colonel; she was now in the reserves. The couple had three daughters, and Connie flew T-38s at Edwards to support tests. I never flew with her, but everyone on base knew who she was. People still referred to Rich as "Connie Engel's husband."

I kept my head down; I just wanted to fly and do a good job. And I did. I flew hundreds of hours in high-performance jets. I ran electronic warfare equipment, tested navigation systems at low altitudes at night, and pulled up to nine g's, maneuvers that raised welts all down my legs where my g-suit pressed the seams of my flight suit into the skin. Other women engineers and pilots were flying high-performance jets, and it frustrated me that in the late 1980s, we were still discussing what women could or couldn't do.

The lack of role models for women was a persistent problem. Connie Engel might have been a good role model for me, but I never got to know her. Other women on the base were the same rank as me, or I outranked them. It seemed I was becoming a role model myself, although I mostly made things up as I went along. A few men became my role models, although they couldn't help me with unique issues that came from being a woman.

For example, the lack of adequate relief facilities in high-performance aircraft. Men used a small device nicknamed a "piddle pack." Women had nothing.

Fortunately, flights in high-performance aircraft were usually only a little over an hour. I was cautious about my fluid intake and never passed up the restroom on my way to a flight. But even that didn't always work.

One warm spring day at Edwards in 1987, I headed out for what I thought was going to be a short flight in an F-16. But the engine start was delayed about a half hour for a dead battery. By the time we reached the end of the runway, I already felt like I could use a restroom.

After about an hour of flying, I relaxed, figuring we would land in fifteen or twenty minutes. Then a KC-135 airborne tanker called on the radio: "Hey, we're sitting up here in the refueling track and we had a mission cancel, so we've got an extra ten thousand pounds of gas. Anyone want it?"

Noooo… I thought. Before I could say anything, the pilot jumped on the radio and said, "Yes, we'll take some!"

"No, stop…," I wanted to shout as we zoomed up to rendezvous with the tanker, but I couldn't get the words out. My overactive imagination held me back as I thought what the pilot might say at the operations desk after the flight if I asked him to land.

"I had a chance to get some gas," I could hear him saying as he jerked his thumb toward me, "but the chick had to pee!"

I worried that any perceived weakness on my part might reflect badly not just on me, but on women in general. I reluctantly decided there was no way I was going to ask the pilot to return and land.

About ten minutes later, we had enough fuel to fly for another hour. I encouraged the pilot to perform maneuvers requiring high power settings that burned fuel more quickly than droning around. After several loops and other aerobatic maneuvers, I suggested we fly low-level, five hundred feet off the ground, another fuel-slurping tactic. A bit later, we practiced strafing and bombing runs, which I had discovered earlier in the flight had the added benefit of significant g-forces—every time we pulled more than two or three g's I felt better. I didn't know if there was a physical reason for that or if the distraction from the g's made me forget my ever-increasing pain.

My strategy worked, with the pilot none the wiser about my situation. About forty-five minutes after refueling, we retreated to the base and landed. As we taxied back to the ramp, I prepared to exit the jet as quickly as possible: I stashed my checklist and my kneeboard in my g-suit pocket and disconnected everything I safely could. By the time the crew chief marshaled us into our parking spot, the only thing connecting me to the jet was my shoulder harness and intercom cord.

As soon as the pilot shut down the engine and popped open the canopy, I told him, in what I hoped was a perfectly calm voice, that I had to use the restroom and would meet him in the debriefing. I disconnected my harness and intercom and saw that the crew chief,

obviously eager to get rid of us, was already moving the crew stand to the plane. I extricated myself from the cockpit and strode across the ramp as fast as I could, given my agony, shedding my g-suit and harness en route. I stumbled into the women's restroom and finally, two and a half hours after we took off…relief. But I had held up my end of the unspoken bargain—I had not become an example of why women should not fly in fighter aircraft.

<div align="center">✳ ✳ ✳</div>

By 1987, women military aviators realized that things needed to change. Until then, most women were happy to just fly, with little thought to their careers. In this way, women were no different from their young male peers, who were also just interested in flying.

But careers are a relentless push upwards for military officers. The oldest women pilots, now majors and lieutenant colonels, were expected to hold staff and commander jobs. They started to realize that the inability to serve in combat or hold combat positions held them back, even for jobs where combat wasn't the primary mission, like airlift and aerial refueling.

In the Air Force, typically tanker pilots are chosen to command tanker squadrons, groups, and wings, and airlift pilots command airlift units, so Air Force women had a viable career path, at least to the level of colonel or brigadier general. Above that, things get dicier. Generals are, by definition, generalists, and if combat experience or training is valued above other experience, fighter and bomber pilots have an advantage in the rise to the top.

In the Navy, female aviators had no career path equivalent to the men. The prohibition from serving on ships limited them to commanding only a handful of specialized shore-based squadrons. Above the squadron level, things looked hopeless. How could a female Naval aviator be promoted to captain, let alone admiral?

As women aviators realized the career impact of the combat exclusion laws, an organization created in the early 1980s primarily as a social group took on more importance. The group began when former WASPs in the Order of Fifinella reached out to the younger military pilots. Through multiple reorganizations and name changes across a decade, the organization became the Women Military Aviators, Inc.

The group's March 1986 newsletter indicated the shift toward advocacy with an excerpt from an essay by Rosemary Mariner. Now a lieutenant commander, Mariner had lobbied for women in combat roles since the 1970s. In 1982, she told United Press International reporter Patricia McCormack why she wanted to fly combat aircraft: "If we are barred from combat we are barred from operational high level, decision-making jobs. When you go into a profession, you want to reach the top. You take the risks along with the rewards." Being barred from taking those risks, Mariner said, "The best we can do is junior varsity."

But Mariner thought too many women aviators were getting out of the military. Her article took them to task for, in her eyes, not taking flying as seriously as their male peers. She acknowledged that women aviators had challenges the men didn't, the main one being that flying on the support side wasn't nearly as rewarding as flying on the combat side. "Add to this low flight time, acceptance problems, a semi-supportive husband, and the alternative of an airline job, and getting out becomes the easiest choice."

Mariner thought women shouldn't be making the easiest choice. They had a debt to repay to those who had come before them, a debt best repaid "by doing your very best, creating new opportunities, and helping the women coming up behind you."

In the next newsletter, Captain Kimberly Krampitz, a navigator at Minot Air Force Base, North Dakota, urged members to heed Mariner's advice: "Maybe I'm naïve, but it seems to me with the advent of nuclear weapons every woman in the world unlucky enough to live in a targeted area has become a combatant. Perhaps some of us realize this fact and want a chance to defend ourselves. Are we already vulnerable now? Yes. Women flying KC-135s pull alert 120 days a year. If 'the button' is pushed, they go to war. After three years of pulling alert, they're eligible for the award of the 'Combat Readiness Medal.' Many of us already have CRMs—yet we continue to face restrictions forbidding us to fly 'combat' aircraft, such as 'reconnaissance' aircraft like the RC-135. (But we refuel them worldwide.) How much longer are we going to accept the double standards that allow us to pull alert but don't allow us to fly 'combat' aircraft? Let's start with lobbying for the things we want. Let's get in touch with DACOWITS, NOW, and WEAL and flood them with letters. Let's write our congressional

representatives, and get some action! Why not expand our newsletter into a 'newsmagazine' dealing with current topics pertinent to women flyers?—and then let's send a copy of this magazine to the JCS, SAC, MAC, TAC, and ATC CINCs, our Senators and Representatives and right to the office of the President of the United States!... Let's change the world of women military flyers!"

The women were fired up at their third convention, held at the Antlers Hotel in Colorado Springs in 1987. In open forums, women complained about career barriers created by the combat exclusion law. Jeanne Holm, the banquet speaker, predicted the law would be lifted by the end of the 1990s. "Anyone who thinks women aren't going to fly in combat are kidding themselves. New opportunities are opening for you. Show a lot of tenacity and sooner or later the doors will open."

Ironically, the best piece of advice came from a man, Lieutenant Colonel W. H. Clover, an Air Force Academy instructor. After urging the women to work with the alphabet soup of organizations on their side, he said, "If you want to be a political force, you have to make people angry."

The women agreed: it was time to make people angry.

<p style="text-align:center">*　　*　　*</p>

It wasn't just women military pilots who realized there was a problem. In early 1987, after receiving a letter from a female ROTC cadet who wanted to fly fighters, Senator Dennis DeConcini had what he thought was a great idea. Why not let Air Force women train in fighter aircraft? The catch: like the female Navy pilots, the women would not be allowed to fly in combat. DeConcini was clear about that: "I want it understood that I continue to believe that women should not be placed in combat situations." However, the senator believed women "could be put to use training other qualified pilots—both men and women. And I am certain there are other creative and practical uses for skilled fighter pilots of both sexes." Apparently DeConcini hadn't talked to female Navy pilots about the lack of "creative and practical uses" the Navy had found for them. The idea quickly died, but it brought attention to the fact that a Dutch woman had recently graduated from the Air Force's pilot training

school that focused on fighter pilots. More than a few people saw the irony in the Air Force training a woman from another country as a fighter pilot while refusing to train one of their own.

In her role at WEAL, Carolyn Becraft honed her soundbites on combat restrictions for easy inclusion in newspaper articles and opinion pieces. The press started to listen. In April 1987, Becraft told the *Chicago Tribune*, "In order to get a reasonable career progression, women must be involved in the main issues of the military, such as combat. Otherwise, they can't advance. It's the same as corporate boardrooms—you can't get there without first having decision-making jobs."

Becraft railed especially hard at the Navy. To have a career in the Navy, "you have to be able to go to sea on ships. But the Navy does not want women on ships, even though women fly Navy support and transport planes and work in communications and police facilities."

Uneven application of combat definitions across the services led Secretary of Defense Caspar Weinberger to establish a task force that came up with a "risk rule" to provide clearer guidance. The 1988 rule stated that "risks of exposure to direct combat, hostile fire, or capture are proper criteria for closing noncombat positions or units to women, providing that the type, degree, and duration of such risks are equal to or greater than that experienced by combat units in the same theater of operations."

But Weinberger's well-meaning attempt to clarify the rules backfired. Instead of opening noncombat positions or units, the rule focused on closing noncombat positions or units. It also wasn't clear how to calculate the risks involved with a particular position or unit, something real-world events would soon demonstrate.

The steady trickle of openings to women throughout the latter part of the 1980s seemed largely disconnected from the risk rule. Instead, commanders in the field lobbied for women. In October 1989, the Military Airlift Command, which owned most of the transport aircraft in the Air Force, asked the air staff to allow women aircrew members to fly airdrop missions. General Hansford T. Johnson, the MAC commander, sent a letter to the chief of staff of the Air Force, General Larry D. Welch, that began, "I believe it is time to open more MAC cockpits to women." He said he personally supported the proposal that had been submitted. He also recom-

mended women be allowed to fly the C-17, a new cargo aircraft coming into the Air Force in a few years.

The Air Force approved women to begin flying airdrop missions. But it came too late for Margie Clark and many of her peers. By then, they were moving on to staff jobs. Many would never become airdrop-qualified.

*　　*　　*

My career was catching up to me as well. In the summer of 1989, I moved back to Wright-Patterson Air Force Base to work in a non-flying job. My direct coworkers included a major who had been a C-5 cargo pilot, a captain who had been a B-52 bomber pilot, and two lieutenants. Our office was made mostly of cubicles; the lieutenant colonel we worked for had a larger office space with some privacy, while the rest of us worked in an open area.

I was no longer wearing a flight suit to work every day, which was a bit of an adjustment. I was used to keeping everything I needed in my flight suit pockets, but now I carried a regulation black Air Force purse that I invariably forgot whenever a group of us left for lunch. The office joke soon became, "Does the captain have her purse?"

I didn't mind the kidding; I laughed at my absentmindedness as well. But then something happened that wasn't so funny.

The new job involved a lot of travel, and at a staff meeting, the lieutenant colonel said, "I can't wait to start traveling with Eileen."

No one said anything. I didn't know what to say; a superior had never said anything like that before. The comment would have been questionable coming from a peer but was out of line coming from my boss. I ignored it; maybe he'd had a slip of the tongue.

Over the next few weeks, the lieutenant colonel made other suggestive remarks around me in front of other people. One day, I went into his office area and told him his remarks made me uncomfortable. I asked him to stop.

"But I like you. I'm just trying to be nice."

I repeated, "You're making me uncomfortable. Please stop."

He didn't stop. A few more weeks went by, more remarks. I thought about going to his boss. Or to the equal opportunity office. I wasn't sure what to do. Reporting the behavior might brand me as a trou-

blemaker. And were his remarks really that bad? Was I overreacting? I didn't think so—I'd just spent the last seven years dealing with male aircrew members who could be a bit rough around the edges. Some of them might have made similar comments at the officers' club on a Friday night after a few beers, but I couldn't imagine them doing it at work.

One day, while walking to lunch with the two pilots I worked with, I mentioned how the lieutenant colonel made me feel. Was I overreacting?

No, the captain said. "We've actually talked about it. You haven't been reacting to him, so we thought maybe you didn't mind."

"Oh, I mind. I just don't know what to do. I don't care about ruining his career, but I don't want to ruin mine as well."

They understood that. To make me feel better, the major said, "He thinks he looks cool when he's doing that, but really, he just looks stupid. No one has any respect for him."

I decided not to report my harasser, unless he crossed a line into something worse, like touching me or suggesting I sleep with him. I felt terrible that I lacked the courage to do anything about it, but such are the dynamics of power in the military.

A few weeks later, I was eating lunch at my desk when the lieutenant colonel walked into our office area. The two pilots were also at their desks. The lieutenant colonel started talking to one of them about a problem we were working on. I turned around and said, "Hey, I have a proposal."

The lieutenant colonel said, "Hey, Eileen's gonna proposition me!"

I turned back to my desk and said, "We won't have any of that."

The major blurted out, "Hey, Eileen, you want me to be your witness in a sexual harassment case?"

Except for the lieutenant colonel, everyone—me, my office mates, people outside our cubicles who overheard the exchange—burst out laughing. I turned back around.

The lieutenant colonel's face was bright red. He slunk into his office. He never bothered me again.

Sexual harassment was of course not new to the military. From Claire Griffith's tormenter to the pornography carried by Kathy Cosand's crews to the man who drove my classmate from officer training, harassers were deeply embedded in military culture. They still are.

As more women entered the military in the 1970s, there were more cases of harassment. What might have previously been viewed as an isolated problem to be swept under the rug at the local level now became a highly visible problem across the Department of Defense. The Defense Advisory Committee on Women in the Services paid closer attention as early as 1980, when Donald Gray, director of equal opportunity in the military, testified that sexual harassment was sometimes used to drive women out of nontraditional fields. He told DACOWITS that a newly assigned woman mechanic "complained that the men she worked with were changing their clothes in front of her and exposing themselves. When she complained to her superiors, her name and phone number were scrawled in latrines and her photo was put in an obscene cartoon and posted." Gray decried the "boys will be boys" attitude that still prevailed in much of the military. Others thought the lack of combat roles for women helped spawn harassment. If women weren't full members of the team, they were fair game for bullying.

The harassment, the lack of career paths, inconsistencies across the services, neglect of issues such as decent-fitting clothes and equipment, and the endless studies about the "impact" of women made some women wonder if it wasn't all a plot to drive them from the military. If the military could make it too hard for women, maybe we would give up and go away. But it was too late to get rid of us. As the 1980s came to a close, another combat operation demonstrated that the military could no longer operate without women.

* * *

In the opening hours of Operation Just Cause on December 20, 1989, First Lieutenant Lisa Kutschera and Warrant Officer Debra Mann piloted two Black Hawk helicopters to ferry infantry soldiers across the Panama Canal for an assault on Panamanian Defense Forces at Fort Amador. As in Grenada, the women weren't technically flying in combat, but PDF soldiers still shot at them. The Army awarded Air Medals to all the pilots in the operation, male and female.

The operation in Panama to remove dictator Manuel Noriega from power stood out from previous operations in the 1980s. It

was a much larger and more complex operation, and it involved heavier casualties; twenty-three U.S. men died during the attack. The operation also used forces already stationed in Panama, including more than six hundred women; nearly two hundred additional women also arrived during the operation. One of those women was Captain Linda Bray, who commanded a military police unit.

On the first day of Just Cause, Bray was supposed to lead thirty soldiers, some of them women, to take over a kennel that held guard dogs, something that should have been a routine police function. But the kennel turned out to be heavily defended by Panamanian soldiers. Despite the "risk rule" that was supposed to keep her unit from harm's way, Bray was suddenly in combat. In the resulting battle, her troops killed three Panamanian soldiers while taking no U.S. losses.

In one account, Bray crashed a jeep into a gate at the kennel during the firefight. Bray told *New York Times* reporter Michael Gordon, "I joined the Army for the excitement, the challenge, experience and loyalty to my country. I haven't been let down a day."

Patricia Schroeder said that Bray's performance proved women could perform in combat. She also said she would introduce legislation to establish a test unit that would examine women in direct ground combat roles; the test would run for four years. As Schroeder pointed out, "This distinction between combat and noncombat units is really a joke."

The Army later backpedaled on Bray's story, claiming she had done nothing close to combat. Some people said she was miles away during the attack. It seemed that the Army wasn't yet ready to admit a woman could defend herself and her troops with a gun in combat, although it was apparently okay for a few defenseless female helicopter pilots to be shot at. It was another example of the women's battle cry: "You know you're in combat when you get to shoot back!"

Women Air Force pilots also participated in Just Cause, flying hundreds of flights in cargo aircraft. But they didn't fly airdrop missions; the restriction wasn't lifted in time for the Panama operation.

*　　*　　*

Kathy and Bob Cosand knew their time at McGuire would eventually come to an end. In 1982, the Air Force reassigned Bob to Altus Air Force Base in Oklahoma as an instructor pilot. Kathy, now a part-time reservist, remained assigned to her unit at McGuire. She commuted from Altus to McGuire for a few days each month to fly. She was grounded for part of the time: their son was born in 1983. After Kathy gave birth, Bob didn't mind staying at home with the baby for a few days each month while Kathy flew in New Jersey.

Cosand continued her quest to not stand out as a woman. She never asked her squadron to pay for her monthly trip to McGuire, even though reimbursement was allowed. Most of the men who commuted didn't need reimbursement; they were airline pilots, and they got free flights to and from Newark as an airline perk. Cosand hoped to eventually fly for the airlines, but with a newborn and plans for another child, an airline job was on hold. She worried if she asked for payment for her commute, it would be a sore spot in the squadron. Instead, she bought cheap airline tickets, but the money she earned as a reservist barely covered her commute costs.

Her arrangement began to fray in 1989, when a new colonel was assigned to her unit. The colonel, from South Carolina, brought with him archaic Southern attitudes about women in the workplace. He especially frowned on women with young children who worked outside the home. After Bob was selected for an embassy assignment in Honduras, the colonel made a new rule that seemed designed specifically to kick out Cosand: if someone moved overseas, they could no longer be in his unit.

She decided to fight. With Bob attending language school in California for a year before the move to Honduras, she had some time. She filed a complaint with the inspector general at McGuire. The investigation concluded that the colonel had the right to bar her from his unit. But the inspector general, her former squadron commander, knew Cosand's abilities and was sympathetic. After he delivered the official bad news, he got up, closed the office door, and said, "I will deny this conversation ever existed. But keep fighting and call your congressman."

The colonel claimed he was concerned about Cosand's ability to respond to an activation if she lived overseas. But she knew she could arrive one day after being called, even though the rules allowed seventy-two hours. And she was certain that squadron members who flew for the airlines wouldn't meet the seventy-two-hour requirement. She told the colonel, "I'm not your problem. Your problem is your Northwest Airlines guys who go fly to Tokyo and spend four days on the ground and then fly back."

Cosand considered the colonel's concerns ridiculous. Her McGuire squadron had never been activated, and there was no reason to think it would be. At least the colonel didn't kick her out right away; as she continued her fight, he allowed her to remain.

But six thousand miles from McGuire, a storm brewed over a tiny country most U.S. citizens had never heard of. That storm would change Cosand's life and the lives of all women aviators in the U.S. military.

CHAPTER 7
On the Brink of Victory (1990–1991)

On August 2, 1990, Iraqi forces attacked Kuwait. Within an hour of the invasion, two aircraft carriers, USS *Independence* and USS *Dwight D. Eisenhower*, steamed toward the Middle East. On August 7, U.S. Air Force fighter aircraft and a U.S. Army brigade deployed to Saudi Arabia, kicking off Operation Desert Shield. Two days later, F-15C fighters armed with air-to-air missiles patrolled the skies along the border between Saudi Arabia and Iraq, lying in wait to shoot down any Iraqi aircraft foolish enough to try entering Saudi Arabia. Within two more days, the Army brigade protected the airport at Dhahran.

Things looked grim. Colonels who had flown combat missions in Vietnam two decades earlier chatted in hushed tones in the hallways of my office building. The C-5 pilot in my office confided that a friend flew a C-5 loaded with twenty thousand body bags to the Middle East.

The U.S. was going up against the fourth largest army in the world. Planners projected the battle to be short and bloody. Casualty estimates ran as high as thirty thousand. And given that the all-volunteer force was now 10 percent female, at least some of those casualties were expected to be women.

Despite the predicted death toll, just about everyone in our office, including me, was eager to get into the fight. At least the pilots had a chance; if things got dire enough, the Air Force might start pulling pilots out of office jobs. As an engineer, my options were limited. Still, I wanted to go, even if all I did was carry around a general's briefcase.

Civilians might find it odd that we were jumping up and down to be in a war. After all, the best military is strong enough to deter anyone from attacking in the first place. But once the shooting starts, everyone wants to be there. It's what they've been training to do for years, even decades.

I never got anywhere close to Saudi Arabia. Like most Americans, even most military members, I watched the conflict unfold on television. But ironically, because the combat restrictions relegated women to support roles, plenty of them were among the first to arrive in the Middle East and the last to leave.

Two days after the start of Desert Shield, Army Captain Victoria Calhoun, a CH-47 "Chinook" helicopter pilot at Fort Bragg, North Carolina, deployed to Dhahran as part of an advance party to conduct reconnaissance and prepare the base for more arrivals. Calhoun found the adventure she had sought for years. The weather was horribly hot. Thousands of microscopic sand pellets from frequent dust storms blasted unclothed skin, and the sand clogged everything—tents, food, weapons, and aircraft parts. Helicopter maintenance was a nightmare.

Calhoun's monstrous Chinook resembled a pudgy semi-truck with two spinning rotors on the top at each end. The helicopter carried people, supplies, and heavy equipment such as artillery pieces. Equipment too big to fit in the helicopter's cargo hold was slung beneath the aircraft using fifty-foot-long cables. The Chinook could carry the equivalent of about five Ford F-150 pickup trucks on a sling.

Figure 22: CH-47 Chinook helicopters similar to those flown by U.S. Army Captain Victoria Calhoun during Operations Desert Storm and Desert Shield. (Courtesy of the National Archives and Records Administration)

The daughter of an Air Force pilot, Calhoun had entered the Army's ROTC program at Mary Baldwin College in Virginia. She was mostly in the program for fun and money—the training involved outdoor activities like rappelling, and the Army paid her a hundred dollars each month. After commissioning, she trained for field artillery, then went to flight school at Fort Rucker, Alabama, and on to West Germany, where she asked to fly the Army's newest helicopter, the UH-60 "Black Hawk." A superior officer denied her application saying, "A woman's not going to get to fly a UH-60 before I do."

Calhoun never forgot the officer's rebuke. She opted for the Chinook and cut her teeth flying in Germany's rugged mountains. She slipped beneath bridges and hugged hillsides as she skimmed a few feet above the ground. The flying was some of the best a pilot could hope for, but Soviet-led forces weren't likely to come crashing into West Germany. In 1989, she requested a transfer to Fort Bragg, home of the Army's elite airborne and special operations forces. She figured if any action happened, it would be from there. She was right. That December, her unit deployed to support the Panama invasion. But her operations officer wouldn't let her go because he didn't think women should be in hostile territory. Even worse, he replaced her with a less-experienced male pilot.

Seven months later, she feared she might also sit out Desert Shield. Calhoun's battalion commander called the unit together to address them about the upcoming deployment. The operations officer who had cut her from the Panama mission asked, "Are the women going?"

What a ridiculous question, Calhoun thought. The battalion commander, superior to the operations officer, looked perplexed. He said, "They have to go; we're not mission capable without them!"

While Calhoun helped the Army settle into Saudi Arabia, Air Force crews began hauling tens of thousands of people and millions of pounds of equipment to the Middle East. Reserve units in the U.S. began activating for the first time since the 1950s Korean War. Units with cargo aircraft were in high demand, and cargo reserve units, where women aviators were concentrated, were among the first to activate.

To those who didn't follow the military closely, activating the reserves might have been seen as an act of desperation. It was not. It

was a carefully orchestrated plan set in motion in the 1970s, when Department of Defense officials realized that failure to activate reserve units contributed to the public's poor opinion of the Vietnam War. A handful of draftees trickling off to war did not garner the same community support as a unit composed of hundreds of neighbors. After Vietnam, the military reorganized so units could no longer fight without the reserves. Entire missions, such as aeromedical evacuation, were transferred to the reserves, along with substantial portions of other missions, such as aerial refueling. "Weekend warriors," especially in the Air Force, regularly flew missions with their active-duty counterparts. No longer viewed as a B-team called in as a last resort, the reserves had transformed into a force as good as, and sometimes better than, their active-duty teammates.

* * *

Army officers weren't the only ones confused about whether women were supposed to deploy. On August 6, Stephanie Wells, a C-5 cargo pilot, called her reserve unit to volunteer to fly missions to the Middle East. The chief pilot told her women were excluded.

The pronouncement shocked Wells. She couldn't understand why women weren't eligible. Maybe the Saudis had requested no women? A female NASA coworker also in her reserve unit was happy about the restriction. Wells didn't understand why. She was desperate to help.

The chief pilot called Wells back at ten thirty the next evening. Women weren't excluded after all. She started packing her bags.

Wells was as ready to deploy as any of the men. She had grown up as a tomboy and in 1975 was the first woman to get an ROTC commission at Iowa State University. She was also the first woman to graduate from Iowa State with a degree in meteorology.

Wells started out in the Air Force as a weather forecaster but applied for pilot training as soon as it opened to women; she was in the third class of women pilots. After a tour as a T-37 instructor pilot at Reese Air Force Base, she transitioned to the WC-130 "Typhoon Chaser," flying out of Guam. As she completed a third flying tour, this time as a T-38 instructor, she realized her career options had narrowed. The WC-130s had limited assignment opportunities, and

the regular C-130s, with their tactical mission, were not yet open to women. Wells took the path to the reserves in 1985 and joined a unit at Kelly Air Force Base near San Antonio that was transitioning to C-5s. The unit had flown C-130s prior to that, so they had never had a female pilot. But Wells soon proved her worth; she quickly became an aircraft commander and qualified to do aerial refuelings. She also landed her dream job: flying as a project pilot with NASA in Houston. She flew T-38 trainers, a modified KC-135 tanker, and a Gulfstream II business jet modified for training astronauts and other support missions.

Wells was eager to be part of the buildup in the Middle East, but she wasn't sure why the U.S. was there. The public reason was that the U.S. was getting rid of an unprovoked attacker, but Wells thought perhaps it had more to do with preserving access to oil. Would the U.S. have gone up against another attacker if the country invaded hadn't been so rich in resources that we needed?

Wells set aside her thoughts. She knew the C-5s she flew were badly needed. The C-5 was massive, nearly a football field in length. It carried outsize cargo such as tanks and large helicopters in its belly. Fully loaded, the aircraft weighed nearly a million pounds. The C-141 that Kathy Cosand flew was smaller and couldn't carry outsize cargo, but there were more C-141s than there were C-5s. Together, the aircraft were the workhorses of Desert Shield.

On August 13, Wells flew her first Desert Shield mission, loading cargo in the U.S. and flying it to the east coast of the U.S. The next day, she flew to Rota, Spain, and then on to Sigonella, Italy. Sigonella was a zoo—aircrews swapped stories about thirty-hour days with only ten hours of crew rest and being crammed into rooms with three people all trying to get some sleep.

Wells and her crew were tired, and she asked for an additional four hours of crew rest—sixteen hours instead of twelve. The planners laughed and said she was lucky to get twelve. With the urgency of war, just about anything that might normally keep a mission from flying was waived: maintenance was deferred, crews flew duty days up to thirty hours, and individual aircrew members could fly 150 hours in a month, above peacetime limits of 125 hours.

Figure 23: Major Stephanie Wells with her crew on a C-5 during Desert Shield/Desert Storm. (Courtesy of the Stephanie Wells Collection)

The transport aircraft flew regular rotation missions from the U.S. to the Middle East, often landing at intermediate stops in Europe. When an airplane landed, the crew stopped, but the airplane kept going with a fresh crew. The crew that had just landed became untouchable for their crew rest, a minimum of twelve hours. In that window of time, crewmembers had to decompress, get a bite to eat, get a good night's sleep, and wake up ready to fly again. The endless grind exhausted even the most energetic crewmembers.

On August 28, while Wells was back in Houston, one of her unit's C-5s crashed on takeoff from Ramstein, Germany. Only one crewmember survived. Wells was selected to notify the aircraft commander's family of his death, since the family lived north of Houston. She called a chaplain from the local Air National Guard unit to accompany her. They donned their service uniforms and arrived at the house at midnight. It was one of the hardest things she ever had to do. She wrote in her diary, "Tough! Tears my heart out. Tears flow. Emotions out of control."

During peacetime, the C-5s might have been grounded after a crash or perhaps had some restrictions put on them while investigators figured out what happened. But with the war, the aircraft kept flying.

Wells arrived home from her gut-wrenching duty at 3:00 a.m. At 11:05 p.m. that same day, August 29, her phone rang: her squadron had been activated for ninety days. She was to report to Kelly no later than eleven the next night. That gave her enough time to rush over to NASA for a T-38 flight the next day. She left after dinner for the four-hour drive to Kelly, feeling a "strange mix of emotions. Sadness, hurt, excitement...honor...worry...pride."

Not all her squadron mates were happy about their activation. Some were airline pilots who took a huge pay cut overnight. Wells couldn't understand their attitude. If they couldn't afford to be called up, why were they reserve members?

*　　*　　*

Desert Shield impacted Kathy Cosand as well. A few weeks after the inspector general had denied her the right to remain in her McGuire unit, she prepared for the family move to Honduras. As she packed boxes, Iraqi forces invaded Kuwait. A friend called and said, "Whatever you do, don't answer the phone."

Cosand laughed. "Caroline, I'm not going to do that."

Three weeks later, as Cosand settled into her new home in Honduras, she heard rumors that one of her sister squadrons had been activated. She hated to leave her two-year-old and seven-year-old, but she talked to Bob about flying some missions: "Most of the boxes are empty and things are going okay, so why don't I volunteer to fly a two-week trip? Maybe if more of us do that, they won't activate us."

Bob agreed, and she called her squadron. It turned out a C-141 was returning to McGuire from Panama; it would stop in Honduras to pick her up. She packed her gear for a two-week trip and headed to the pickup point, but the promised aircraft overflew the airport and didn't land.

Seething, Cosand returned home and called her squadron. When the scheduler came on the line, she ranted: "Hey, I'm not going to make it to fly tomorrow. They overflew. I thought this was

all in place. I thought they were all briefed. I thought…. Basically, they screwed me over."

She paused long enough for the other officer to get in a word.

"Well, Kathy, I'm glad you called." The scheduler read her unit's activation order. She now had seventy-two hours to get to McGuire on her own.

"Oh, crap. I'll do what I can. I think I'll be there tomorrow."

Cosand launched into high gear. After a few panicked moments, U.S. embassy personnel got her onto a commercial flight the next morning at 6:00 a.m. In Miami, she dashed to the Continental Airlines counter, spotted a flight leaving for Newark an hour later, and said, "I don't care what it takes—I need to be on this airplane."

In Newark, she hopped on a bus and strode into her squadron about four in the afternoon. Spying the colonel who was trying to kick her out of her unit, she lit into him with everything she had in her five-foot, four-inch frame.

"Okay, I'm here from Honduras after whoever told those people to overfly. You guys really did a number on me with that. I'm here. Now I want to know where all the airline pilots are."

None of the airline pilots had arrived; none would even make the seventy-two-hour timeline.

Cosand flew to Zaragoza, Spain, shuttling equipment and people to Saudi Arabia. Working thirty-hour days, she and her crew flew 150 hours in sixteen days. Although exhausted, Cosand enjoyed what she was doing. Aeromedical evacuation flights of injured or wounded personnel touched her the most: whenever she carried patients, she went back to talk to them, holding their hand to reassure them before returning to the cockpit, hoping they would make it.

Three months after she was activated, Cosand's nemesis colonel approached her at the squadron. He admitted he had been wrong: "I've learned a valuable lesson from this. The next time someone asks me to let them prove what they can do, I'm going to try to at least give them the opportunity."

Cosand thought, *Okay, so maybe this worked.* She remained in her unit at McGuire.

* * *

As transport airplanes poured into Saudi Arabia, so did aerial refueling tankers and other support aircraft. In addition to refueling other aircraft, the KC-135s and KC-10s also hauled cargo. The tanker crews were all volunteers. KC-135 pilot Captain Christina Vance Halli volunteered to deploy because she was bored with her job at Minot Air Force Base, North Dakota. At Minot, a frigid and remote location, the blonde Los Angeles native mostly sat on alert status, ready to refuel B-52 bombers should they embark on a long journey to drop nuclear weapons on Soviet targets.

The fall of 1990, Halli was selected to fly Desert Shield missions to transport cargo and troops to the Middle East. Before deploying, she received training on what to do if her tanker was attacked by enemy forces during a one-week "Tanker Tactics" course at Edwards Air Force Base. She recalled the "tactics" as "When told to do so, break away, get down low, and fly really fast! That was the maneuver!" The training hardly seemed worthy of a week-long course, but she enjoyed the time at Edwards.

During her Desert Shield deployments, Halli carted fuel and people across the Pacific and then had a flight to Europe. After a few deployments, she was back to sitting alert again in dreary Minot. But the deployments had given her a taste for more.

* * *

A few days after being activated, Stephanie Wells jumped on a C-141 as a passenger, along with four other crews from Kelly. They picked up four more crews at Travis Air Force Base in California and headed to Hawaii. Crammed into the back of the packed C-141, Wells passed the time reading classified information she'd been given about the buildup, along with pointers about Saudi customs and chemical warfare threats and gear.

Her first mission out of Hawaii was a long one—fourteen hours to U-Tapao, Thailand, with two refuelings. Abeam Guam, she took on 170,000 pounds of fuel from two tankers, spending seventeen minutes hooked up to the first tanker and eighteen minutes on the second.

Wells still wasn't sure how she felt about the potential for war, but she set aside those feelings to do her duty, which she wrote "is exciting, a change of pace, and makes me feel alive." She fretted about leaving her cat for three months but wrote, "It has gotten me into a positive mindset about myself, and whatever I do at the end of it career-wise, I'll feel better about."

After flying several other missions, she flew from Torrejón, Spain, to Dhahran on September 19. Her aircraft carried a helicopter for a general, and she did an aerial refueling over the Red Sea. She loved the refuelings, except for the changing communications requirements. She and other crews were no longer sure what was okay to say over the radio—how much fuel they wanted, for example—leading to confusion.

As the ground crew at Dhahran unloaded the general's helicopter, the hydraulic winch attached to it went awry. The helicopter shot five feet down the ramp and screeched to a halt, ripping off the skids. It barely missed a loadmaster. The helicopter body slammed onto the ramp, and the tail boom smashed onto the tarmac. The helicopter was a tangled heap.

Wells made some phone calls and filled out paperwork, but no one seemed too concerned: "Got to expect some losses in a big operation."

By early October, enough coalition forces were in place to blunt an Iraqi attack into Saudi Arabia. But President George H.W. Bush and other coalition leaders wanted more. They wanted Iraqi forces out of Kuwait, and Saddam Hussein didn't appear willing to leave, despite nearly universal world condemnation, along with a United Nations-imposed trade and financial embargo.

An offensive operation to dislodge Iraqi forces needed much more coalition equipment and personnel, so the stream of transport aircraft into Saudi Arabia continued unabated. The United Nations Security Council set a deadline for Iraq to withdraw: January 15, 1991.

Later in October, Wells flew a load of Army helicopters to King Fahd. They landed after dark. The ground crew was not happy to see them.

"Who are you and why are you here?"

Wells said they had been told to deliver the aircraft.

"We don't want your helicopters. We can't unload them."

After much discussion and many phone calls, the ground crew agreed to take the helicopters. It took another three hours to unload them.

By the time Wells and her crew were ready to depart, the sun was coming up. After they were airborne, Wells finally understood why the ground crew didn't want the helicopters. Looking down at King Fahd, she saw a sea of helicopters, probably one thousand aircraft, parked in every available space at the airport and spilling onto the surrounding sand.

Wells still enjoyed the flying, but she began to wonder more about what was going to happen. The word was that she would likely be activated for at least another ninety days, maybe even a full year. She wrote in her diary: "We keep shoving more people and supplies into Saudi; Saddam won't back down; Bush won't back down. We're in a stalemate with the chessboard still filled with pieces. I have mixed varying feelings about all this, philosophically. The liberal internationalist/isolationist side of me says we shouldn't be there at all—it's not our business. The aggressive side of me says we should get in there and do it now and quit wasting time. But when I think of the casualties which will undoubtedly result which will not be me, I feel guilty. I find it easier (and since I have no choice), to just go with the flow—whatever happens."

Wells also mused as to why she was so upbeat: "I think it is mainly because almost all of the usual forms of emotional stress are removed from my life right now. I can't be ambitious so I can't be frustrated. I'm doing only one job—and an easy one at that—and have lots of time off, so I can't feel stretched. I'm overseas a lot and I'm flying a lot, which I enjoy, so I'm happy." She was taking advantage of her newfound time—reading books, playing the piano, and riding her bike when she had a few days back in Houston.

In the middle of November, her squadron was extended another ninety days. Wells found her morale slipping, but mostly because other pilots became intensely negative. "They bitch and piss and moan.... Worse, they get obstinate and insulting and refuse to cooperate with the mission flow, which thereby affects everyone else.... Negative attitudes are infectious."

By the end of November, as the stalemate with Iraq continued, more troops flowed into Saudi Arabia. Landing at Dover Air Force Base, Delaware after a trip, Wells and her crew expected to go home to Texas for a few days, but they were told to turn around and go back to the Middle East. Another one hundred thousand troops from all over the U.S. were going over, and she took a few hundred who were waiting to load at Dover. Her next cargo included medical supplies, including blood. A few days later, she flew seventy tons of one-thousand-pound bombs destined for Diego Garcia to be loaded on B-52 bombers there. Things were getting scary, and also unsafe: she grew more exhausted with each passing day.

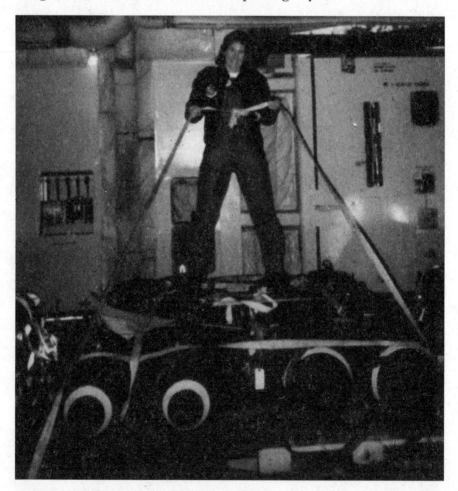

Figure 24: Major Stephanie Wells with a load of bombs on a C-5 during Desert Shield/Desert Storm. (Courtesy of the Stephanie Wells Collection)

Then she landed at Cairo for a day off. She had expected a four-star hotel but wound up in a tent. But the change of pace was exciting, and someone had arranged for a driver and van to take them anywhere they wanted. A tour of the pyramids on camels and horses and surprisingly good food at the tent city chow hall helped refresh her.

She spent Christmas flying from Frankfurt to Riyadh and back again. But no one minded working on Christmas. The crew bought each other little gifts. On the ground in Riyadh, they found that the U.S. troops hid their Christmas tree in a tent so they wouldn't offend the Saudis. Wells gave the ground crews a tour of the C-5 and handed each of them liter bottles of beer she had hidden in the crew relief area before they left Frankfurt. The ground crews stashed the verboten alcohol inside their pants to carry it off the plane.

<p align="center">* * *</p>

Wells flew to Bahrain on January 15, the deadline for war. Everyone suited up in their chemical warfare gear. The Iraqis didn't budge. The deadline passed. Nothing happened.

The next morning, Wells was the most frightened she had been since she'd been activated. The war seemed inevitable, but when? She wrote, "During the intel brief before our departure I actually felt the dry-mouth adrenalin surge of anticipation. Enroute, I got all my chem warfare gear out of the bag and ready. We listened intently to all six of our radios for broadcasts indicating the balloon was going up." Still nothing happened.

The next morning, Wells wrote, "THEY DID IT! Our loadmaster was right. A massive attack began at 2330Z...with apparent initial success. As I figured, the nervousness of anticipation is gone. Even my attitude has shifted towards 'Go get 'em, boys,' and get this thing over with."

Desert Shield turned into Desert Storm.

<p align="center">* * *</p>

One of the first women to make it into the war was Air Force Captain Sheila Chewning, a weapons controller sitting with other officer and enlisted aircrew in the back end of an airliner-sized aircraft distin-

guished by a gigantic disc-shaped radar antenna mounted on top of the fuselage. The huge "AWACS" radar could track aircraft from much longer distances than the smaller radars carried by fighter aircraft.

AWACS stood for Airborne Warning and Control System, and five of the aircraft had arrived in Riyadh on August 8 along with the F-15 air superiority aircraft. Chewning had arrived about a month later. She and the other AWACS crew acted as airborne traffic controllers of military aircraft, searched the skies for enemy aircraft, and helped other aircraft find aerial refueling tankers, among other things. After the Air Force opened AWACS aircraft to women in 1983, Chewning had been one of the first women to become an AWACS controller.

On January 17, 1991, Chewning was the senior controller onboard an AWACS that controlled eight F-15s as they escorted friendly aircraft to targets in Baghdad and swept the skies for enemy aircraft.

The F-15s had just finished an airborne refueling when Chewning spotting a dot on her radar console. She identified it as a threat and called on the radio, "We've got an enemy."

Actually, two enemies, inbound from the north.

Chewning relayed the enemy's distance and bearing to the F-15 pilots. The two lead pilots found the enemy and confirmed there were two targets.

"Same."

"Same."

Everyone remained calm, but Chewning sensed the pilots were preoccupied with something. She later learned that displays in the F-15 cockpits had lit up with indications the enemy was targeting them with ground fire.

Chewning watched the enemy aircraft turn back to the north and assumed they were running back to safer territory. But then the aircraft turned around and headed straight for the F-15s.

One of the pilots called, "Locked on." He was now tracking the enemy aircraft with his radar.

Chewning waited. There was nothing to do except watch her screen while the pilots launched their missiles. The dots marched toward each other. The pilots said nothing. Finally, she couldn't take it anymore and radioed, "Status."

A few seconds later, the enemy dot vanished. The pilots called, "Splash One, Splash Two." Both aircraft had been shot down.

During training missions, Chewning had never thought about what the dots meant. Since nobody got shot down in training, the dots never disappeared. Now she had a weird feeling as the realization hit her: *We just killed someone.*

She turned to the controller next to her and said, "The dot just went away."

Even with the reality of war sinking in, Chewning later recalled to the *Air Force Times*, "We really felt like we were doing our jobs."

At one minute after midnight on January 17, Kathy Cosand prepared to do her job. She was getting ready to take off from Ramstein Air Base in Germany with forty-four thousand pounds of cluster bombs. It was snowing. Her C-141 was badly overweight.

Cosand and her crew watched the snow fall as they waited for their takeoff clearance. Then a call came on the radio: "All missions are canceled." The airspace over Saudi Arabia was shut down as coalition fighters and bombers kicked off Desert Storm. Cosand and her crew remained in their airplane as planners decided what to do with them. She fretted. With the impending war, she was authorized to fly her airplane at its "emergency war weight." But the extra tonnage meant if one of the airplane's four engines quit while taking off from the short runway, she would most likely crash. Remembering the C-5 crash from the previous October, she thought, *If we lose an engine, not only are we going down, but we have forty-four thousand pounds of cluster bombs. This is going to be ugly.*

About 2:30 a.m., she got the call to take off.

With the C-5 crash and the enormity of her cargo weighing heavily in her gut, Cosand taxied her 170-ton aircraft onto the icy runway and lumbered into the sky. But when they arrived over Italy, whoever was calling the shots in the air war had apparently decided he didn't want cargo airplanes in his airspace that night. Cosand turned back to Ramstein. The most stressful takeoff of her career had been for naught.

As Cosand prepared to take off, Stephanie Wells woke at 1:00 a.m. in Torrejón to watch the war unfold on CNN. Bush addressed the nation at three in the morning, then she slept until nine. At ten, they were alerted, but the aircraft commander she was flying with

turned down the mission, claiming he'd slept only two hours. Wells couldn't believe it. She wrote, "He's a coward…. I think he's a wimp. Command post thinks he's scared to fly into combat and doesn't press him. We go back to bed."

Two days later, Wells flew with another crew into Jubail. Adrenalin coursed through her body. She hadn't been able to get rid of it, even with lots of extra running. The adrenalin surged as they neared Jubail, close to the front lines of the war. She suggested the aircraft commander turn off the landing lights and make a short approach, but he did neither. After unloading the M60 tank they carried, they waited for fuel. Wells napped in the plane until an alert woke her. As she donned her gas mask, it occurred to her that perhaps sitting in an aircraft near thousands of gallons of fuel might not be the best place to be during an attack. And what good would a gas mask be at that point?

Back and forth, back and forth, Wells went with the C-5s. By early February, things began to slow down, and on February 13, she managed to get home for a few days while her father underwent surgery.

* * *

The day after Desert Storm started, Christina Halli raised her hand again to deploy. After spending a couple of weeks flying aerial refueling and cargo missions from the Azores, she and her crew flew a trip to Greece. Security was tight, and Halli was advised of an unusual approach to the landing: lights out on both the aircraft and at the airport, and no talking on the radio. She was also to fly a preset pattern. This was in the days before GPS, and her young navigator had to find the airport in the pitch dark. He directed Halli to the runway like an air traffic controller, calling out commands such as "Turn to a heading of 270" or "Turn a little to the left" until the faint outline of the airport materialized in the distance.

Halli descended to a few hundred feet above the water. She flew much faster than for a normal approach. With no moon and few surface lights, it looked like they were flying into a black hole. Once over the runway, the darkness obscured the visual cues she relied on to pull up the tanker's nose for the landing. Using her periph-

eral vision, she made a best guess, flying "by the seat of her pants," feeling her way for the last fifty feet down to the runway. It was an uneventful touchdown and rollout.

The airport looked like a ghost town. No marshaller showed them where to park. The ramp was empty, so the crew stayed inside the cockpit, wondering what to do next. After a few minutes, a sedan with its lights off drove onto the edge of the ramp. Halli and her crew climbed down from the airplane, and a man wearing a flak jacket approached and told them to low-crawl across the ramp to his vehicle.

Halli thought, *These guys are getting serious.*

A few days later, Halli piloted a KC-135 tanker headed toward Iraq. Although it was night, she had the lights out on her aircraft. So did the other two dozen aircraft trailing nearby. The gaggle of tankers and fighters was invisible to anyone on the ground. The aircrews talked to no one, not even to each other.

Halli led the flight of four fighter aircraft assigned to her for refueling. Her tanker and the other aircraft in the strike package had departed from Incirlik Air Base in Turkey thirty minutes earlier. As Halli neared the Iraqi border, the boom operator lay prone in the rear of the fuselage and extended the refueling boom. One at a time, Halli's fighters slid in, maneuvering below and behind the larger aircraft, inching closer and closer until the operator plugged the boom into the fighter and fuel flowed.

Halli kept an eye on the border. Only fighter aircraft were supposed to enter Iraq. She would turn back as the fighter pilots scoured the skies for enemy aircraft or dropped bombs on targets such as supply lines or power plants. The Iraqis would try to shoot down any aircraft inside their airspace, but the U.S. pilots were well prepared to defend themselves. If the Iraqis launched a surface-to-air missile at a fighter, equipment onboard the aircraft chirped in the pilot's helmet to warn him; lights also flashed on his instrument panel. If needed, a pilot dumped chaff, small bits of metal that confused enemy radars, or ejected flares that confused heat-seeking missiles. He also launched missiles or fired guns at anyone or anything that threatened him.

Halli longed to fly one of the fighters. Her four years at the Air Force Academy had been studded with tales of combat bravery, especially stories about legendary fighter pilots like the maverick

and mustachioed Robin Olds, whose "Wolf Pack" of F-4s shot down seven North Vietnamese MiG-21s in a single engagement. There were no legendary tanker pilots.

As one of the top graduates in her pilot training class in 1985, Halli was qualified to fly fighters but of course couldn't. The next best thing was being part of the team that refueled them so they could drop bombs on their targets and return to their base.

The fighters also needed tankers for unforeseen events, such as when a plane leaked fuel from combat damage or a pilot burned up fuel reserves as they maneuvered to avoid a threat. Tanker pilots sometimes flew deep into enemy territory to refuel another pilot in trouble. Although Halli was barred from engaging the enemy, no rules prevented her from flying into Iraq. She wouldn't hesitate to put her own life at risk to help a fellow pilot. Halli never crossed the Iraqi border, but another woman, Captain Anne Weaver Worster, entered enemy territory four times during Desert Storm, once flying her tanker as far as 250 miles inside Iraq.

At Iraq's northern border, Halli started a U-turn as she watched the fighters enter Iraq and split up for their individual targets. She and the other tankers then flew racetracks in the sky, waiting for the strikers to return in an hour or two. EC-130 jamming aircraft loitered nearby; their onboard operators jammed enemy radios, protecting the striking aircraft as they penetrated hundreds of miles into Iraq. The EC-130s also carried linguists, who coded and decoded messages and translated enemy transmissions. The Air Force found that women were excellent linguists, and they made up a significant chunk of the career field. Other support aircraft usually carried one or two female aviators, but the back of an EC-130 was often packed with women.

The orbits kept the defenseless support aircraft far from Iraqi anti-aircraft artillery and surface-to-air missile sites. But the enemy still shot at the larger aircraft, including once when a surface-to-air missile exploded above a tanker.

Time passed slowly while the fighters were in Iraq. While they waited, Halli and her crew pulled out their secret boredom-fighting weapon: unshelled pistachios, ubiquitous and cheap in Turkey. Each tiny nut took a long time to extract and consume. As Halli munched, she observed the light show in the distance. First, Iraqi anti-aircraft

artillery lit up the sky as the fighters neared their destination; explosions from the ground followed as bombs and missiles pummeled the targets. The end of the light show signaled that it was time for her to prepare for the fighters' return.

With help from her male navigator, Halli maneuvered her tanker to a rendezvous point in the sky. The boom operator lay on his stomach again and extended his boom. The fighters shed their cloaks of darkness one at a time as they neared the tanker. In an intricate dance in the Syrian sky, thirsty aircraft gulped down fuel for their triumphant return to Incirlik.

During her two-month Desert Storm deployment, Halli flew twenty-nine combat support missions, earning an Air Medal. Flying in the strike packages out of Incirlik was itself a reward. Tankers flying from other bases in the Middle East met their fighters in the sky; they had no idea who was on the receiving end of the boom or what their mission was. The fighter and tanker crews at Incirlik briefed together, lived together, and partied together. As Halli recalled to me: "We were all one big happy family. At the end of the war, we had a little air show, put all our aircraft on the ramp at Incirlik, walked around, drank beer, and high-fived. There was that real sense of closeness because we were all in this together."

<p style="text-align:center">∗ ∗ ∗</p>

In Saudi Arabia, everyone was vulnerable whether they held combat or support jobs. On the second day of the war, the Iraqis started launching Scud missiles. The missiles weren't terribly accurate, but they were lethal when they managed to hit something. On February 25, 1991, twenty-eight soldiers were killed and ninety-eight others wounded when a Scud landed on their barracks at Dhahran. About half the fatalities were reservists; three were women.

All aircrews were prepared for the omnipresent threat of the Scuds, which might carry chemical weapons. During one flight, Kathy Cosand received word of a "black flag" Scud alert as her aircraft neared Saudi Arabia. Taking her eyes off the burning oil fields in the distance, Cosand donned her bulky chemical warfare gear. It took at least thirty minutes, a difficult feat in the cramped C-141 cockpit. On the ground, Cosand and her crew dashed to a bunker, where they

bided their time for several hours in the suffocating gear as their aircraft was refueled and reloaded for the return flight.

The women aviators had expected to encounter hostile fire, but they had not expected hostile hosts. The Saudis treated the U.S. women as they treated their own: the U.S. women had few liberties and couldn't do their jobs at times. Saudi air traffic controllers sometimes ignored radio calls from female pilots. Saudi ground crews refused to deal with Technical Sergeant Donna Davis, a C-5 flight engineer who operated systems such as the engines, fuel, and pressurization on the complex cargo aircraft. She had joined the Air Force right after graduating from high school in 1974, so she was used to being one of a handful of women in her unit. But she didn't expect the unprofessional treatment the Saudis dished out. One of her duties as a flight engineer was to order fuel and supervise the C-5's refueling, but Saudi refuelers ignored her when she ordered fuel. They wouldn't hand her paperwork after a refueling was complete. After a few tries, Davis gave up. The C-5 crews flew with extra people because of the long duty days, so she asked the male flight engineer on the crew to take care of the refueling.

Other customs interfered with mixed-gender aircrews remaining together overnight in Saudi Arabia. During routine missions to Europe or Asia, crews stayed near each other in the same quarters. But the Saudis separated the men and women, sometimes stashing the women in hotels and whisking the men away to a tent city. Donna Davis was once housed in a large tent a half-mile from the rest of her crew. When her aircraft commander received word of an unexpected early takeoff, he trudged to her tent at 3:00 a.m. to retrieve her, an unnecessary delay for an urgent mission.

The rules also dampened the women's ability to relax with their teammates during layovers. A male relative was required to accompany a woman outside her quarters, so the oldest male member of a crew became an honorary brother. The women had to cover up with a black robe, although the rules regarding hair coverings were ambiguous at first. Once when Davis was out with a group of men and women, they were approached by two policemen, one carrying a knout, a rope with a big knot.

The civilian policeman demanded, "Why are these women's heads not covered?"

Davis's "brother" replied, "We didn't know they needed to be."

With no scarves available, the group returned to their rooms. Someone in the U.S. chain of command decided the women couldn't leave the hotel. But one woman needed to retrieve an engraved bracelet she had purchased at a market during a previous outing. She covered her head with a tablecloth to make it past the religious police.

To keep the peace, U.S. men played along with the Saudi chauvinism, but they pushed back at times. As Davis walked through a hangar after a flight, she passed two male airmen, one U.S. and one Saudi, working on an airplane. She overheard the Saudi airman say, "See, the U.S. is weak; you have your women fighting for you."

The U.S. airman retorted, "Yeah, and who did you call to save you?"

Figure 25: An airman moves equipment during Desert Storm. (Courtesy of the National Archives and Records Administration)

* * *

After air forces demolished much of the Iraqi defenses, the ground war began on February 24. That day, Major Marie Rossi, the company commander of one of Victoria Calhoun's sister units, appeared on

CNN, saying, "This is the moment that everybody trains for—that I've trained for—so I feel ready to meet the challenge."

On the second day of the ground war, Calhoun and her Chinook lifted elements of the 101st Airborne Division to Forward Operating Base Cobra, ninety-three miles inside Iraq. She never saw anyone shooting at her, but the missions inside Iraq allowed her to log twenty-two hours of combat time, just like her male counterparts. She came within ninety miles of Baghdad during one mission.

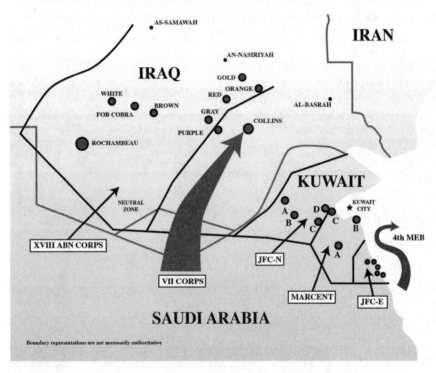

Figure 26: Ground assault in Desert Storm, February 1991; U.S. Army Captain Victoria Calhoun ferried troops and equipment to Forward Operating Base (FOB) Cobra, located inside Iraq. (Courtesy of Mary Skomerza)

Offensive operations ended at 8:00 a.m. on February 28, but not the danger. Marie Rossi, the pilot who had appeared on CNN, died the day after the cease-fire when her helicopter collided with an unlit radio tower during an early morning flight.

Thirty thousand women deployed during Desert Shield and Desert Storm. The combat exclusion law did not keep women from

harm's way: women logged combat time, thirteen died, twenty-one were wounded, and two became prisoners of war.

The war dispelled any remaining doubts about the capabilities of women under the pressure of combat. Their performance also shot down other myths. Since the 1970s, naysayers had attacked women on the unsubstantiated grounds that they were too weak, they would hurt unit cohesion, or they would get pregnant or claim family issues to avoid deploying. None of those predictions came true.

During their deployments, both men and women left behind families, including small children. Donna Davis left her son with her parents, only returning home for a short respite at Christmas. Sometimes childcare took creative juggling. Reserve Captain Peggy Phillips had three small children and an airline pilot husband, also an activated reservist. The couple served in the same unit at McChord Air Force Base in Washington State. Their commander allowed them to work their schedules so that while one was flying on a trip, the other did office work and could be at home during the evenings.

Gender-bending moments occurred as well. When tanker pilot Halli volunteered to deploy, the male navigator on her crew didn't want to go—his wife was pregnant. Since the deployment was voluntary, he was replaced with another navigator, the exact scenario in reverse the naysayers had predicted.

After the war ended, because women flew transports or other support aircraft, they were still not treated as equals. Combat troops headed home. Cargo pilots, first into the theater, were also the last out, with many months of unglamorous and unheralded flights that returned people and equipment to the U.S.

Kathy Cosand hauled back many Marines, who amused her as they opened shoeboxes to show off scorpions they had collected for fighting. At Riyadh, she discovered they had built a pool out of sandbags, large enough to swim in. The combat units were feted upon their return home, and after dropping a group off in El Toro, California, Cosand felt left out: "There was this big party going on and I was thinking, 'What about us? We're not done. We have to go back and get more of your buddies.'"

For Stephanie Wells, it was also more back and forth until finally, on May 15, her squadron deactivated. She arrived back in the U.S. at Westover Air Force Base on May 21. As with Cosand's

arrival, the crowd was there for the ground troops, not the aviators. Wells still appreciated the greeting, even if it wasn't for her. She wrote in her diary, "The Welcome Home setup they had at Westover was something to behold. Giant American flag, red carpet, grandstand, free everything, and lots of young girls to hug those troops as they came home. There was quite a crowd to greet a flight of them which arrived at 2:00 a.m. I admit to having more than a few tears in my eyes."

<p style="text-align:center">✳ ✳ ✳</p>

In the wake of Desert Storm, it was clear that women were part of the team. The U.S. military could no longer go to war without them. Americans also became more accepting of the idea that women could serve in hostile areas. Reservists played an outsized role in the public's acceptance: unit activations became local stories, and people watched their neighbors, not just Johnnie but also Susie, head overseas to fight the enemy. Communities were proud of their women for serving, not horrified that they had gone to war.

Thrilled by their performance and the public's newfound acceptance, women aviators and their supporters thought the tide had turned; perhaps the archaic 1948 law would finally be repealed. The timing was perfect: within a few days of the war's end, the House Armed Services Committee began hearings on the 1992 defense budget. It would be easy to slip a provision into the budget authorization bill that changed the law, and representatives Pat Schroeder and Beverly Byron did just that. Schroeder introduced an amendment to repeal the combat aircraft exclusion, and Byron introduced a second amendment to repeal the law prohibiting women on combat ships.

Carolyn Becraft was hopeful, but even as the stars aligned, she girded for battle. She was as shocked and thrilled as others when the defense authorization act, including the amendments to repeal, passed out of the committee with a 100 percent vote. On May 22, 1991, Becraft was even more amazed when the full House voted to repeal the combat exclusion laws.

Figure 27: Carolyn Becraft, as Deputy Assistant Secretary of Defense for Personnel Support, Family, and Education, mid-1990s. (Courtesy of the Office of the Secretary of Defense)

The House repeal was only the first step, but women aviators were ecstatic. Captain Jackie Parker, the Air Force's first female test pilot, called me days later with the news that a general was already trying to get her into an F-16 fighter unit in the New York Air National Guard. I had been an instructor flight test engineer at Test Pilot School when Jackie had been a student, and I thought if anyone could fly a fighter, she could.

Parker had been a stellar pilot from her earliest days in the Air Force. When she arrived for pilot training at Reese Air Force Base in 1980, she announced that she would graduate at the top of her class, would become a T-38 instructor pilot, then a C-141 pilot, then a test pilot, and then an astronaut. Stephanie Wells, who at the time was Parker's instructor, was used to the outsized egos of student pilots, so she was skeptical of the brash pronouncement. In the decade since, Parker had done everything but become an astronaut. The last goal eluded her only because she was an inch too short for NASA. An F-16 would be a nice consolation prize.

Figure 28: U.S. Air Force Captain Jacqueline Parker, the U.S. Air Force's first female test pilot, with an F-4 at Edwards Air Force Base, 1989. (Courtesy of the U.S. Air Force)

But before Parker or any woman could fly an F-16, the Senate had to repeal the combat exclusion law. Then President Bush had to sign the bill to make it official. And plenty of people were determined to keep that from happening.

The House vote gobsmacked both the Department of Defense and anti-feminist Elaine Donnelly, who was opposed to women in the military at all. Even in the wake of Desert Storm, she claimed the military was being "feminized" by women who hurt military readiness. Donnelly and her supporters regrouped.

Donnelly's hard lobbying against women in combat roles quickly made a dent. Senator John McCain, who had originally supported repealing the law, wobbled. Given his stature on defense-related matters, the Senate vote was in jeopardy.

The House vote was the Hail Mary pass the women aviators had needed for decades, but with a few yards to go before dancing in the end zone, Becraft felt the momentum slipping away. She called Rosemary Mariner. Less than a year earlier, Mariner had broken yet another barrier when she became the Navy's first woman to command an aviation squadron, VAQ-34, at Point Mugu, California. Although the electronic warfare squadron flew an attack aircraft, the A-7, the jets were used for training other pilots, not for actual combat. Mariner hadn't made it into Desert Storm, but she had trained male pilots who had.

Becraft told Mariner, "This is what you gotta do. This is important for you aviators. You can't have one fifty-year-old Army dietician fighting for you. You gotta do it."

"It" was a letter writing campaign. Becraft sent Mariner and Air Force Lieutenant Colonel Kelly Hamilton a list of members on the House and Senate Armed Services Committees and told them that Women Military Aviators members needed to write to all the lawmakers. "You need to say these laws restrict me from what I can do. They are allowed to do that. They are citizens."

Hamilton, a KC-135 tanker pilot assigned to a staff job in Hawaii, bought a fax machine to keep up with the hundreds of letters she sent Congress and other organizations. As a former WMA president, she helped strategize the overall campaign for the repeal; phone calls from the mainland often woke her in the middle of the night.

While the women aviators wrote letters, the opposing team put up a formidable defense. Phyllis Schlafly and other anti-feminists pushed their views in conservative newspapers, and their views extended well beyond repeal of the combat exclusion laws. To them, allowing women in combat was an all-out assault on the American family and society. A June 18, 1991, *Washington Times* article quoted Schlafly, president of the conservative Eagle Forum: "The oft-stated goal of the radical feminists is a totally gender-neutral society, and the military is the cutting edge of this fantasy." Opening combat aircraft would lead to the "slippery slope" of drafting women and forcing them to serve on future battlefields.

McCain and Warner had back-pedaled, but at the start of the June 18 Senate Armed Services Committee hearings on the House bill, Senators William Roth and Edward Kennedy announced that they supported the bill.

But the Schlafly and Donnelly lobbying had shifted the momentum. All four service chiefs testified at the Senate hearings that they opposed women flying combat aircraft or serving on ships other than hospital ships. General Merrill McPeak, the chief of staff of the Air Force, admitted that, while there was "no military reason to exclude women from flying combat missions," he would still "choose a male pilot over a female even if choosing the woman would result in more combat effectiveness." He added, "I admit that doesn't make much sense, but that's the way I feel about it." McPeak was also conflicted; he conceded that "if a woman passes…and wants to fly the F-15, then in my judgment we should not erect a policy barrier against her doing that in the Air Force."

At least McPeak admitted his personal views made no sense. Marine Corps Commandant General Robert H. Barrow was unapologetic about his emotional appeals. He claimed that putting women into combat units would "destroy the Marine Corps…something no enemy has been able to do in over two-hundred years." He blasted the women aviators as well: "They have their own agenda, and it doesn't have anything to do with national security."

A senior military woman sitting in the gallery noted, "I think the general's agenda has more to do with maintaining the macho image of the Marines than with national security."

Testimony from other witnesses that day, men and women from all four services, was a mixed bag. Even those in favor of the repeal admitted there might be an adjustment period, especially with modifying ships to accommodate women. But there was very little discussion related to the actual topic: women flying combat aircraft. Most of the testimony was from soldiers and Marines convinced that women would ruin their combat units. No senior military women were called to testify and, with the exception of Defense Advisory Committee on Women in the Services chair Becky Costantino, there was no testimony from experts who had studied women's issues.

With the House bill now stalled, Roth and Kennedy introduced a new bill, but the committee tabled it. In its place, other committee members resurrected the timeworn method of stalling decisions about women: another study. Once the study was done, the Senate would consider changing the combat exclusion law. With the summer recess looming, it looked like the clock would run out before Roth and Kennedy could propose another bill.

The two senators weren't ready to give up. The Senate would be debating the 1992 National Defense Authorization Act on July 25, and Roth and Kennedy co-sponsored an amendment to that bill. The amendment did not have to go through committee; it would be voted on by the full Senate. But the opposition's strong defense made passage uncertain.

Then the opposition made an unforced error. On July 18, the *Washington Times* published an article by reporter Suzanne Fields, who had recently flown in the back seat of an Air Force F-15 fighter airplane at Langley Air Force Base in Virginia. Fields described the F-15 as giving her "a dandy show, with loops and swoops, rollouts, 'lazy 8s' and turns at 4 G's." At the end of the flight, she wrote, "I felt like a well-wrung orange peel" with her "face as green as my flight suit." Rather than chalk up her exhaustion to inexperience, her takeaway was that male pilots were right to be skeptical that women could deal with the physical demands of flying a fighter.

Heather Wilson, a 1982 Air Force Academy graduate, Rhodes Scholar, future congresswoman, and future secretary of the Air Force, was steaming after she read the article. Wilson had left the Air Force after deciding the service was not a viable career path, given the restrictions put on her. She had even turned down pilot training

because she knew she couldn't fly combat aircraft. By 1991, she was involved with politics and was a member of the Defense Advisory Committee on Women in the Services.

Wilson believed the *Times* article was yet another example of the misconceptions about the abilities of military women. With Senate hearings only a week away, she sent word to the WMA membership: "Activate your Rolodexes!"

Carolyn Becraft called Rosemary Mariner with a similar plea: "Get your women and come to Washington."

The fight was on.

CHAPTER 8
A Weighted Door: The Presidential Commission (1991–1992)

The *Washington Times* article spurred women aviators back into the game with a roar birthed from rage. Wilson and Becraft's plea spread across the WMA phone lines: "Come to Washington in uniform to tell your story. If you can't do that, write letters to your representatives." For those who made it to Washington, the plan was to visit the offices of all one hundred senators, armed with facts and stories about how the combat exclusion law hurt both their careers and military readiness. Rosemary Mariner told the women they would have to be on leave, but to wear their uniforms anyway.

Becraft rounded up women's organizations: DACOWITS, NOW, the National Women's Law Center. She developed fact sheets to leave with Senate staffers, making sure every point on the sheets could be legally backed up.

Dozens of women aviators and their supporters, including some men, flooded into Washington. Becraft teamed with Heather Wilson and the leaders of the women's organizations to divvy up the office visits. The women's organizations took the liberal senators, Wilson took the conservatives, and Becraft took what was left. Each group had at least one military woman during the visits. Since the military women were in uniform, they couldn't lobby, but they could "educate" while the nonmilitary women said, "The Senate must repeal the law."

Lieutenant Commander Trish Beckman, a naval flight officer in a flight test assignment at Patuxent River, Maryland, called Commander Lucy Young and asked, "Can you come to Washington and educate Senate staffers on your accomplishments?" Young, an airline pilot, had flown A-4 strike aircraft in the late 1970s and early 1980s, training male pilots to fly. Hearing from a woman who had actually qualified for combat tasks, even if she couldn't execute those tasks in combat, would be huge.

Young's airline schedule had only a small window for her to come to Washington, but with victory so close, she wasn't about to miss the chance to help. On July 24, she donned her summer white uniform, flew into Washington National Airport, and caught a cab to the Hart Senate Office Building. There, she met Beckman and several other women, and they headed down the street to the American Café to talk strategy over lunch. Young joined a small group at the Senate building to tell her story: she had flown the A-4 for years, she was qualified in air combat maneuvering, and she could land on carriers. She had also flown C-9 cargo aircraft as a reservist during Desert Shield and Desert Storm.

Young and the other women were on the Hill by eight thirty the next morning to attend a press conference Kennedy and Roth held at nine thirty to announce their amendment to the defense authorization bill. Reporters packed the Senate's Dirksen Office Building for the "pep rally," which was designed to counter arguments made by opponents.

Roth went first. "We are here to talk not about whether we are to have women flying combat missions, but whether we want the best pilots flying combat missions.... We want the best person in the cockpit of a stealth fighter or an F-16, not the second best or the third.... Our legislation gives the Secretary of Defense maximum flexibility to fill the job with the best-qualified person."

Roth decried the proposed study. "The Senate Armed Services Committee, instead of adopting our proposal, has called for a study commission. We don't need a commission to study the issue." He also pointed out that women aviators who talked to him about making a change weren't doing so out of concerns for equality or for their careers. "These women talk to me about serving America to the best of their ability." Repealing the ban on combat aircraft simply gave

women "the chance to compete for...these positions, nothing more and nothing less."

Kennedy spoke next and pointed out that the laws weren't unfair to just women; they were unfair to men "because they force them to bear an excessive share of the burdens of military service. They are unfair to the country because they often operate to keep the most qualified personnel from critical military positions."

He then addressed the ridiculousness of the laws. "The issue is not whether women should be in combat; they already are.... The issue is not whether women should be shot at, they already are.... The real issue is whether women can shoot back."

Former WASP Barbara Ward Lazarsky piled on: "We don't need a new commission."

Becky Costantino, chair of the Defense Advisory Committee on Women in the Services, spoke last. She noted that DACOWITS had pushed to repeal the laws since 1979, and that the majority of military women favored doing so. She took Schlafly and Donnelly to task by pointing out that the legislation was very narrow, focused on just combat aircraft. "It's...an area very separate from anything related to hand-to-hand combat. Discussions of areas aside from aircraft are simply diversionary tactics...." She urged the Senate to support the new legislation, "to take a step of vision and courage."

After the press conference, Lucy Young and other aviators spoke to Barton Gellman with the *Washington Post*. Young showed Gellman a picture she carried in her wallet of the A-4 she had flown. She lamented leaving active duty because of career limitations. An Air Force captain, Terry VandenDolder, also talked about leaving active duty to join the reserves and fly for the airlines. She had been fighter-qualified during pilot training but was assigned to cargo aircraft.

On July 31, the Senate met to debate the defense bill, including the Roth-Kennedy amendment to repeal the combat exclusion law. Carolyn Becraft sat in the gallery, expecting a huge fight. Jeanne Holm was too nervous to attend; she was sure the amendment would fail.

Before the vote, Senators John Glenn and John McCain introduced an amendment of their own, to do the study the committee had recommended. Now there were two amendments to vote on, and

they appeared to be in opposition. Repeal now? Or do a study and vote to repeal later?

The debate raged on both amendments for an hour and a half, then abruptly died. The vote on the Glenn-McCain amendment came first. It passed, 95–3. The study had passed.

Glenn moved to table the Kennedy-Roth amendment, but the Senate voted 69–30 to keep it in. They then approved the amendment with a voice vote. After all the drama, the vote was over in just a few minutes.

The Senate moved on to their next topic, as if the historic vote to allow women in combat aircraft had been some routine resolution. It took Becraft and others in the gallery a few minutes to realize they had won.

The repeal was front-page news. But the major milestone was only a partial victory. The repeal did not force the Air Force and Navy to put women in combat aircraft; it merely allowed them to if they wished. The commission to study the issue muddied things, and Pentagon officials were vague about what they might do.

Figure 29: Some of the women who fought to kick open the door to fly in combat, pictured in 1995 at the ground-breaking of the Women in Military Service for America Memorial. Front Row (L to R): Ann Patrie (Army), Rosemary Mariner (Navy), Kelly Hamilton (Air Force), Sue Davies (Navy), Trish Beckman (Navy). Back Row (L to R): Kim Corcoran, Kate Clinton, Peggy Carnahan, Kim Olson, Marcy Atwood (all Air Force). (Courtesy of the Kim Corcoran Collection)

On December 5, 1991, President Bush signed the defense bill into law, officially repealing the 1948 combat exclusion law. The women aviators had prevailed. But one obstacle remained: the fifteen-member commission gearing up to study the issue. In the meantime, women aviators again put their hopes on hold.

But before the commission had their first meeting, a raucous event on the other side of the country thrust the plight of women aviators to the forefront in a way no one had expected.

* * *

On Thursday, September 5, 1991, the Tailhook Association, a professional organization for naval aviators, kicked off their annual symposium at the Las Vegas Hilton hotel. Educational and professional development sessions abounded over the next three days. Aviators who had participated in Desert Storm described their experiences, including shooting down enemy aircraft.

On Saturday afternoon, the annual Flag Panel convened to round out the conference. The panel consisted of one Marine Corps general and eight Navy admirals, including Vice Admiral Richard M. Dunleavy, who was the deputy chief of naval operations for air warfare, the Navy's senior naval aviator. The Flag Panel was always well attended; it was an opportunity for junior officers to raise ideas and ask questions in relative anonymity since they wore civilian attire.

At some point during the panel, a woman naval aviator asked when women might receive combat assignments.

Dunleavy said, "Hoo boy." A few people laughed.

The admiral continued. "If Congress directs [the secretary of the Navy] to allow qualified women to fly combat aircraft, we will comply."

The answer didn't satisfy anyone. One man in the audience said he strongly objected to women in combat aircraft; the audience burst into loud cheers and applause. But women didn't think Dunleavy had gone far enough; saying he would comply if directed to do so wasn't exactly a ringing endorsement.

The buzz about Dunleavy's comment continued, but everyone seemed ready to move on to the hospitality suites set up throughout the hotel by Navy squadrons.

Even Air Force aviators knew about the suites. A couple of years earlier, as I drank beer with three male pilots on a Friday night at the Edwards officers' club, one of them suggested a weekend trip to Tailhook. The men began making plans; it wasn't clear if I was invited.

I asked, "Can I go?"

All three said, in unison, "No."

Seeing the startled look on my face, one of them added, "It's too crazy."

"Oh, come on," I pleaded. "I spent two years at Holloman. I saw plenty of crazy stuff at the o-club there."

"No. This is raunchy stuff. Way crazier than anything you ever saw at Holloman."

No one would describe the antics I took part in at Holloman as "raunchy." Perhaps they had been when strippers were allowed at the club, but they had been banned in the early 1980s before I arrived.

Wow, I thought. *Tailhook must be pretty wild.*

It was. The event had always involved large amounts of alcohol and strippers, but in the early 1980s, some squadrons started moving their parties into the hotel hallways. Drunken aviators made cat calls at women who stumbled into the circus or rated them according to their attractiveness. By the late '80s, the juvenile behavior had escalated to gauntlets where men grabbed women's breasts and crotches. Suites on the third floor had a particularly bad reputation for rowdiness and misogynist behavior.

That Saturday evening, September 7, Lieutenant Paula Coughlin, a thirty-year-old helicopter pilot and admiral's aide, mistakenly found herself near a third-floor gauntlet as she looked for some dinner companions.

Some men in the gauntlet recognized her and yelled, "Admiral's aide, admiral's aide!"

At the same time, one of the men grabbed Coughlin's buttocks so hard that he lifted her off the ground and pushed her forward a step. Hands pawed and grabbed her everywhere. One man put his hand down her bra. Coughlin turned her head to the left and bit the man's forearm. She fought back for about twenty feet along the line until she spotted an open hotel room and escaped.

Coughlin was stunned. She complained to the admiral she worked for, but he blew her off. She then wrote a letter to Admiral

Dunleavy, who contacted the chief of naval operations. An investigation began.

On October 29, Gregory Vistica, a reporter with the *San Diego Union-Tribune*, broke the Tailhook story. At that point, the Navy was investigating more than Coughlin's accusations; at least four other women had come forward, including one who was underage. On October 11, the Tailhook president had sent a letter to commanders in the field decrying the reported events. But the president didn't seem to fully grasp the seriousness of the allegations. He didn't send the letter until naval investigators contacted him, and he waxed sorrowfully at the conclusion of his letter: "We have to figure out a way to have a great time responsibly or we will jeopardize the very future of Tailhook altogether."

Tailhook participants would soon have a lot more to worry about than the future of their organization. The five women in the original complaint were the tip of the proverbial iceberg that all of naval aviation was about to crash into.

*** * ***

In January 1992, with the Tailhook scandal unfolding but before the Presidential Commission assembled, Senator Roth was tired of waiting. He threatened to put forth new legislation to force the services to let women start flying combat aircraft before the commission completed its study. Beverly Byron was also frustrated nothing had changed. Christopher Jehn, in charge of Department of Defense manpower, insisted the issue was "more complicated than simply lifting the combat-exclusion law." The Pentagon dug in, refusing to assign women to combat aircraft.

Elaine Donnelly supported the slow approach: "Once again… the true objective here is not enhancement of military readiness and a strong national defense, but the advancement of liberal feminist causes and social experimentation in the military."

Rosemary Mariner scorned the commission as another delaying tactic. She wrote to the WMA membership: "It is clear in both the language, floor votes and extensive press coverage, that Congress did not intend to study, or in other manner, delay the combat assignment of female aviators."

Mariner pushed back on concerns about bonding as having "no basis in fact.… Those people of either sex who can't keep their emotions out of the cockpit shouldn't be flying in the first place."

She drove home her point about the committee: "The concept of 'we must do a study' is a common political ruse to diffuse accountability and staff action.… It ignores the tons of detailed individual records of flight and officer performance. Contrary to those who claimed that there aren't any studies, it ignores the stacks of DoD, DACOWITS, service studies and reports that have been published every year since the inception of the All-Volunteer Force. Selective ignorance does not justify wasting the taxpayer's money to study something Congress did not request."

But outrage wasn't enough to stop the commission.

* * *

On a July day in 1992, Air Force test pilot Jackie Parker sped north toward Chicago on Interstate 65. Strands of her bobbed blonde hair fluttered in the breeze through the 300ZX's open T-top.

She was headed for a building at Northwestern University that housed the Presidential Commission deliberating the fate of women military aviators. As an uninvited guest, she wasn't sure she'd get to testify that day, but it was worth a shot.

Rosemary Mariner had phoned Parker at her home in Dayton, Ohio, the evening before: "Jackie, the Presidential Commission is having a hearing in Chicago. You've got to get up there and see if they'll let you testify."

Mariner knew several Navy women aviators were testifying in Chicago, one of a series of meetings that summer, but she thought it would be good for Air Force women who had flown fighters to speak as well. Parker fit the bill: as part of her test pilot training, she had flown F-4 and F-16 fighters and A-7 and A-37 ground attack aircraft.

Parker told Mariner she would try to make the six-hour drive. She called her supervisor to request a short-notice leave. He was comfortable with the idea of women flying in combat, so there was little discussion, just, "Go, go!"

Parker pulled into the Northwestern campus in the early afternoon, wearing civilian clothes. Since she wasn't an invited witness,

she was technically lobbying and couldn't appear before the commission in uniform.

She entered the building and found empty halls and closed doors.

Then she spotted an Air Force lieutenant colonel in uniform. She marched over and learned his name was Mike Lynch; assigned to the Pentagon, he provided liaison support to the commission. Parker introduced herself and, after summarizing her credentials, began to harangue him.

"I don't understand why you haven't called either me or Eileen Collins to testify! We're the only two women pilots in the Air Force who have flown in fighters. Is it possible for me to testify?"

Lynch, taken aback by this somewhat insubordinate not-in-uniform junior officer, leaned back and eyed Parker up and down. After pausing for a few seconds, he said, "We don't take walk-ins."

Before Parker could respond, he added, "How tall are you, anyway?"

Startled by the question, the five-foot, three-inch Parker straightened up to her full height and stammered, "Well, I had to get a waiver to get into pilot training."

After pondering a moment, Lynch relented, "Okay, we're going to have a panel in Dallas on biometrics in August. Maybe you can come to that."

Lynch didn't promise Parker anything, but the truth was that he had been trying to find her for several weeks. Someone on his staff had heard that Parker was the smallest pilot in the Air Force. Lynch wanted her to tell the commission that her size hadn't prevented her from becoming a successful pilot, but he'd had trouble tracking her down. And now here she was, standing in front of him, like manna from heaven. Angry manna, that is.

Now all he had to do was get her on the schedule in Dallas.

* * *

Mike Lynch's assignment to the commission had been pure luck. He wasn't a career personnel officer. With a degree in psychology, he had been a drug and alcohol officer and then entered the recruiting business. In 1990, he landed in the Pentagon in a job where he oversaw

the policies the Air Force used to decide who to bring into the Air Force and where they would be assigned. He often became involved in arcane issues such as deciding whether to allow the enlistment of a reservist with 150 tattoos. The potential reservist was a woman, but the issue had nothing to do with gender. The Air Force simply had no policy governing tattoos, so Lynch had to write one.

Lynch already had women's issues under his umbrella and was the Air Force's liaison to the Defense Advisory Committee on Women in the Services, but in October of 1991, his role expanded when his boss, Lieutenant General Billy Boles, told him he was assigned as the liaison officer to the Presidential Commission.

One of Lynch's first jobs was to prepare a briefing about the Air Force's current demographics and policies regarding women: how many, which career fields were open to them, that sort of thing. As Lynch dug, he discovered that, even in 1991, women weren't assigned to Shemya Air Force Base, located on a remote island in Alaska. The reason: there was only one dormitory. Digging further, Lynch learned that the dorm had four floors; it would be easy to designate one small part of the building for women, and it would be easy to change the sign on one of the bathrooms. But just as in Vietnam, no one wanted to make the change. Too hard. Boles was incredulous when Lynch told him about Shemya. The base opened to women.

Lynch formed an opinion about the commission early on. He believed the Bush administration stacked the membership to produce the outcome they wanted: no women in combat aircraft. The commission was supposed to be neutral, with an equal number of members holding conservative and liberal viewpoints, seven each. But members were also required to be knowledgeable about military issues, which drove the commission to pursue retired generals and admirals. Bush administration officials assumed that even "liberal" retired officers would have unfavorable views about women serving in combat.

But there were several ringers, the main one being the fifteenth member of the commission: the chair, a recently retired Air Force four-star general, Robert T. Herres. A 1954 Naval Academy graduate, Herres had entered the Air Force because he thought he would have a better chance to fly. By Air Force standards, Herres was either a renaissance man or a unicorn. His wide-ranging career

included piloting both fighter and bomber aircraft, tours as a test pilot, and command positions in research and development and strategic bombing organizations. He led NORAD, the organization that tracks Santa Claus every Christmas Eve, and was the first commander of the U.S. Space Command when it activated in 1985. His final assignment was vice chairman of the Joint Chiefs of Staff.

Another ringer was Thomas V. Draude, a retired Marine brigadier general, who commission organizers must have been certain would be against women in combat aircraft. After all, the Marines still did not have a single female pilot, given that all their aircraft were used for combat. But the commission had overlooked one item: Draude's daughter was a Navy pilot.

When Draude, who had served in the Gulf War, found out his daughter had qualified for flying jets in the Navy, he wasn't quite sure what to think. But then someone called her a "good stick," and Draude said, "I found myself bursting with pride."

It would be a busy year for Mike Lynch and the other service representatives to the commission. The committee developed seventeen "issues" ranging from quotas, standards, and pregnancy policies to the actual issue at hand, combat, with conscription tossed in as well. The service reps found people to research the issues and testify.

After several months of meetings in Washington, D.C., the committee spread across the country, hoping to take the pulse of public feelings on women in combat. The first of those meetings was in Chicago—"The Midwestern Perspective"—where Lynch had met Jackie Parker. Next was Los Angeles for "The West Coast Perspective" and an earful from Navy pilots. Then it was on to Dallas—"The Southern Perspective"—in late August.

When committee members weren't listening to testimony, they jetted about the country and overseas, taking twenty-seven trips to military bases, an aircraft carrier, and the U.S. Military Academy at West Point. They also examined policies in other countries, including the Netherlands, Denmark, the U.K., and Israel, and spoke with high-ranking Russian officers at Harvard University.

Lynch's research on pregnancy in women aviators and anthropometrics was eye-opening: not only were the services inconsistent in their approaches, each service had internal inconsistencies. For example, there was no department-wide policy on how long women

could fly after becoming pregnant. Each service set their own standards, resulting in everything from immediate grounding to flexible rules that depended on the type of aircraft a woman flew.

Another area of concern was lighter-weight women who flew ejection-seat aircraft. Lynch learned that women below a certain weight had to carry a "lead sled" to add to the seat to help protect them in the unlikely event of an ejection. But Lynch was curious. Many small men flew ejection-seat aircraft; how many men were impacted by the same problem? A lot, it turned out. Percentage-wise, women were more likely to be below the weight standard, but the total number of women impacted was small since there were so few of them. In sheer numbers, more than three times as many men as women did not meet the minimum weight for their aircraft. Once Lynch discovered the problem, he worked to ensure that ejection-seat requirements for a new training aircraft could accommodate smaller pilots, both female and male.

As the commission panels developed research topics, Lynch noticed questions were often framed in a way that tried to presume a foregone conclusion. Elaine Donnelly was especially adept at the practice. In her opinion, women couldn't make good military members because they were either sick all the time, pregnant, or too busy raising children. She asked Lynch to evaluate how much work women missed due to illness compared to men.

Lynch asked the personnel experts at Randolph Air Force Base in Texas to pull the data, and, indeed, women did on average take slightly more time off for illness. But Lynch, trying to keep politics out of the analysis, thought the answer was too one-dimensional. After all, people miss work for all sorts of reasons besides illness, such as injuries, personal issues, or family emergencies. He asked the people at Randolph to pull additional data and discovered that men, on average, lost more work time for injuries. Overall, the two categories of missed work offset each other. And that didn't even begin to factor in the amount of work men missed because of disciplinary issues, but Lynch didn't go there. He kept the focus on the question at hand: health issues.

While much of the testimony was as dry as the lakebed floor at Edwards, there were moments of entertainment. Testifying on June 8, Lieutenant General Buster Glosson, an Air Force fighter pilot who

had flown in combat in Vietnam, flatly rejected the notion of women flying in combat. He stated that air combat came down to "stamina and cohesion," neither of which women had, despite all data to the contrary. He said that during Desert Storm, young men regularly flew seven-to-nine-hour missions, much of it over hostile territory. And did it day after day. Surely women didn't have the stamina for that. Apparently he hadn't heard, or didn't want to hear, that women flying transports and tankers regularly worked thirty-hour shifts with minimum crew rest for days on end and survived quite well.

But, protested Colonel Richard F. Jones, chief of flight medicine at the Pentagon, "combat aviation differs predominantly [from noncombat aviation] in the one area, in my mind, and that is that the combat pilot has to fly, fight, and win." He made it sound as if female pilots could not walk and chew gum at the same time.

<div align="center">✳ ✳ ✳</div>

By the time the commission arrived in Dallas, Elaine Donnelly's agenda was clear to Lynch: she didn't think women should have anything to do with the military. She was certain, without evidence, that women were disruptive, they hurt unit morale, and they couldn't even do their jobs well. There were plenty of people who shared her point of view.

In Dallas, Donnelly raised the "lost time" issue yet again. This time it was about pregnancy. Her thinking was that, since women who flew were in their childbearing years, they would be constantly grounded for pregnancy and need time off to care for children. It was the old Jacqueline Cochran diatribe against women, this time wrapped in the authority of a Presidential Commission. But the women aviators of the 1990s had something the Mercury 13 didn't: data on pregnancy. The data showed that, aided by modern birth control, most women who flew military aircraft waited to have babies until they were older and in staff jobs that no longer required flying. Lynch watched Donnelly's face fall when she saw the data shoot down one of her suppositions.

Throughout the commission, General Herres remained above the fray. One day after listening to the never-ending concerns among some committee members, he suggested to Lynch that the Air Force

offer the committee members rides in military aircraft and a visit to the Air Force's survival school in Washington State. Lynch passed the request up his chain of command, where it was quickly approved. He didn't expect the retired military members to be interested in the rides and visit, but he was surprised when Elaine Donnelly was the only one who took him up on the offer.

Donnelly flew in the back seat of an F-15 at Nellis Air Force Base and visited the survival school during the weeks between the Chicago and Los Angeles meetings. During the next meeting, Herres asked her about her flight, and she gushed for ten minutes about how great it was. When she paused to take a breath, Herres said, "Now you understand why women want to fly those aircraft." While other commission members snickered, Donnelly sputtered and turned red.

<p style="text-align:center">* * *</p>

As the Presidential Commission traveled around the country that summer, I headed to my new assignment as an Air Command and Staff College (ACSC) student at Maxwell Air Force Base near Montgomery, Alabama. The six hundred students were divided into smaller seminars of about fifteen students each, with each seminar a careful mix of people from different career fields, genders, ethnicities, services, and countries.

The seminar leaders, mostly recent ACSC graduates, were of similar age and rank to the students, which created a collegial atmosphere more like a civilian college than a typical military school. Academic freedom rules encouraged open debate and opinions contrary to Department of Defense and service policies.

Changes abounded at the school and across the Air Force. The collapse of the Soviet Union and U.S. success in Desert Storm had rendered much of the school's traditional curriculum to the dustbin. The new commandant, Colonel John Warden, whose air warfare theories had driven the one-sided victory in Iraq, dreamed of converting us into air power acolytes. The Air Force had also recently implemented a major reorganization that ensured the dominance of fighter pilots for decades: a single command, Air Combat Command, headed by a fighter pilot,

now owned all fighter and bomber aircraft. Photocopied sheets of paper documenting the latest hot topic replaced neatly bound volumes of obsolete materials.

One of our first assignments was to write a paper advocating a position on an issue, and the more controversial, the better. Given the chaos from recent world events, Bill Clinton's campaign promise to allow openly gay military members, and the Presidential Commission studying women in combat, there was plenty of fodder. Our seminar leader had to approve our topics, and I asked to advocate for women in combat. One of my male classmates asked to advocate against women in combat.

I was a little nervous about my request; I had no idea how our seminar leader, a major named John, felt about women in combat. He was a fighter pilot and an Air Force Academy graduate who attended when the first women were admitted. His wife was also in the Air Force, in a career field heavy with women. He might go either way on the issue, but would he give me a lousy grade if he disagreed with me? This was an academic environment; I figured he would grade my paper on the strength of its arguments, not his own beliefs. I took the plunge.

A few days later, John gave us our assigned topics. Before he read the list, he said, "I normally wouldn't allow two people to write about the same topic. But I think the women in combat issue is very important, and we have one who is pro and one who is con. So, I'm going to allow it. But I'm not going to tell you which side I'm on until after I've handed back the papers."

My opponent was a tanker pilot. He had obviously flown with many women, and he didn't fly fighters or bombers himself, so his stance seemed curious to me.

I called Jackie Parker to discuss the issues from her perspective. I chased down previous student papers on the topic. I called the wing commander of the lone woman U-2 pilot in the Air Force; he raved about her performance. I wrote up my findings and turned in the paper.

A week or so later, I learned I had done well. But what I really wanted to know was John's position.

After returning our papers, he said, "I'm for women flying in combat aircraft." My opponent's face fell. I felt giddy.

John continued: "The biggest issue people seem to have with women in combat is unit cohesion. But men don't just bond with men. And women don't just bond with women. People bond. Period." I wished he was testifying before the Presidential Commission.

<p style="text-align:center">*　*　*</p>

Coming into the next to last commission meeting in early November 1992, Lynch and the other service reps agreed on one thing: they had no idea what the commission was thinking. There was an inkling the commission might recommend that the Air Force open some fighter aircraft, but that was it. The Navy was still dead set against women on combat ships. The Army and Marines were convinced that putting women into combat would destroy both services.

The commission deliberated and voted on each of the seventeen issues one at a time. Combat aircraft came early. The commission noted that women were fully capable of flying combat aircraft and competing with men. Yet, with all the evidence presented to the contrary, too many members still believed integrating women into male units would cause problems with unit cohesion. They were also still squeamish about women POWs.

By a vote of 8–7, the commission recommended "current DoD and Service policies with regard to Army, Air Force and Naval aircraft on combat missions should be retained." That was bad enough, but the commission went even further, recommending that Congress reenact the sections of the combat exclusion law they had repealed.

Curiously, the commission recommended opening combat ships to women. When Carolyn Becraft heard about the mixed vote, she decided the commission had lost all credibility. It made no sense to recommend opening combat ships but not aircraft.

On November 3, the last day of the commission's votes, U.S. citizens cast their own votes. A few hours after the commission wrapped up deliberations, Bill Clinton defeated George H.W. Bush in the presidential election, 370 electoral votes to 168.

Clinton had pledged to allow women in combat during his campaign, but it was far from a major issue for him. A campaign brochure titled "Fighting for the Forgotten Middle Class" said nothing about military issues. The official 1992 Democratic Party

Platform briefly mentioned gay rights in the military but was silent on women in combat. In a Veterans Day speech after he was elected, Clinton said he would make good on his campaign promise to allow gay military members to serve openly. He said nothing about women in combat.

The commission delivered their final report to President Bush on November 15. Jackie Parker and the other women who had pushed for combat roles again put their dreams on hold.

CHAPTER 9
A New Administration (1993-1995)

On a January night in 1993, Second Lieutenant Jeannie Flynn, a student pilot at Laughlin Air Force Base near Del Rio, Texas, arrived at the officers' club for one of the most important events of her Air Force career: Assignment Night. That evening, she and dozens of other student pilots at Laughlin and other training bases would select the airplanes they would fly after graduating on January 22.

Flynn, the third of four daughters, had come from an Air Force background. She was very young when her father had retired from the Air Force, but the flying bug still bit her. She took her first flight in a small airplane in high school and flew in the back seat of a fighter aircraft in the late 1980s as an ROTC cadet at the University of Texas. She loved the thrill of the ride but didn't think she would ever get the chance to pilot such an aircraft. After obtaining a degree in aerospace engineering, she received a master's degree in aeronautics and astronautics at Stanford before heading to pilot training in January 1992.

By then, the combat exclusion law had been repealed, although the Presidential Commission to further "study" the problem was just getting underway. During her training, Flynn decided she wanted to fly the F-15E, an aircraft that had both an air-to-ground, bomb-dropping mission and the coveted air superiority mission, shooting other aircraft from the sky with missiles or guns. Before

Assignment Night, she did her homework and found that the prohibition against her flying the aircraft was now only based on policy, not law. With the Clinton administration sweeping into power, she hoped the policy might soon change.

Assignment Night was run via teleconference by Roger Brady, who had been a T-38 instructor with the second class of women pilots and was now a colonel at the Air Force's personnel center at Randolph Air Force Base. Brady had sent a list of the aircraft available, along with the base of assignment, to the wing commanders at each pilot training base to share with the students so they knew their options before the meeting. The students chose their aircraft in the order they graduated in their class, rotating from base to base: the top pilot at Laughlin would choose first for this class, followed in turn by each of the other bases, then the second pilot at Laughlin would choose, and so on until every pilot had an aircraft.

It was a bad time to be at pilot training. With the post-Cold War drawdown that began in 1990, there were few fighter aircraft available. In the past, fighter pilot hopefuls might become a first assignment instructor pilot in a T-37 or T-38, but FAIP slots were also now scarce. Other pilots were shoved into a program called "banked pilots," where they went off to desk jobs for three years or so until an aircraft opened. In addition, many current FAIPs had been held back from expected fighter assignments, creating some disgruntled instructors who took their misery out on the students.

Captain Kevin Price arrived at the officers' club at Reese Air Force Base, along with his wife. The two would just watch the show and munch on popcorn; Price already knew he would be flying the F-16 fighter. He had been a backseater, a weapon systems operator in F-4s with the Air National Guard in Terre Haute, Indiana. When the unit transitioned from F-4s to single-seat F-16s, they sent him and other backseaters to pilot training.

But the stakes were high for the twenty-five-year-old Flynn. As the top graduate at Laughlin, she would choose first.

After a few introductory remarks, Brady said, "Laughlin, you have the first assignment."

A distinctly female voice came on the line: "I'll take the F-15E."

Flynn's gutsy move startled Price and others in the room at Reese.

Brady swallowed hard and read his response from a piece of paper. "Current U.S. policy does not allow women to fly combat aircraft. Would you please make another choice?"

It was the response Flynn had expected. She was ready with a choice that wouldn't make waves: "I'll take the KC-10 to March."

Brady knew the exchange was going to happen. Flynn's wing commander had called him the day before.

"Hey, Roger. We're gonna have assignments tomorrow. We've got a woman who finished first in the class. She's gonna ask for a fighter."

Brady groaned. "Please, I don't need this pain." Rumors were flying all over about the Clinton administration changing the policy, and Brady knew it was just a matter of time before it happened. He tried putting his colonel's hat on. "What's she doing that for? She can't do that."

The wing commander said, "She's smart. She's just putting her marker down. She knows it's gonna change. And when it does she wants to be able to say, I was there, there was a fighter, and I could have had it if the [policy] had changed and I want my shot."

Brady was okay with that, but he figured he'd better tell his boss, a general. This was the sort of thing that could, as people say, wind up on the front page of the *Washington Post*. The general wasn't concerned about women flying in combat aircraft—he knew it was inevitable. But he didn't like bad news. Brady told him he had every-thing under control. Everyone would be nice, and it would be okay. The general wasn't happy, but he gave his blessing. Brady called the wing commander back and told him Flynn could go ahead, but she needed to have her second choice in her hip pocket.

Flynn was pleased that it was on record that she wanted the F-15. She later told Chuck Dent, a reporter with the *San Angelo Standard-Times*, that if the policy changed, "I'll be more than willing to volunteer."

Flynn also noted that some of her superiors had counseled her that fighting the policy might damage her career. But she was sanguine about her choice, telling Dent: "I might win it, but I might also give myself a miserable career. I thought about it and…I am not doing it to cause problems and I don't think I am causing problems by just asking for my first choice."

After graduating from pilot training, Flynn drove to March Air Force Base, but before she started her KC-10 tanker training, someone told Brady, "You need to get that woman back. She's going to be a FAIP." The Air Force wanted to keep their options open regarding women; if the Air Force spent money on Flynn's KC-10 training, it would be harder to justify pulling her out if a fighter opened for her. If they sent her to be a T-38 first assignment instructor pilot, the transition would be easier.

But if the new administration didn't act soon, Flynn might be the last woman in the Air Force to fly the high-performance T-38. An overhaul of Air Force pilot training was about to further dash the hopes of women pilots.

* * *

For decades, the Air Force had trained pilots to a one-size-fits-all standard. All pilots flew two jet trainers: first the T-37, then the T-38. All pilots had to demonstrate proficiency in aerobatics, tight formation flying, and other skills whether they flew large aircraft or nimble fighters after they graduated.

In the early 1990s, the Air Force decided to transition to a dual-track system, similar to the one used by the Navy. In the new system, all students would start in the T-37, but after a few months, more skilled students would shift their training to the T-38s; after graduation, they could expect to fly combat aircraft—fighters or bombers. Lesser-skilled pilots or those who preferred to fly tankers or cargo aircraft would train in a business jet-type aircraft where they focused on crew management and the challenges of flying cargo and troops around the world.

As the Air Force began moving to the new training system in the early 1990s, they announced that they were considering only allowing women to go into the "tanker/transport/airlift" track. No matter how good they were, women would not be allowed to train in T-38s. After all, if they couldn't fly in combat aircraft, what was the point of wasting training resources on them?

Women were aghast. They couldn't fly fighters, but at least they had been able to fly the T-38 as instructors, and some had become "career trainers," pilots who spent all or most of their career training

other pilots how to fly. Was the Air Force planning to close off the career trainer route to women?

No, the Air Force said. We're getting rid of all career trainers, male or female. And first assignment instructor pilots too.

It is unlikely that Air Force leadership pursued dual-track pilot training and eliminated FAIPs to deliberately keep women out of high-performance jets, but the outcome would be the same, especially if they simultaneously eliminated career trainers.

In an *Air Force Times* interview on December 8, 1992, General McPeak tried to explain the twisted logic behind the changes: "The fighter/bomber track is aimed at producing pilots who will go into fighters and bombers.... We have [also] decided...that we don't want our pilots to be instructed by first assignment instructor pilots.... So the place that we would send women after they graduate at the end of the fighter/bomber track went away. It disappeared." In other words, if you're a woman, it sucks to be you.

In December 1992, with the election settled, the Air Force decided to continue with FAIP assignments for women only until July 1993 to give the Clinton administration time to determine whether to allow women into combat aircraft. And if Clinton didn't honor his campaign promise, there was still a chance a new secretary of the Air Force might decide to continue the FAIP program. In January 1993, McPeak promised the Defense Advisory Committee on Women in the Services that women could become FAIPs for another six months, a promise they would not forget.

* * *

In late March 1993, Les Aspin, now secretary of defense, testified at a House Armed Services Committee hearing that he favored opening combat cockpits and ships to women. Of course he did; he had been a leading proponent while committee chairman. Pat Schroeder urged him to stop stalling: "They're limiting more and more of the entry-level [aviation] positions to women. I hope they open them all up soon. To have invested in women and then throw them overboard doesn't make sense."

A few days later, things started coming to a head. Admiral Frank B. Kelso II, the chief of naval operations, announced that he wanted

to open more jobs to women immediately, with a long-range goal of allowing women to serve in combat aircraft in four years. Fearing a backlash from the other services, the Navy hadn't yet submitted their proposal to Aspin.

There was much speculation that the Navy was making the move to deflect fallout from the final report on the Tailhook investigation, which was about to go public. The report was bad. Eighty-three women and seven men had been assaulted during Tailhook, and those were just the ones investigators had been able to find. Recommended charges included "indecent assault, indecent exposure, conduct unbecoming an officer, and failure to act in a proper leadership capacity." In addition, fifty-one people had made false statements to investigators. Dozens of pages documented lewd behavior, along with a generally misogynist attitude toward women in the Navy, including officers who wore T-shirts with "WOMEN ARE PROPERTY" stenciled on the back. The previous secretary of the Navy, H. Lawrence Garrett III, had resigned the previous summer, and two admirals had retired. It looked as if a vast swath of other Navy senior leaders were about to get the axe.

Some people, including Rosemary Mariner, believed the combat restrictions had contributed to the Tailhook behavior in the first place. She had previously told *New York Times* reporter Eric Schmitt, "Until you remove all the combat restrictions on women, you're going to continue to have this problem. If the institution says you're not good enough to fight or doesn't want you to, it's natural for people to think you're inferior."

But Aspin couldn't just let the Navy open up combat aircraft; such a move would open the Department of Defense to a slew of lawsuits from women in the other services. He would have to open all combat aircraft to women, regardless of their service. Two days later, Aspin's job got even harder. The *Baltimore Sun*, which had broken the story about the Navy wanting to open combat cockpits to women, ran a story on the Air Force's seemingly backwards step with the two-track pilot training system. The article revealed that "the service also intends to stop allowing women to serve as supersonic jet flight instructors, preferring to use experienced combat pilots, all of whom are men."

Tanker pilot Kelly Hamilton mourned the decision. "We already have women who are not able to pursue a career path they're qual-

ified for. You have people being told you have nowhere to go from here. Under the new program, they'll say you're not qualified because you don't have the training. The concern I have as an aviator is that people are going to get cut out of the loop. It's called clearing the decks, really."

With the Navy and the Air Force both hurtling toward decisions at opposite ends of the combat spectrum, Aspin said he would develop a consistent policy across all the services by October 1. The Air Force said they would be flexible; if the rules on combat aircraft changed, then women would of course be able to once again train in T-38 aircraft as long as they were accepted into the fighter-bomber track.

But why wait until October? Aspin could change the policy with a memo. What was taking so long?

Carolyn Becraft thought she knew. Clinton's campaign promise to allow openly gay service members had pushed women in combat to a secondary issue. Within a few days of Clinton's swearing-in, he held a two-hour meeting with the six joint chiefs, who all expressed extreme concerns with changing the policy that prohibited gay people. The meeting was front-page news, and the issue lingered, relegating articles about women in combat to inner pages. Becraft was furious, but there was little she could do.

On Sunday, April 18, 1993, the Defense Advisory Committee on Women in the Services gathered at the Tysons Corner Marriott in Falls Church, Virginia, for the first day of their annual spring meeting. Women Military Aviators members turned out in force, decked out in their dress uniforms. Many of them sat together in the front row, including Rosemary Mariner and her husband, Tommy, who were next to Lieutenant Kara Hultgreen, a Navy pilot who flew EA-6B electronic jammer aircraft out of Key West. Air Force aviators included tanker pilot Kelly Hamilton and Anne McGee, a KC-135 tanker navigator.

The aviators had already developed questions they wanted to ask on combat policies and had agreed on a strategy for engaging high-ranking officers. Questions about a specific service policy would be asked by a woman who was not in that service, to reduce the possibility of negative impacts on the woman's career. Navy women would ask about Air Force issues. Air Force women would present Army issues. Army women would ask about Navy policies. The women

intended to remain respectful and put the senior officers at ease. In reality, it was a trap.

The meeting began with the usual humdrum introductions and pleasantries. Then General McPeak spoke. Knowing DACOWITS members had concerns about eliminating the career trainer route, he addressed that first.

"First, some reports have implied that the Air Force is changing the way we do pilot training in order to bar women from flying high-performance jets…. The essential point that gets obscured is that the Air Force is changing [pilot training] to improve…not to exclude women."

Women pilots in the audience bristled.

McPeak then went through a lengthy explanation about why the single-track pilot training was "not an effective use of training resources." He justified the elimination of first assignment instructor pilots by saying it was a matter of raising training standards and cutting costs.

The women didn't buy it.

McPeak agreed that eliminating FAIPs was a step backwards for women. He reminded DACOWITS that he had agreed to allow women to become T-38 FAIPs for another six months in case the new administration opened up combat aircraft to them.

He continued: "If we receive direction to open bomber and fighter assignments to women, we can do so on a moment's notice. The procedures are ready. All we need is the go order from the boss."

The women were about to explode. But they had to wait a few more minutes while McPeak made a few perfunctory remarks about sexual harassment issues that had risen at the Air Force Academy. Few in the audience paid any attention.

As soon as McPeak finished his remarks, Navy pilot Kara Hultgreen sprang to her feet to begin the carefully planned assault. She asked, "Congress already changed the law one-and-a-half years ago, so why not open bombers and fighters to women?"

McPeak said, "My view is that the impact of women in combat will not be healthy. My concern is with the morale and cohesion of our combat units. I think it would be a mistake to open fighters and bombers to women."

"If I were a woman, I'd be upset about that," he continued. "But it's still a nagging worry for me. I have a culturally based hang-up. I can't get over this image of old men ordering young women into combat. I have a gut-based hang-up here. And it doesn't make a lot of sense in every way. I apologize for it."

A male Navy pilot asked, "Have you ever flown with a woman?"

No, the general admitted.

"Well, neither I or the aircraft care about what gender the pilot is, just their ability to fly."

Hultgreen then asked, "You said you are standing by for guidance. Have you made a recommendation to the secretary of defense?"

For a few seconds, McPeak looked as if he was going to put Hultgreen in her place. Then, apparently remembering he was a lion in a den of angry lionesses, he said, "I have not been asked and I have not volunteered my views, but he knows my views since I testified before the committee when he was chairman of the House Armed Services Committee."

McPeak, now off-balance, struggled to find common ground. "I think it is a mistake, but we are ready to implement if we get the go-ahead. There is legitimate disagreement on this subject. I hope we can disagree openly on this. I believe it will adversely impact unit cohesion. But I expect to receive further guidance from the administration and if so, we will salute smartly and open bombers and fighters to women."

But why wait if the Navy was already starting to move out? McPeak's dragging his feet was only slowing everyone down.

Hultgreen asked McPeak if he had ever served in a unit with women pilots. He admitted he hadn't. His entire career had been spent in combat units.

"Then how can you be so sure that cohesion will suffer if women are assigned to combat units?"

"It's not clear to me that you have to experience a bad thing to know about a bad thing."

The audience gasped.

Navy Lieutenant Commander Lori Melling, an F-18 test pilot, tried another tack.

"You say that it is unit cohesion that makes you oppose women in tactical aviation squadrons, correct?"

"Yes."

"And you had men and women flying together in tanker and transport squadrons, including AWACS, during Desert Storm. Did you have a problem with unit cohesion in those squadrons?"

McPeak hesitated. "Not that I'm aware of."

"So, why do you think that your fighter pilots are any less professional than the rest of your male pilots?"

McPeak hesitated again. "I'm dealing with a human relations problem, and not all human relations problems yield to logic. I can't offer a syllogism of how I arrived at this view."

Another woman asked, "Is cohesion your only concern?"

"Yes. I'm widely quoted on my personal views on this problem as having no empirical basis for my belief. War itself is a highly illogical activity." After muttering something about Robert E. Lee and the Civil War, he ran out of steam. "It's very hard to explain."

After decades of accusing women of being too emotional to be good pilots, the women had reduced one of the top male pilots in the world to an emotional mess.

Outside, reporters besieged the women for sound bites. Chuck Vinch, a reporter for *Stars & Stripes*, captured the two decades of frustration that spilled out.

Hultgreen: "He admitted that his whole premise is illogical. It's nonsense to say unit cohesion would suffer. I can say confidently that every man in my squadron would say 'I would fly with women in combat' without hesitation."

Captain Annette Totten, an Air Force intelligence officer: "That's pretty disappointing coming from someone who has proven to be such an innovator in so many ways in terms of restructuring the Air Force."

Lieutenant Linda Heid, a Navy EA-6B pilot: "If a woman is physically, emotionally, and mentally capable, she should be in the job, case closed."

But even as McPeak publicly denounced the idea of women in combat, the Air Force was quietly preparing for the inevitable.

* * *

About a week after the McPeak meltdown, Roger Brady's new boss, General Henry Viccellio Jr., called Brady at home about ten o'clock at night.

"Hey, Roger, you need to meet me at the personnel center."

"Sure. See you first thing in the morning?"

"No, now."

The drive was only a few minutes; both Brady and Viccellio lived on the base. When Brady arrived, another colonel, who worked in assignments, was also there.

Viccellio said, "The policy on women flying fighters is going to change in a few days. And the day they do it, General McPeak wants to roll out the first ten." It would be a big splash, and a big picture for the press.

The three men piled the records of all the women pilots in the Air Force onto the floor next to their office chairs. The women they selected had to meet two criteria: they had to have graduated high enough in their class that they would have gotten a fighter had they asked for one, and they had to not be too senior so they wouldn't be at a disadvantage with their peers. Brady understood that second part very well: he had gone to pilot training as a captain and had spent the next ten years catching up. There weren't that many records, and it only took them about an hour and a half to identify ten qualified women, including Jeannie Flynn.

Three of the ten women declined to become fighter pilots; they either weren't interested, or they were far enough along in their career that they didn't want to switch aircraft. McPeak wound up with seven women.

On April 27, Sharon Preszler, a C-21 business jet pilot at Andrews Air Force Base in Maryland, arrived home after a red-eye flight from Hawaii to find four messages from one of the colonels she worked for on her answering machine. When she reached him, he gave her a phone number and told her to call another colonel at the Pentagon. He had no idea what it was all about.

The colonel at the Pentagon asked, "Do you want to go fly the F-16?"

Preszler could hardly believe her ears. Of course she did. She had graduated third in her pilot training class a year earlier and had been denied a fighter.

The colonel seemed a bit uncertain if her fighter was going to actually happen, but he told her to come to an office in the Pentagon the next day—and to wear her flight suit. She drove across the Potomac River the next morning and arrived at the Pentagon at 6:45 a.m. for an 8:00 a.m. meeting. After wandering the halls of the massive building for a bit, she found the office. Two other women pilots, also in their flight suits, were there: Jeannie Flynn and Captain Martha McSally, who was a T-37 instructor pilot at Laughlin Air Force Base. The three women spent the rest of the day training on how to deal with the media.

That afternoon, April 28, Aspin and the four service chiefs, clad in their finest service dress festooned with rows of medals, filed into the press conference in the Pentagon briefing room at four o'clock. Aspin went first, announcing that he had ordered the services to open combat cockpits to women, along with allowing them to serve aboard most Navy ships.

Army General Gordon Sullivan, Navy Admiral Kelso, and Marine Corps General Carl Mundy spoke. Then McPeak stepped up to the microphone. After being the most public opponent among the service chiefs to women in combat aircraft, McPeak did as he had said: he saluted smartly and moved out.

McPeak told the assembled reporters: "We've heard the decision of the secretary, support it fully and are prepared to implement it immediately. We've already identified the first seven women pilots who will enter fighter…training, and after a short break if those of you who are interested will come back, I have brought three of these young women aviators with me. Come back and we'll have a short press conference where you can talk to them."

In response to a question about how he had come to terms with the new policy counter to his views, McPeak said, "Well, we had a discussion period in which my views were asked, and I gave my honest opinion. If I hadn't, I think the secretary should have fired me. Now the secretary's made a decision and it's my job to implement that decision as well as I can, and if I don't do that, he should fire me for that. So, the discussion period's over, we're in the mode

now of carrying this out in the best possible way and we will do that."

Another reporter asked, "Are you comfortable with this decision you have to carry out?"

McPeak answered, "I'm comfortable with it. I had a full opportunity to state my view. The secretary made a decision, so I'm comfortable with it, and there's always a small chance that I was wrong."

Yet another reporter tried to goad McPeak into sharing his personal views: "What were your concerns? Is it G forces? Is it stamina? Is it the physical strain of high-performance flying, or killer instinct, blood loss?"

But the secretary had won, and McPeak was a gracious loser. "I would prefer to duck it. We had…" He trailed off as laughter filled the briefing room.

"We had a discussion. The secretary made a decision. I support the decision 100 percent, and if you'll give us about two minutes, I'll be right back with the first three women fighter pilots."

Figure 30: General Merrill McPeak introduces the first three U.S. Air Force women fighter pilots, Captain Sharon Preszler, Captain Martha McSally, and Lieutenant Jeannie Flynn, on April 28, 1993. (Courtesy of the National Archives and Records Administration)

After all the bickering, McPeak seemed almost gleeful as he introduced the trio, who strode into the room dressed in their flight suits adorned with colorful embroidered unit patches.

First up was Jeannie Flynn, who had been denied her F-15E during pilot training. She would go to the Air Force's Lead-In Fighter Training (LIFT) course at Holloman Air Force Base. After completing that training, she would learn to fly the F-15E. Preszler would be the second woman to attend LIFT and would fly the F-16 afterwards. McSally would fly the A-10 attack aircraft after her LIFT course.

A photo in papers the next day showed McPeak smiling at a frizzy-haired Flynn, who beamed as she spoke to reporters. He may not have agreed with the decision, but his face said everything: he was proud of his pilots.

Flynn was ecstatic to get a second chance to fly the F-15E: "It's definitely a challenge…it's front line; you're the one that's out there fighting."

McSally made sure that reporters understood what the women had been saying for years: "This is opening a whole new door. It's not so much an equal opportunity issue. It's got to do with trying to have the most effective force for the military. If you have better qualified women than men when the assignments come up, then you would have the most effective force if those women go above the men behind them."

McPeak's introduction of the women upstaged the other services. The Navy and Army barely rated a mention in most media coverage, although both said they would also open combat aircraft. For the Army, that meant Apache and Cobra helicopters, and for the Navy that meant carrier-based aircraft.

After the press conference, the three Air Force women moved on to talk shows and other media interviews. Kelly Hamilton, who had given many interviews during her career as she advocated for selection processes that focused on the most highly qualified candidate over gender, joined Jeannie Flynn on *Larry King Live*. The two women marked the beginning and end of the tale: Hamilton, who had joined the Air Force unable to fly at all, and Flynn, a fighter pilot, a goal that seemed unimaginable two decades earlier. Hamilton who, placing her career in jeopardy, had fought for the right to fly her tanker during Desert Storm, and Flynn, who could now fly one of the fighters Hamilton might refuel. A portion of a Hawaii State Senate Certificate presented to Hamilton in 1992

had said, "Lt. Col. Hamilton has forced open the door to allow other women to follow her lead." It was finally time for Flynn and the others to go through the door.

<p style="text-align:center">∗ ∗ ∗</p>

On October 8, 1993, the Women Military Aviators convention kicked off at the Omni International Hotel in Norfolk, Virginia. The guest list included a who's who of women aviators currently in the military, WASP, and powerful women such as Jeanne Holm and Sheila Widnall, who had been installed as Bill Clinton's secretary of the Air Force in August. With her appointment, Widnall had become the first woman to serve as a service secretary.

At the Saturday evening banquet, Widnall talked about the WASP and reviewed the events that led up to the opening of combat cockpits to women. She also urged the WMA members to mentor the women coming up behind them and thanked the WASP for helping to blaze the trail for her to become the most powerful woman in the Department of Defense.

The celebration really got going in the hospitality suite after the banquet. There, the reality of the win set in. Jeanne Holm, still trim at seventy-two, relaxed and confident in a tailored sapphire-blue suede suit and three-inch heels, held court as the younger women admired the trailblazer.

Kelly Hamilton, who had followed the general's career as she rose through the ranks, asked a question that had been bothering her since 1975. "Why weren't you more outspoken on the combat exclusion law?"

Holm said, "You only fight wars you can win—timing was the key."

For most of the women, it was a bittersweet victory. They had won but would never reap the benefits gained. Those who gained were younger women. But no service had announced that training women in fighters was an "experiment." The women were on the A-team, and they were here to stay.

* * *

On February 14, 1994, Jeannie Flynn graduated from her F-15E training class at Luke Air Force Base near Phoenix, Arizona. General McPeak immediately brought her back to the Pentagon for another press conference. He proudly introduced Flynn, once again wearing her flight suit, as the first woman fighter pilot in U.S. history.

Flynn said, "I realize that not every person wanted this to happen, but I also know that at this time, that's irrelevant.... What really matters is just that you're qualified and that you're competent in your job."

Flynn was the first female fighter pilot in the U.S. but not the first female combat pilot. The Army had taken that honor when Second Lieutenant Charlene Wagner graduated from her Cobra attack helicopter pilot training in June 1993.

The Navy wasn't far behind. On February 19, 1994, Lieutenant Shannon Workman, a pilot on EA-6B jamming aircraft, completed her nighttime carrier qualifications on the USS *Eisenhower* to become the Navy's first female combat-ready naval pilot.

Enlisted women training for combat aircrew positions received much less publicity. In December 1993, Senior Airman Christine Kelly completed her training to become a loadmaster on an Air Force special operations aircraft, the AC-130 gunship. There were no press conferences at the Pentagon.

Women flying in combat aircraft was no longer big news. But the debates still had some life in them.

* * *

On October 25, 1994, Navy Lieutenant Kara Hultgreen, the woman who had taken on General McPeak, was killed when her F-14 fighter crashed as she attempted to land on an aircraft carrier off the coast of Southern California. The radar intercept officer in the rear cockpit ejected as Hultgreen lost control, but it was too late for her.

What happened after the accident was unprecedented. Within days, some of her fellow aviators began a smear campaign, faxing news outlets information that claimed to prove Hultgreen was a

sub-par aviator who had only been allowed to fly the F-14 because she was a woman.

For evidence, the attackers pointed to Hultgreen's failure to qualify to land the F-14 on an aircraft carrier on her first try. But that wasn't unusual: one-quarter of all pilots failed on their first try with the F-14. It was a hard aircraft to land. And Hultgreen passed on her second attempt. The Navy's senior leadership, embarrassed by the attackers' behavior, backed Hultgreen.

The attacks on Hultgreen's reputation were especially egregious since accident investigators hadn't yet analyzed what had gone wrong. It turned out that one of the F-14's engines had a problem, and she failed to fully execute the emergency procedures, which led to the loss of control. But she only had about four seconds to do everything right, and when Navy investigators presented the same scenario to other pilots in a simulator, nearly all of them also crashed.

The brouhaha over Hultgreen's death died down, but plenty of people still had a problem, including a major I worked with in my new job at the Pentagon. We worked in a cubicle farm, and at least once a week, I overheard Russ pontificating that women shouldn't be flying combat aircraft. The first time I heard him, I figured he was blowing off steam, and I ignored it. Despite his convictions about women, I liked him. He had flown combat missions in Desert Storm, and he had great stories. But after a while, the constant harping got to me.

One Friday afternoon, the office gathered in the break area for our traditional nachos and beer. I rode the bus to and from work, so I didn't worry if I wanted to drink a little.

That day, I felt a bit brave as the alcohol from two beers kicked in. About a dozen of us stood in a circle around a table. Russ was opposite me. During a lull in conversation, I looked across at him and said, "Hey, Russ. I've been meaning to talk to you about something. I really get tired of hearing you talk about how women shouldn't be flying combat aircraft."

A colonel stood near me, and his eyes widened.

Russ looked startled, then recovered. "Well, I don't think women should be flying in combat." The colonel looked at Russ, then back at me.

"But do you know how it makes me feel? I don't care what you think privately or talk about privately, but you shouldn't be talking about it at work. It's a settled issue."

"Well, it's not settled in my mind."

"But it's settled in the Air Force's mind. So, stop talking about it."

The conversation remained civilized, but the colonel's eyes grew larger with each volley. He didn't say anything. And I didn't need any help.

I finally said something like, "Let's just agree to disagree. But I would appreciate it if you wouldn't talk about it at work."

Everyone started eating nachos again. I knew I hadn't changed Russ's mind, but I felt better for having said something.

On Monday, Russ came up to me and said, "I talked to my wife this weekend about what you said, and she said you are right. I shouldn't be talking about this at work. I apologize."

I hadn't expected this. "Apology accepted," I said, and we shook hands.

A few days later, the colonel asked me to come see him in his office.

"I wanted to talk to you about this thing with Russ."

"It's not a thing. He apologized on Monday. It's okay."

"Are you sure? You two were really going at it there for a while."

"It's okay. He said I was right, and he apologized."

"Well…" The colonel seemed reluctant to let it go. Another woman in the office had recently filed a sexual harassment complaint. Was he worried I might file another one?

"It's fine. Really. Trust me, I'm not planning on filing any complaints."

That seemed to satisfy him.

* * *

Figure 31: Martha McSally, the first U.S. woman fighter pilot to fly a combat aircraft in combat, in 1995 as a captain, pictured with an A-10 as a lieutenant colonel in 2004. (Courtesy of the U.S. Air Force)

In January 1995, Captain Martha McSally became the first woman fighter pilot in the U.S. to fly a combat mission when her A-10 unit deployed to Kuwait. For security reasons, the event received no publicity, but years later, she recalled, "I was a young and new fighter pilot and here I was in Kuwait. On my first flight over Iraq, we were enforcing the no-fly zone, and as I crossed the Kuwait/Iraq border, I'll never forget the feeling I had that I had asked for this and now I was here."

EPILOGUE

In March 2022, I attended the Women in Aviation conference in Nashville, Tennessee. I like to think that the original "fly girls" from the 1920s—young women pilots who rejected societal norms of the time—would be thrilled by the results of what they set in motion. About five thousand people attended the conference; about 80 percent were women. Attendees came from all over the world and represented all aspects of private, commercial, and military aviation: pilots, flight attendants, mechanics, air traffic controllers, engineers. I moderated a Women Military Aviators panel on non-pilot flying careers in the U.S. military. Between my panel members and the audience, we had at least a dozen specialties: naval flight officer, flight test engineer, loadmaster, refueling boom operator, sensor operator, gunner on special operations aircraft, and flight attendant. Those are just the ones I remember.

The number of women in military flight suits at the conference made it clear that women no longer have limits on their military careers. The women were confident and proud of their service. They were a lot like me at their age.

Kathy Rambo Cosand, who retired from the reserves as a colonel, was honored at the conference. Four-star general Jacqueline Van Ovost, a 1988 graduate of the Air Force Academy, graduate of USAF Test Pilot School, and now commander of U.S. Transportation Command, unveiled a painting of Cosand that will hang in the halls of the Pentagon.

Wally Funk, one of the Mercury 13 denied the opportunity to become an astronaut, was also honored. Funk achieved her dream of

spaceflight on July 20, 2021, when she made a sub-orbital flight on Blue Origin's New Shepard spacecraft. A representative from the National Aeronautic Association presented her with the 2021 Katherine and Marjorie Stinson Award, given annually to recognize a living person for an outstanding and enduring contribution to the role of women in the field of aviation, aeronautics, space, or related sciences.

Jacqueline Cochran passed away on August 9, 1980. She is buried in the Coachella Valley Public Cemetery in California.

My aunt Florence died in November 2008; she was buried with military honors in the Fort Logan National Cemetery in Denver alongside her husband, Bob. She does not share a grave with Bob; as a veteran, she was entitled to her own spot.

Jeanne Holm passed away on February 15, 2010. She is buried in Arlington National Cemetery.

Carolyn Becraft later served in two high-level positions in the Department of Defense. She was deputy assistant secretary of defense for personnel support, families, and education, and then assistant secretary of the Navy for manpower and reserve affairs. She remains active in social issues.

Margie Clark Varuska retired from the Air Force as a lieutenant colonel and became an airline pilot. She is still active in WMA.

Rosemary Mariner passed away on January 24, 2019, after a battle with cancer. The day after her funeral, eight female naval aviators flew four F-18E/F fighter aircraft over her grave in a traditional missing man formation, now a missing woman formation, a tribute to one of the women who had done so much to make their careers possible.

Jeannie Flynn, now Jeannie Leavitt, did not have a miserable career. After her highly visible entry into the F-15E, she kept a low profile and worked her way up the fighter pilot career ladder. She was promoted to brigadier general on July 3, 2016. When this book went to press, she was a two-star general and the Air Force chief of safety.

Some former women combat pilots are involved in politics. Tammy Duckworth is a senator from Illinois. Martha McSally formerly served in the House and Senate.

The first generation of women military aviators has spawned the second. Both Kathy Cosand and Connie Engel have daughters who are Air Force pilots.

The success of women in combat aircraft led to the opening of ground combat positions in the Army and Marines as well. In August 2015, Army Captain Kristen Griest and First Lieutenant Shaye Haver became the first women to complete the Army's intense Ranger School. Since then, more than one hundred women have completed the course.

There are still challenges. Stories of misogynists inside and outside the military fill my Twitter feed almost daily. Women (and increasingly, men) juggle competing demands of service, family, and personal life. Women still deal with many of the same equipment issues my generation dealt with four decades ago. I laughed as an F-18 backseater at the WIA conference told me that another woman aviator's biggest thrill on a recent eight-hour flight was that she managed to pee during the trek.

Women and people of color are still underrepresented in the ranks of military aviation. Fixing this problem isn't just about equality. It's about ensuring that the military has the best people available to recruit and retain. That isn't possible if more than half the young people in the U.S. don't believe that military aviation is a viable career for them. Many don't think it's possible because they've never seen a pilot who looks like them, while others don't feel welcomed into the community when they take a trip to the local airport.

Both the civilian and military sides of aviation are making strides to increase the diversity of their workforce. Youth programs, targeted recruiting, mentoring, and increased numbers of role models are starting to make a dent. I am optimistic. In the 1950s, women made up about 6 percent of doctors in the U.S., which is about the same percentage of U.S. pilots that women are now. Women physicians now make up more than a third of the workforce, and the number continues to climb. If they can do it, so can we.

Just as my generation stood on the shoulders of the fly girls from a century ago, I hope this book will inspire younger women to consider careers in aviation and the military. I also hope it will inspire women of my generation to write their own stories. There are thousands of stories waiting to be told. And millions of young girls waiting to be inspired.

APPENDIX A
Military Primer

U.S. military personnel consist of officers and enlisted members. Enlisted members are usually high school graduates, but most have not graduated from college, at least when they first enter. Officers are required to have college degrees. Officers who serve in professions such as doctors, dentists, nurses, and lawyers are "non-line" officers; they must be certified in their professional field before receiving their military commission and compete separately for promotions from the "line" officers who serve in specialties such as aviation, personnel, engineering, and maintenance.

Enlisted personnel may supervise other enlisted members, but only officers can supervise both enlisted personnel and other officers. To maintain good order and discipline, officers may not socialize with enlisted personnel outside of the workplace, except for official functions and limited activities such as sports and clubs. These rules are often relaxed during deployments and temporary duty assignments.

Only officers can command a unit. Command positions are critical to an officer's career growth and are highly coveted at all levels.

Officers have ten separate grades, O-1 through O-10. Ranks are second lieutenant through general for all the services except the Navy and Coast Guard, where ranks are ensign through admiral. The grade structure is shown below, with equivalent ranks for Navy and Coast Guard in parentheses, followed by a typical promotion/service timeline:

O-1: Second lieutenant (Ensign), 0–2 years

O-2: First lieutenant (Lieutenant, junior grade), 2–4 years

O-3: Captain (Lieutenant), 4–10 years

O-4: Major (Lieutenant Commander), 10–15 years

O-5: Lieutenant Colonel (Commander), 15–20 years

O-6: Colonel (Captain), 20–30 years

O-7: Brigadier General (Rear Admiral, Lower Half), 24+ years

O-8: Major General (Rear Admiral, Upper Half), 27+ years

O-9: Lieutenant General (Vice Admiral), 30+ years

O-10: General (Admiral), 30+ years

Most officers who remain for at least twenty years retire as lieutenant colonels; about 10 percent of all officers retire as colonels. Fewer than 1 percent retire as generals.

Each service is organized differently and uses different names for organizational units, but there are equivalencies. For example, a company in the Army is roughly equivalent to a flight in the Air Force. The typical Air Force unit structure is:

Flight: 30–50 people, led by a captain or young major

Squadron: About 200 people, made up of 3–5 flights, usually commanded by a lieutenant colonel called the "squadron commander"

Group: About 500–600 people, made up of 3–4 squadrons, always commanded by a colonel called the "group commander"

Wing: 2,000+ people, made up of 3–4 groups, always commanded by a colonel or brigadier general called the "wing commander"

The Army, Navy, and Marines follow different organizational structures, except for flying units, which are similar to the Air Force structure.

The primary mission of fighter aircraft such as the F-22 and F-15 is air superiority, accomplished by shooting other aircraft from the sky. Fighter aircraft still carry guns, but missiles are the primary weapons of modern air combat. Some fighter aircraft, such as the F-35 and F-16, can also attack targets on the ground by dropping bombs or launching missiles. Fighter aircraft are small and agile, and typically have one or two crewmembers.

Attack aircraft, such as the A-10, focus on attacking ground targets, as do bomber aircraft such as the B-1, B-2, and B-52. The Air Force is the only U.S. service that flies bomber aircraft, which carry conventional or nuclear weapons, or both, depending on the aircraft. Bomber aircraft are much larger than fighter and attack aircraft and can carry many more weapons; they have two to four crewmembers.

Transport aircraft, such as the C-17 and C-5, are airliner-sized and carry military equipment and passengers around the world. Aerial refueling aircraft, such as the KC-135 and KC-46, are designed to transfer fuel to other aircraft to extend the range of those aircraft. Also called tankers, these aircraft carry passengers and cargo when needed.

Helicopters come in many shapes and sizes and support missions such as attacking ground targets, combat search and rescue, VIP transport, and missile field surveillance.

Other aircraft support various missions: training, special operations, reconnaissance, and air battle control, among others.

The crew size on transport and other support aircraft varies widely, anywhere from two people to dozens.

APPENDIX B
Timeline for Women in the U.S. Military

(Characters in *The Fly Girls Revolt* are highlighted in bold)

1861: U.S. secretary of war appoints Dorothea Dix to organize and recruit women nurses.

1865: Army discharges all female nurses.

1898: Congress authorizes Army to appoint women nurses as civilian contractors.

1901: Congress establishes the Nurse Corps as an Army auxiliary.

1908: Navy establishes a Nurse Corps.

1917: Navy admits women to the Naval Reserve. Marine Corps follows in 1918.

1918: Enlisted women in the Navy, Marines, and Coast Guard demobilize.

1925: Congress changes wording of Naval Reserve Act to make only "male citizens" eligible to ensure women cannot enlist in the Navy.

1941: **Representative Edith Nourse Rogers** authors a bill to create a Women's Army Auxiliary Corps (WAAC).

May 12, 1942: Congress passes bill to establish the WAAC, led by **Oveta Culp Hobby**.

1942: Bills pass to authorize women's components for the Navy, Marine Corps, and Coast Guard.

September 1942: The Women's Flying Training Detachment (WFTD) led by **Jacqueline Cochran** and the Women's Auxiliary Ferrying Squadron (WAFS) led by **Nancy Harkness Love** created to employ women as civilian pilots.

June 1943: Bill passes to establish a Women's Army Corps (WAC) giving women full military status.

August 5, 1943: WFTD and WAFS merge to form the Women Airforce Service Pilots (WASP) led by **Jacqueline Cochran**.

December 20, 1944: WASP disbanded.

September 1947: Armed Forces Unification Act creates the Department of Defense and the U.S. Air Force.

June 2, 1948: Congress passes the Women's Armed Services Act to provide permanent status to women in the armed forces.

September 1951: Secretary of Defense George C. Marshall forms the Defense Advisory Committee on Women in the Services (DACOWITS).

1952: **Jeanne Holm** is the first woman to attend Air Command and Staff College.

November 8, 1967: President Johnson signs legislation that opens the door for promotion to general and admiral ranks.

1969: Air Force opens ROTC to women.

June 11, 1970: Army promotes the first two women to brigadier general: Anna Mae Hays and Elizabeth P. Hoisington.

1971: First woman, **J. Leslie Farr Holley** (later Kenne), commissioned through ROTC.

March 22, 1972: Equal Rights Amendment clears Congress.

February 1973: The draft ends.

1973: Navy accepts first group of eight women into pilot training.

1975: Navy pilot **Rosemary Mariner** becomes the first female tactical jet pilot.

October 1975: **J. Leslie Farr Holley** (later Kenne) graduates from U.S. Air Force Test Pilot School as a flight test engineer.

Summer 1976: Women begin attending service academies, including **Margie Clark** (later Varuska).

Fall 1976: First ten women attend USAF pilot training, including **Kathy Rambo** (later Cosand).

November 23, 1977: Congress grants military veteran status to the WASP.

May 1980: First women graduate from the service academies.

1983: Colleen Nevius, a Navy helicopter pilot, graduates from the U.S. Naval Test Pilot School.

1989: **Jackie Parker,** a C-141 cargo pilot, graduates from the U.S. Air Force Test Pilot School.

1991: Women participate in the Persian Gulf War, including **Victoria Calhoun, Donna Davis, Kathy Cosand, Christina Vance Halli,** and **Stephanie Wells**.

May 1991: House of Representatives repeals the ban on women flying aircraft in combat.

Spring/Summer 1991: **Carolyn Becraft** organizes women military aviators and others to support repeal of the combat ban in the Senate.

July 31, 1991: Senate repeals the ban on women flying aircraft in combat and passes legislation to establish a Presidential Commission to further study the issue of women in combat.

November 1992: Presidential Commission recommends against women flying in combat.

November 3, 1992: Bill Clinton elected president.

April 28, 1993: Services ordered to train women for combat aircraft.

July 1993: Air Force First Lieutenant **Jeannie Flynn** (later Leavitt) reports to fighter pilot training.

January 1995: **Martha McSally** becomes the first U.S. woman to fly a combat aircraft in combat.

BIBLIOGRAPHY

Chapter 1

Interview with author: Sharon Halford.

Interview: May, Geraldine P., Colonel and Colonel Emma Jane Riley. File No. 436, U.S. Air Force Academy, May 1989.

Nolen, Stephanie. *Promised the Moon: The Untold Story of the First Women in the Space Race*. Toronto, Canada: Penguin Canada, 2002.

Cochran, Jacqueline and Maryann Bucknum Brinley. *Jackie Cochran: The Autobiography of the Greatest Woman Pilot in Aviation History*. New York: Bantam Books, 1987.

Landdeck, Katherine Sharp. *The Women with Silver Wings: The Inspiring True Story of the Women Airforce Service Pilots of World War II*. New York: Crown, 2020.

"U.S. Aviatrix to Help Ferry Bomber Plane." *New York Times*, June 17, 1941.

Dwiggins, Don. *They Flew the Bendix Race: The History of the Competition for the Bendix Trophy*. Philadelphia: J. B. Lippincott Company, 1965.

"F. W. Fuller Breaks Bendix Race Mark." *New York Times*, September 4, 1937.

Laura Greening Myers. "Mary Webb Nicholson." Find a Grave. https://www.findagrave.com/memorial/22990113/mary-webb-nicholson, accessed March 28, 2022.

"ROGERS, Edith Nourse." History, Art & Archives, United States House of Representatives. https://history.house.gov/People/

Detail/20569, accessed April 27, 2022.

"New Bill Provides for Women's Army." *New York Times*, December 31, 1941.

"Women's Auxiliary Favored for Army." *New York Times*, January 22, 1942.

"Bill for Women's Auxiliary Corps of 150,000 Passed by the House." *New York Times*, March 18, 1942.

Holm, Jeanne. *Women in the Military: An Unfinished Revolution.* Novato, California: Presidio Press, 1992.

"Senate to Vote on Army Corps." *New York Times*, March 20, 1942.

Baldwin, Nona. "WAAC Will Begin Recruiting Soon." *New York Times*, May 14, 1942.

Baldwin, Nona. "Mrs. Hobby Slated to Head the WAAC." *New York Times*, May 15, 1942.

Baldwin, Nona. "Mrs. Hobby Sworn as WAAC Director." *New York Times*, May 17, 1942.

"Letters, Telegrams, Phone Calls Pour in from Thousands Seeking to Join WAAC." *New York Times*, May 26, 1942.

Greenbaum, Lucy. "10,000 Women in U.S. Rush to Join New Army Corps." *New York Times*, May 28, 1942.

"Rush to Join the WAAC Is Looked for on Holiday." *New York Times*, May 30, 1942.

"Questions Floor WAAC Recruiters." *New York Times*, May 29, 1942.

"Ability to March Required in WAAC." *New York Times*, May 18, 1942.

"WAACs May Give Lives, Mrs. Hobby Tells Corps." *New York Times*, July 24, 1942.

"WAAC Will Train as Soldiers First." *New York Times*, July 9, 1942.

"436 Commission as WAAC Officers." *New York Times*, August 30, 1942.

"Fort Oglethorpe." *New York Times*, April 21, 1943.

Darnton, Eleanor. "WAACs Fight Back." *New York Times*, June 27, 1943.

Pfau, Ann Elizabeth. *Miss Yourlovin: GIs, Gender, and Domesticity During World War II.* New York: Columbia University Press, 2008.

O'Donnell, John. "Capitol Stuff." *New York Daily News*, June 9, 1944.

"Stimson Condemns Gossip about WAAC." *New York Times*, June 11, 1943.

"WAACs Now in Army; Name Becomes WACs." *New York Times*, July 3, 1943.

"Women Will Form a Ferry Command." *New York Times*, September 11, 1942.

"First of the WAFS Pass Ground Tests." *New York Times*, September 12, 1942.

"Named to Direct Women's Air Work." *New York Times*, September 15, 1942.

"Air Ferry School Opens for Women." *New York Times*, November 24, 1942.

"More Women Join in War Aviation." *New York Times*, November 18, 1942.

"Women War Pilots Named the WASPs." *New York Times*, August 21, 1943.

Carl, Ann B. *A Wasp Among Eagles: A Woman Military Test Pilot in World War II*. Washington, D.C.: Smithsonian Institution Press, 1999.

Roosevelt, Eleanor. "My Day, September 1, 1942." *The Eleanor Roosevelt Papers Digital Edition* (2017), https://erpapers.columbian.gwu.edu/browse-my-day-columns, accessed January 20, 2022.

"Three Die When Plane Crashes at Avenger Field." *Taylor Daily Press*, August 31, 1943.

Ray, John W. "Women Who Would Be Warriors." Air War College Report No. 452. Maxwell Air Force Base, Alabama, April 1978.

Pearson, Drew. "CAA Trained Pilots Get Runaround from Army." *Lock Haven Express*, March 15, 1944.

"WASP Shut-Down Begun by the Army." *New York Times*, June 28, 1944.

Memo, General H. H. Arnold to Jacqueline Cochran. October 1, 1944. Jacqueline Cochran: Papers, 1932-1975. WASP Series. Box 12. Eisenhower Presidential Library.

Press Release. November 16, 1944. Jacqueline Cochran: Papers, 1932-1975. WASP Series. Box 14. Eisenhower Presidential Library.

"National Security Act of 1947." Office of the Historian, Foreign Service Institute, United States Department of State. https://

history.state.gov/milestones/1945-1952/national-security-act, accessed March 14, 2022.

Chapter 2

Interview with author: Claire Griffith.

Interview: Jeanne M. Holm Collection (AFC/2001/001/04293), Veterans History Project, American Folklife Center, Library of Congress. Available at https://memory.loc.gov/diglib/vhp/bib/4293.

Interview: May, Geraldine P., Colonel and Colonel Emma Jane Riley. File No. 436, U.S. Air Force Academy, May 1989.

Maves, Norm, Jr. "Maj. Gen. Jeanne Holm a Fighter from the First." *Sunday Oregonian*, October 7, 1990.

Jung, Helen. "Opening up the Boys Club." *Oregonian*, March 7, 2010.

Holm. *Women in the Military: An Unfinished Revolution.*

"Maj. Gen. Jeanne Home, USAF (retired)." *Salem Statesman Journal*, March 27, 2001.

Seydel, Carie A. "Flight of the WASP." *Airman*, June 2001.

Holly, Hazel. "Hamilton Field Launches Drive to Recruit More WAF Officers." *San Francisco Examiner*, September 16, 1951.

Historical Summary—Office Director WAF, 1 July 50–31 December 50. Ref K141.33. Air Force Historical Research Agency.

Memorandum for the Chief of Staff, Subject: WAF Program. December 6, 1950. Ref K141.33. Air Force Historical Research Agency.

"College Exec, Ex-Navy, to Head WAF." *Air Force Times*, June 9, 1951.

"WAF Get New Head Today." *New York Times*, June 12, 1951.

"WAFs Are Embittered: A WAVE Will Lead Them." *New York Times*, June 17, 1951.

"Ex-WAF Chief Mum." *San Antonio Light*, June 24, 1951.

"48 Women Enlisted to Aid Recruiting." *New York Times*, August 12, 1951.

"Marshall Decries Shifts on Defense." *New York Times*, September 18, 1951.

"80,000 Women Set as Need in Services." *New York Times*, September 19, 1951.

"Service Goal is Set at 112,786 Women." *New York Times*, September

20, 1951.

"U.S. Task Stressed on Armistice Day." *New York Times*, November 12, 1951.

Cochran and Brinley. *Jackie Cochran: The Autobiography of the Greatest Woman Pilot in Aviation History.*

Qualifications for Astronauts, Hearings Before the Special Subcommittee on the Selection of Astronauts of the Committee on Science and Astronautics, U.S. House of Representatives, July 17 and 18, 1962. Washington D.C.: U.S Government Printing Office.

"S. Viet Nam WAFCs Answer to WAFs, WACs." *Jefferson City Daily Capital News*, February 23, 1966.

Miller, Joy. "First Female Officer in Viet Nam, Major's Stateside in Teaching Job." *Montgomery Advertiser*, April 26, 1966.

Anderson, Jack. "Should We Send Out Women Soldiers to Vietnam?" *Parade*, January 2, 1966.

Kenaston, Nancy. "AF Women to Serve in Viet Nam; Col. Jeanne Holm Visits Eglin." *Playground Daily News*, December 8, 1966.

History of the 315th Air Division, PACAF, 1 July 1967 to 31 December 1967, Volume 1 of 5. Ref K-DIV-315-HI. Air Force Historical Research Agency.

"Nurse Gets 3 Combat Medals." *Middletown Journal*, October 8, 1968.

Oliver, Ione. "Only Woman Operations Officer in Combat Zone." *San Bernardino Sun*, October 10, 1969.

"Major Archer Nominated for 'Unsung Heroine' Title." *Redland Daily Facts*, July 25, 1969.

Glaser, Vera. "Air Force Gals Get Uniform." *Lima News*, April 10, 1968.

Smith, Kelly. "GI Dress Planning Top Secret." *Jefferson City Post Tribune*, April 27, 1967.

Delong, Edward K. "WAF Skirts Are Rising Despite Midi." *Cedar Rapids Gazette*, July 23, 1970.

Chapter 3

Interviews with author: Carolyn Becraft, Claire Griffith, Roy Martin, and Jeff Peer.

History of the Women in the Air Force, 1 January 1969-30 June 1969. Ref K141.33. Air Force Historical Research Agency.

Interview: Jeanne M. Holm Collection. Library of Congress.

Maves, Norm, Jr. "Maj. Gen. Jeanne Holm a Fighter from the First."

Nordheimer, Jon. "Coed Air Force Cadets Think Equality is Lure." *Cumberland Sunday Times*, December 28, 1969.

"Air Force Coeds' Hemline Discreet But It's Creeping." *Corpus Christi Caller Times*, November 23, 1969.

"Lt. Gen. Leslie F. Kenne, USAF, Retired." State of Alabama Engineering Hall of Fame. https://engrhof.org/members/lt-gen-leslie-f-kenne-usaf-retired, accessed December 20, 2021.

"Two Officers Get Stars and Kisses." *New York Times*, June 12, 1970.

Moffat, Peace. "Women Made the News in 1971." *Austin Daily Herald*, December 28, 1971.

"Woman General Plugs Assets of Air Force for Girl Grads." *Middletown Journal*, July 28, 1971.

Lazar, Kay. "Fight for Equality Recalled: Hub Woman Battled Military in Lawsuit for Fair Benefits." *Boston Herald*, March 16, 2003.

"Officer Asks Benefits—for Husband." *New York Times*, December 25, 1970.

"Female Officer's Claim of Dependent Mate Denied." *Air Force Times*, March 7, 1959.

"Air Force Backed on Sex Bias Case." *Air Force Times*, April 7, 1972.

Frost-Knappman, Elizabeth and Kathryn Cullen-DuPont. *Women's Rights on Trial*. Detroit: New England Publishing Associates, Inc., 1997.

"A 'Flaming Feminist' Lauds Court." *New York Times*, May 22, 1973.

"Air Force Woman Wins Benefit Suit." *New York Times*, May 15, 1973.

Willenz, June A. *Women Veterans: America's Forgotten Heroines*. iUniverse: 2000.

"Air Force Captain, Unwed, Has Baby." *New York Times*, December 4, 1970.

"460 F2d 1372 Struck v. Secretary of Defense." *Federal Reporter*. https://openjurist.org/460/f2d/1372/struck-v-secretary-of-defense, accessed April 29, 2022.

"10-1972 Struck v. Secretary of Defense." Supreme Court Case Files, Powell Papers. Washington & Lee University School of Law

Scholarly Commons. https://scholarlycommons.law.wlu.edu/cgi/viewcontent.cgi?article=1617&context=casefiles, accessed April 29, 2022.

"Court Backs Air Force's Ouster of an Unwed Pregnant Officer." *New York Times*, November 16, 1971.

"Air Force Mother to Press Case Against Ouster." *New York Times*, December 6, 1970.

"Air Force Drops Effort to Oust Woman Captain." *New York Times*, December 2, 1972.

Rostker, Bernard. *I Want You! The Evolution of the All-Volunteer Force*. RAND Report MG-265-RC. July 12, 2006.

Shanahan, Eileen. "Equal Rights Amendment Is Approved by Congress." *New York Times*, March 23, 1972.

Franklin, Ben A. "Lag in a Volunteer Force Spurs Talk of New Draft." *New York Times*, July 1, 1973.

"Z-Gram #116; dated 7 August 1972." Naval History and Heritage Command. https://www.history.navy.mil/research/library/online-reading-room/title-list-alphabetically/z/list-z-grams/z-gram-116.html, accessed April 27, 2022.

"Navy Seeks 8 Women to Volunteer as Pilots." *New York Times*, November 8, 1972.

"First Woman Gets Navy Wings." *Abilene Reporter-News*, February 23, 1974.

"Did You Know? Another First." *Naval Aviation News*, April 1974.

Goldstein, Richard. "Rosemary Mariner, Pathbreaking Navy Pilot and Commander, Is Dead at 65." *New York Times*, February 1, 2019.

"Female Navy Aviator Starts Training at Virginia Beach." *Cumberland Evening Times*, July 24, 1974.

"Army to Graduate Woman Aviator." *Huron Daily Plainsman*, June 3, 1974.

"Edwards to Graduate First Woman as Test Pilot Today." *Bakersfield Californian*, July 2, 1975.

"SCHROEDER, Patricia Scott." History, Art & Archives, United States House of Representatives. https://history.house.gov/People/Listing/S/SCHROEDER,-Patricia-Scott-(S000142)/, accessed April 27, 2022.

Hearings Before the Subcommittee No. 2 of the Committee on Armed

Services, House of Representatives, Ninety-Third Congress, Second Session on H.R. 9832 to Eliminate Discrimination Based on Sex with Respect to the Service Academies and H.R. 10705, H.R. 11267, H.R. 11268, H.R. 11711, and H.R. 13729 to Insure That Each Admission to the Service Academies Shall Be Made Without Regard to a Candidates Sex, Race, Color, or Religious Beliefs. Report HASC-94-9, 1975.

McLucas, John L., Kenneth J. Alnwick, and Lawrence R. Benson. *Reflections of a Technocrat: Managing Defense, Air, and Space Programs During the Cold War.* Maxwell Air Force Base: Air University Press, 2006.

"Air Force Will Take Women Pilots." *Hayward Daily Review*, November 21, 1975.

History of The Women in the Air Force 1 July 1975-31 December 1975. Ref K141.33, Air Force Historical Research Agency.

Famiglietti, Len. "20 Women Officers to Train as Pilots." *Air Force Times*, January 12, 1976.

Holm, Jeanne M. "Women and Future Manpower Needs." *Defense Management Journal*, Winter 1970.

Chapter 4

Interviews with author: Carolyn Becraft, Roger Brady, Margie Clark (Varuska), Dave Clary, Kathy Rambo (Cosand), Bruce Deane, Anne Martin Fletcher, and Karen Wilhelm.

Ricks, Chip. *Beyond the Clouds.* Wheaton, Illinois: Tyndale House Publishers, 1979.

"Women Soon to Train as Noncombat Pilots." *Air Force Times*, January 12, 1976.

Famiglietti. "20 Women Officers to Train as Pilots."

Ray. "Women Who Would Be Warriors."

"They'll fly by the seats of their skirts." *San Antonio Express*, August 24, 1976.

"Militarization of the WASPS." PBS, https://www.pbs.org/wgbh/americanexperience/features/flygirls-militarization-wasps/, accessed April 30, 2022.

History of the 332D Flying Training Wing, 1 January – 30 June 1977, Volume 1—Narrative. Mather Air Force Base, California. Air

Force Historical Research Agency.

"In anticipation for tomorrow's CSO Sapphire Event celebrating the first female navigators, hear in their own words what it was like to break through the glass ceiling of women in the cockpit," Facebook, March 10, 2022, https://www.facebook.com/12thFlyingTrainingWing/videos/668976584325268, accessed March 18, 2022.

"Women Navigators Not Much Different." *Ontario Daily Report*, October 12, 1977.

History of the 63rd Military Airlift Wing. Norton Air Force Base, California. April-June 1978. Ref: HAF-CHO(AR)7101. Air Force Historical Research Agency.

"Women Ranked Highly at Academics." *Sunday Herald*, May 18, 1980.

"Second Academy Class Occurs." *Indiana Evening Gazette*, February 23, 1979.

Bondarook, Nina. "25,000 Attend Graduation." *Colorado Springs Sun*, May 29, 1980.

Wilson, Dru. "Top Woman Cadet Sighs, 'It's All Over.'" *Colorado Springs Gazette Telegraph*, May 29, 1980.

Fosse, L. Elisabeth. "Air Force Class of '80: Momence Woman Makes History." *Sunday Journal*, May 25, 1980.

Chapter 5

Interviews with author: Margie Clark (Varuska), Anne Martin Fletcher, Karen Wilhelm.

"Readiness of Military Women Will Be Reviewed." *Air Force Times*, March 30, 1981.

Parker, Laurie. "Memo on Women: Make 'Fullest' Use." *Air Force Times*, February 15, 1982.

Carolyn Becraft. Women's Equity Action League, WEAL Box 9, Texas Woman's University.

Holm. *Women in the Military: An Unfinished Revolution*.

Chapter 6

Interview with author: Gail Wojtowicz.

Boyne, Walter J. "El Dorado Canyon." *Air Force*, March 1999.

"Women in Combat." *Newsweek*, November 11, 1985.

Garamone, Jim. "Warner Praises Women's Role in Libya Raid." *Air Force Times*, May 12, 1986.

Hayden, Sara. "The History of WMA." *WMA Quarterly: A News-letter of the Women Military Aviators*, Summer 2003.

Gibney, Jim. "Women Pilots to Service in Combat by Decade's End, Ex-General Says." *Denver Post*, September 6, 1987.

Cantwell, Rebecca. "Women Pilots Air Complaints on Flight Posts." *Rocky Mountain News*, September 6, 1987.

Dalton, Pat. "Senator Urges Fighter Training for Women." *Air Force Times*, July 13, 1987.

"Women in Combat: Legislation and Policy, Perceptions, and the Current Operational Environment." Military Leadership Diversity Commission, Issue Paper #56, November 2010. https://diversity.defense.gov/Portals/51/Documents/Resources/Commission/docs/Issue%20Papers/Paper%2056%20-%20Women%20in%20Combat.pdf, accessed March 13, 2022.

Letter, Hansford T. Johnson to Larry D. Welch. October 30, 1989. Carnahan Papers, Texas Woman's University.

McKay, Karen. "Sexism, Law Still Obstacles." *Air Force Times*, May 12, 1980.

"Debra Mann and Lisa Kutschera." The Pioneers, last updated September 18, 2002. https://www.ctie.monash.edu.au/hargrave/mann_and_kutschera.html, accessed March 13, 2022.

Gordon, Michael R. "For First Time, a Woman Leads G.I.'s in Combat." *New York Times*, January 4, 1990.

Chapter 7

Interviews with author: Carolyn Becraft, Victoria Calhoun, Sheila Chewning, Kathy Cosand, Donna Davis, Christina Vance Halli, Peggy Phillips, Amy Hermes Smellie, and Stephanie Wells.

Conduct of the Persian Gulf War: Final Report to Congress. Washington, D.C., 1992.

Warrick, Joby. "AWACS Proves to be Gulf 'Trump Card.'" *Air Force Times*, March 26, 1991.

Eskind, Amy. "A Post-Gulf Memorial Day, 1991." *Washington Post*. May 26, 1991.

Holm. *Women in the Military: An Unfinished Revolution.*

Hallion, Richard P. *Storm over Iraq: Air Power and the Gulf War.* Washington, D.C.: Smithsonian Institution Press, 1992.

Zamichow, Nora. "Navy Fighter Pilot Flies in Face of Sexism." *Los Angeles Times*, June 25, 1990.

Email, Kelly Hamilton to author, April 27, 2022.

McConagha, Alan. "Family is at Stake, Critics Claim." *Washington Times*, June 18, 1991.

"Military Chiefs Cold to Women in Combat Role." *San Antonio Express-News*, June 19, 1991.

Fields, Suzanne. "Foes of Women in Combat Reload for Senate Fight; Why the Fuss? This Lady Takes Ride to Find Out." *Washington Times*, July 18, 1991.

Chapter 8

Interviews with author: Carolyn Becraft, Mike Lynch, Jackie Parker, and Lucy Young.

Holm. *Women in the Military: An Unfinished Revolution.*

Scarborough, Rowan. "Kennedy, Roth Back Female Fliers." *Washington Times*, July 26, 1991.

"News Conference with the President's Advisory Committee on Women in the Service, Speakers: Senator Edward Kennedy (D-MA), Senator William V. Roth, Jr., (R-DE) and Others." *Federal News Service*, July 25, 1991.

Schmitt, Eric. "Senate Votes to Remove Ban on Women as Combat Pilots." *New York Times*, August 1, 1991.

The Tailhook Report: The Official Inquiry into the Events of Tailhook '91. New York: St. Martin's Press, June 1993.

Schmitt, Eric. "Wall of Silence Impedes Inquiry into a Rowdy Navy Convention." *New York Times*, June 14, 1992.

Vistica, Gregory. "Women Reportedly Abused by Navy Pilots at Seminar." *San Diego Union-Tribune*, October 29, 1991.

Maze, Rick. "DoD Pleads for Time on Women in Combat." *Air Force Times*, February 10, 1992.

Gellman, Barton. "Female Navy Pilots Seek Combat Roles." *Washington Post*, as printed in *Vancouver Sun*, July 29, 1991.

The Presidential Commission on the Assignment of Women in the Armed

Forces: Report to the President, November 15, 1992.

"1992 Democratic Party Platform." The American Presidency Project, UC Santa Barbara. July 13, 1992. https://www.presidency.ucsb.edu/documents/1992-democratic-party-platform, accessed April 29, 2022.

Baer, Susan. "Clinton Reaffirms His Promise to End Military's Ban on Gays." *Baltimore Sun*, November 12, 1992.

Chapter 9

Interviews with author: Carolyn Becraft, Roger Brady, Sharon Preszler, and Kevin Price.

Dent, Chuck. "Flynn Graduates as No. 1 but that Won't Guarantee Choice." *San Angelo Standard-Times*, January 22, 1993.

Transcript: Merrill McPeak interview with *Air Force Times*. Carnahan Papers, Texas Woman's University. December 8, 1992.

Talking Paper: "Rated Requirements Update." Carnahan Papers, Texas Woman's University. December 17, 1992.

Sia, Richard H. P. "Air Force to Stop Training Women in Combat Planes." *Baltimore Sun*, April 7, 1993.

Cushman, John H., Jr. "Top Admiral Backs Full Combat Roles for Women in the Navy." *New York Times*, April 5, 1993.

Schmitt, Eric. "Aspin Is to Set Women's Role in All Services." *New York Times*, April 8, 1993.

Schmitt, Eric. "Military Cites Wide Range of Reasons for Its Gay Ban." *New York Times*, January 27, 1993.

Transcript: Chief of Staff of the Air Force General M. McPeak Speeches, March 1-June 1993, Book VII of XIII. Ref K168-03-258, 1 April 91-18 Oct 94. Air Force Historical Research Agency.

Vinch, Chuck. "AF's McPeak Riles Women's Group." *European Stars & Stripes*, April 19, 1993.

Emails: Kelly Hamilton to author, April 21, 2022, and April 27, 2022.

Weintraub, Beverly. *Wings of Gold: The Story of the First Women Naval Aviators*. Guilford, Connecticut: Lyons Press, 2021.

"Military Open Combat Flying to Women." *Arlington Heights Daily Herald*, April 29, 1993.

Transcript: Defense Secretary Les Aspin News Conference, April 28, 1993. Ref K168.03-876, part 2. Air Force Historical Research Agency.

Burns, Robert. "Women Get Shot at Top Gun Status." *Madison Capital Times*, April 29, 1993.

WMA Convention File, October 8-11, 1993. Peggy Carnahan Papers. Texas Woman's University.

Delgado, Ray. "First U.S. Woman Fighter Pilot Ready to Take Wing." *Los Angeles Times*, February 16, 1994.

Schmitt, Eric. "Navy Women Bringing New Era on Carriers." *New York Times*, February 21, 1994.

Background Paper: Women in Combat, January 3, 1994. Peggy Carnahan Papers. Texas Woman's University.

Perry, Tony. "Crash Kills First Female F-14 Combat Pilot." *Los Angeles Times*, October 27, 1994.

Schmitt, Eric. "Pilot's Death Renews Debate Over Women in Combat Role." *New York Times*, October 30, 1994.

"A Gender-Neutral Tragedy." *New York Times*, March 2, 1995.

Bergquist, Carl. "1st Air Force Female Pilot in Combat Reflects on Career." December 6, 2006. https://www.af.mil/News/Article-Display/Article/128823/1st-air-force-female-pilot-in-combat-reflects-on-career/, accessed March 27, 2022.

INDEX

N

O

ACKNOWLEDGMENTS

Like any military operation, a book takes a team. I would first like to thank the primary members of that team: my editor at Post Hill Press, Alex Novak; my agent, Leah Spiro, who helped pull together my idea for the story into a proposal; and Stephanie Slewka, who helped edit the proposal and final manuscript.

A book like this also takes an incredible amount of research. Having lived some of this story, I was familiar with the basic outline. But I supplemented that knowledge with interviews, newspaper and magazine articles, and archival material. Thank you to Women Military Aviators, Inc., for connecting me with many of the women I interviewed. Thank you also to Shelia Bickle at Texas Woman's University for access to WMA and WEAL archival materials, Sylvester Jackson at Air Force Historical Research Agency for access to materials I had not seen previously quoted, and Ruth Kindreich at the U.S. Air Force Academy for sending me transcripts of more than a dozen interviews. I also want to thank retired Colonel Walt Hines, who graciously ran over to AFHRA to photocopy an article I missed during my visit, and Jack Waid at Air Force Materiel Command for chasing down several photos of old uniforms.

This book would not have been possible without the many people who took the time to tell me their stories. They are listed here in alphabetical order because no story is more important than another; woven together, they make up the tapestry of the final product. Many thanks to: Carolyn Becraft, Roger Brady, Vicky Calhoun, Sheila Chewning, David Clary, Kathy Rambo

Cosand, Donna Davis, Bruce Deane, Anne Fletcher, Claire Griffith, Sharon Halford, Christina Vance Halli, Mike Lynch, Roy Martin, Anne McGee, Jackie Parker, Jeff Peer, Peggy Phillips, Kevin Price, Amy Hermes Smellie, Margie Clark Varuska, Stephanie Wells, Karen Wilhelm, Gail Wojtowicz, and Lucy Young. And an extra shout-out to Stephanie Wells for sharing her Desert Shield/Desert Storm diary.

Finally, to my friends and loved ones who didn't hear much from me during the final six-month push to finish the manuscript, thank you for your patience.